GAME MODELING USING LOW POLYGON TECHNIQUES

GAME MODELING USING LOW POLYGON TECHNIQUES

Chad and Eric Walker

CHARLES RIVER MEDIA, INC.
Hingham, Massachusetts

Publisher: Jenifer L. Niles
Production: ElectroPublishing, Inc.
Printer: InterCity Press, Rockland, Massachusetts
Cover Design: The Printed Image
Cover Image: Chad and Eric Walker

CHARLES RIVER MEDIA, INC.
20 Downer Avenue, Suite 3
Hingham, Massachusetts 02043
781-740-0400
781-740-8816 (FAX)
info@charlesriver.com
www.charlesriver.com

This book is printed on acid-free paper.

Chad and Eric Walker. Game Modeling Using Low Polygon Techniques.
ISBN: 1-58450-055-7

Library of Congress Cataloging-in-Publication Data

Walker, Chad Gregory, 1976-
  Game modeling using low polygon techniques / Chad Gregory Walker and
George Eric Walker.
    p. cm.
  ISBN 1-58450-055-7 (paperback with CD : alk. paper)
  1. Computer art--Technique. 2. Artists' preparatory studies. 3.
Three-dimensional imaging. I. Walker, George Eric, 1976- II. Title.
  N7433.8 .W35 2001
  794.8'1--dc21

                    2001003701

Printed in the United States of America
01 02 7 6 5 4 3 2 First Edition

Acknowledgments

There were a number of people involved in the creation of this book, and we would like to take the time to express our thanks to them. First we'd like to thank Mom and Dad for their encouragement and love through the years and allowing us to live out our dreams. We'd also like to thank Sheila and Dario Gonzalez for their constant support and helpful editing, as well as Chris Haigood for his continuous encouragement in creating this book. A thanks also goes out to the guys at Ensemble Studios for inspiring us to continue our skills as 3D modelers and pursuing to be the best. Thanks guys! Of course, we have to thank David Fugate, our agent, and Jenifer Niles, our editor, for putting up with us and making this project even possible. Thanks y'all!

Chad and Eric Walker

Dedication

To the Almighty Father and his Son Christ Jesus, without whom we—and ultimately this book—would not be possible.

Contents

Foreword

So you want to make a living as a game artist? The crucial words being *make a living*.

If you want to develop the skills necessary to land a job making a living as a game artist, then you are looking at the right book. I should know for I have spent the last ten years hiring computer game artists. I have sifted through thousands of demo reels, resumes, Web sites, CDs, and resume submissions on every imaginable type of media. In short, if you master what Chad and Eric Walker have laid out in *Game Modeling Using Low Polygon Techniques* then you will increase your odds of getting a job in the game industry astronomically.

This book will help you win the war against the term "starving artist." I have always hated this term because I was always the kid looking out the window or drawing cool pictures, and it was predicted that I would probably be an artist when I grew up (the word "starving" implied by the worried look in my parents' eyes and their wringing hands). With computer technology being what it is today, artists have become more and more in demand as the personal computer has brought with it the computer game, the Internet, and a host of other technologies that demand more and newer content. This book will not only help you develop 3D assets that are applicable to games, but also for the Web sites that are increasingly turning to 3D content so viewers can see their products in real time 3D.

Keep in mind that the fate of the starving artist doesn't need to be yours. You can expect above poverty level salaries as a computer artist and this book is definitely the place to start.

Luke Ahearn, Art Director
The Army Game Project

Introduction

Welcome reader! If you have ever wanted to learn how to create those amazing low polygon 3D models used in today's hottest video games, then you have come to the right place. *Game Modeling Using Low Polygon Techniques* is your first and last step in learning to create game-ready 3D models. Through our simple, step-by-step methods, we will teach you the necessary instructions, organizational techniques, and proper use of your 3D applications, to provide you with a complete working knowledge of low polygon modeling. *Game Modeling Using Low Polygon Techniques* has been designed to benefit anyone interested in making 3D models, from the amateur all the way to the professional. This book establishes solid foundations and principles for modeling low polygon 3D objects — from the initial sketch phase to final development — which can be used in a game. Our belief is that a visual media requires a visual book. This book offers both written descriptions as well as in-depth visual references consisting of more than 500 images, which can be found on the companion CD-ROM. By presenting a complete set of comprehensive step-by-step images for each concept, the book provides an animated style that matches the techniques you'll be learning. Detailed "how to" guidelines are included to teach you about the conceptual phase, and to explain how to create U.V. mapping coordinates (a technical term for where the skins are placed on a model), and texture your models correctly. With these tools, you'll be prepared to branch out and work on your own creative ideas.

To keep things focused, we selected a set of very basic tools necessary for modeling your characters and creating their textures. Because of our careful choices, a wide range of 3D applications may be used to apply these methods and techniques with little difficulty. If you follow the exercises in the sections ahead, you will be prepared to design, model, and texture each of the awesome characters and models covered in the book.

So start up that computer, grab a comfortable chair, and get ready to create a whole world of characters that utilize some of the simplest techniques and industry-proven tips and tricks.

We hope this book serves you well in your future projects and that you come away with a true understanding of *Game Modeling Using Low Polygon Techniques.*

Good Luck!

1

Concept Art

Every game, model, or project begins with an idea. Ideas can be anything from a simple image of a character to a complete game concept or story. Bringing these ideas to life involves a variety of phases and the first phase is what we call "concept art." Concept art is the phase where you put your ideas down on paper and begin to see them evolve into real characters and objects. In the beginning, any little doodle, tight sketch, or even a full-blown painting will help you produce the look and feel of the characters and worlds you want to create. If you are not an artist, don't worry. We have provided pictures in the book, which you can photocopy and draw on, or you can pull up the drawings from the CD-ROM in any type of 2D drawing program and work on them there. Drawing should not limit your ideas or keep you from continuing to develop concept art. One great idea would be to use a friend who can draw pictures or check on-line with artists from around the world. You might be surprised at how many artists would enjoy working on a computer game project.

Concept art is an *invaluable* element in the creation of games, because the more time you spend drawing your ideas, the more time you will save when developing the 3D models. Concept art can also help you conceptualize everything from a simple rock on the road to an evil villain, or even an entire world with levels. Don't underestimate the power of a sketch — they're *essential*. Now let's get started!

Sketching Basics

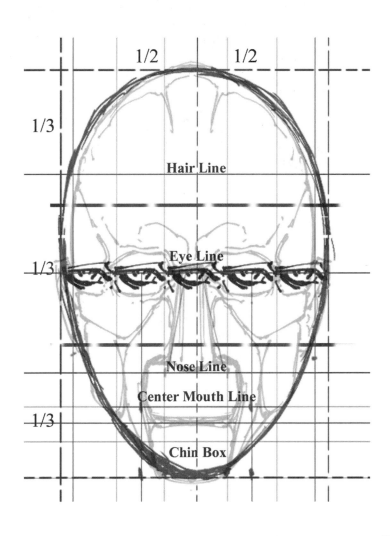

1/2   1/2

1/3

Hair Line

Eye Line

1/3

Nose Line

Center Mouth Line

1/3

Chin Box

TOOLS OF THE TRADE

For any artist, the tool you draw with can be as important as the kind of car you drive. The medium you choose to illustrate with can be as simple as a pencil and notebook paper, or it can go as far as to include oil paintings and sculpting clay. The supplies, tools, and much more can be found in nearly any local art or craft store, such as M.J. Designs, Hobby Lobby, or Art Grafixs. If you are a designer or programmer and have not had the opportunity to draw, fear not. We have included in this book and on the CD-ROM a full set of pictures that will give you a place to build your confidence and ease you into the world of drawing. Be sure to take full advantage of the drawings in this book by printing them from the CD-ROM and drawing on them, or by pulling up the drawings in Photoshop or another type of 2D drawing program. This is also a great opportunity for you to use that friend who can draw, or there may even be an art group at the company you work for that can help out. Don't be afraid to ask friends for help. Many people would jump at the chance to lend a hand in creating sketches or models that could be used in a computer game. The following is a list of art supplies that most artists can't go without:

ON THE CD

- **Pencils** (wood or mechanical .05 preferred)
- **Pens** Sharpie's, Pilot Pens, Rapidiographs
- **Hunt Crow Quills** #97- #102
- **Higgins Black Magic Ink** Any type of ink will do, but this ink is definitely one of the best out there.
- **Erasers** Maybe. Remember you're an artist now; we only make happy mistakes. No need to erase those.
- **Markers** Pantone markers are really good to use for color separations.
- **Watercolors and Oils** This is only if you feel comfortable with these mediums; they can be time-consuming, but they are very rewarding.
- **Paper** There are many thicknesses and grains for paper. The best kind would be a bound sketchbook so that the work you do stays in one place and is easy to keep up with.
- **Templates, Rulers, French Curves** Great tools for drawing straight, smooth, and curvy lines. Also, French curves are great for aiding with any type of curved line you are attempting to draw.
- **Modeling Clay** Any form of clay, which might help you to better visualize the object that you have in mind. Try using Super Sculpey, since it doesn't dry out and can be reused.
- **A Nice Desk for Drawing** Remember, you're going to be there a while so make sure it's comfortable.
- **White Board** Great for roughing out ideas in a large group.

- **An Anatomy Book** Always a handy tool to have, especially for those that need a little help now and then on anatomy.
- **Reference Material** This is any and everything that gets your brain jumping with ideas. It could range from toys, cartoons, the real world, comic books, or even your favorite computer games.
- **Friends** Some of us may need a little help from our fellow friends. Maybe they can throw a new thought your way or even keep you focused on your tasks.

Now that we have all the tools, let's get started drawing.

PLANNING YOUR SKETCHES

The first step in sketching your ideas is to jot down a list of the pictures you want to create. Writing them down first also helps you keep an organized checklist of what you have done and what is still to come. As you can see from the sketch list, this is a big job.

SKETCH LIST

- Ancient Barbarian
- Female Marine
- Civil War Soldier
- Cartoon Hero
- Cartoon Villain
- Horse
- Stegosaurus
- Car
- Sci-Fi Van
- Mech Robot

When you begin listing the characters you may need in your world, be sure to include everything. By keeping a concise list, you won't have to keep adding new objects you may have forgotten — plan carefully. Including a brief description of each drawing is also very helpful. For example, under Cartoon Hero, you may include a description of his looks, height, clothing colors, and even his personality, also referred to as a Character bible. If someone else will be drawing the character for you, especially if you work in a company with different task groups, having all the details in the description will ensure that you get back what you had originally conceived.

The next step is to draw each item on the list according to the description and specs. Remember, if there are several different people drawing your images, there may be many revisions before you get exactly what you want. This phase can be time-consuming and sometimes frustrating, but it's the opportunity to get your ideas sketched just right so that when you go to model them, you are completely ready.

GENERIC HUMAN PROPORTIONS

Computer games usually include a variety of human characters and to model these cool characters, we need to understand the basic principles of human figures. The best way to get a grasp of what a human looks like is to go stand in front of a mirror. Stare at yourself or a friend, and begin studying what makes you, you. Notice that you and a friend may be completely different heights, weights, and color. Begin observing people at a local mall or movie theater. Small features like eyebrows and hairstyle can completely change the look of an individual. Our differences are what make us unique individuals. It helps to provide us with a sense of who we are and what we will become. It's amazing how different we all are when you actually take the time to observe others. But it does bring about the point that we are all generally the same. Most people have a set of arms and legs, two eyes, one mouth, and a nose. In general, there is a set principle for what a person looks like. The following information provides a solid starting point, including the front, side, and back view sketches of a male and female character (See Figures 1.1, 1.2, and 1.3). By using generic proportions and defined measurements for each figure, they can be accurately drawn and reused for a number of different projects.

Each figure can have different proportions and measurements. These listed are simply the most standard sizes for artists to use.

GENERIC MALE SKETCH

One really important point to remember when drawing a person is to use the head as a form of measurement. The head is an oval-shaped object, like an egg. When sketching the head, split it through the vertical center, so you can take half of that measurement and use it to determine the horizontal length. The length of the head should be three times half the width of the face. This will provide you with a proportionate oval-shaped head. In Figure 1.2, we have all the basic proportions of the head marked for you to use.

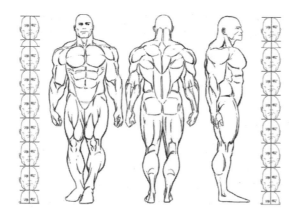

FIGURE *Front, back, and side sketch of male figure.*
1.1

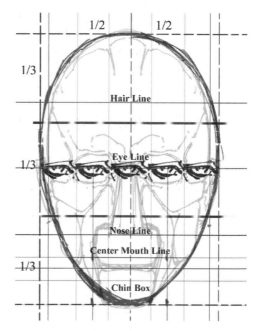

FIGURE *Shape and proportion of the human*
1.2 *head.*

The male figure can stand anywhere from seven and a half heads to eight and three-quarter heads tall, for the full-figure length. So, using the head as the measuring tool, the males' basic proportions and lengths are as follows:

The Body: From the shoulder line down to the bottom of the stomach line is three heads. If you follow the lines across the pictures, you will notice that they divide at the bottom of the chest, the belly, and the crotch.

The Neck: At the base of the neck to the top of the chin, you have about half a head length when the neck is straight.

The Legs: Three to four heads long, from the great trochanter (the pelvis area) to the anklebone. The legs are isometric, so to find the knees, divide the legs through the center. Also, feet are usually one and one-third heads long and half a head wide.

The Arms: Two and three-quarter heads long. The arm starts at the collarbone and ends at the wrist. To find the elbow, just draw a line from the belly over on a slow arch up. Hands are three-quarter heads long. It's basically the distance from your chin to your hairline. The width of the hand is one-quarter of the head wide.

These are the basic measurements for drawing a male figure in proper proportion.

GENERIC FEMALE SKETCH

As with the male, it is best to use the head as the form of measurement. The female figure can stand anywhere from seven and a half heads to eight heads tall for the full-figure length. So, using the head as the measuring tool, the female's basic proportions and lengths are as follows:

The Body: From the shoulder line down to the bottom of the stomach line is two and one-half heads. If you follow the lines across the pictures, you will notice that they divide at the bottom of the chest, the beginning of the oblique, and the crotch.

The Neck: At the base of the neck to the top of the chin, you have about one-quarter to a half a head length when the neck is straight. A half a head length would only be present with some actresses and most models.

The Legs: Three to four heads long, from the great trochanter (the pelvis area) to the anklebone. The legs are isometric, so to find the knees, divide the legs through the center. Females, in general, have a smaller leg width and tend not to have hairy legs. Think of them as soft cylinders rather than a set of bulging muscles. The underlining anatomy of a female is exactly the same as a male except that the definitions tend not to be as showy. When drawing a female be sure to keep in mind that you want her soft, smooth, and elegant. Also, feet are usually one and one-third heads long and half a head wide.

The Arms: Two and three-quarter heads long. The arm starts at the collarbone and ends at the wrist. To find the elbow, just draw a line from the belly over on a slow arch up. Hands are three-quarters of a head long. It's basically the distance from your chin to your hairline. The width of the hand is one-quarter of the head wide.

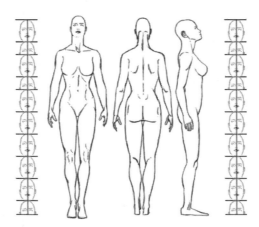

FIGURE
1.3 *Front, back, and side sketch of female figure.*

All of these measurements closely resemble the measurements of the male figure, except that the distance of the waist is only one-half of a head and the limbs are more slender and soft.

When coming up with your next wave of characters, simply make photocopies of these characters, and then draw your costumes, weight differences, and the characters' distinct features on these figures. This technique will help you create new ideas quickly and more efficiently. For those who have difficulty drawing, you now have a definitive human to use with your own costume and characteristic ideas. The next sets of characters to be covered in Chapter 2 were designed using this very method.

CHAPTER

2

Sketching Characters

HUMAN CHARACTERS

Now it's time to put our new art tools, paper, and imagination to use! Let's begin drawing the characters that we have on our checklist from Chapter 1.

ANCIENT BARBARIAN

The first character we are going to sketch is the Ancient Barbarian. For those who need measurements and proportions, please refer to Figures 1.1 or 1.3 on pgs. 7 and 8, where we sketched the male and female characters. We want to come up with an Ancient Barbarian, so we need to define how we imagine him to look. He's an older guy with a battle-scarred look; he has three black circle tattoos on his forehead that give him a tag mark (a mark, feature, or look that makes a character unique and distinguishable), and he's a little heftier than most men. The Barbarian also has a skirt and a set of black armbands that go all the way up each arm. Since he is probably an outdoor type of guy, he should have a big set of boots as well. Look at Figure 2.1 to see how we have interpreted the character from this description into an actual image.

Remember to use the front, side, and back view principle when providing character concepts. Since the model is in 3D, knowledge of what the character looks like from all angles provides the modeler with the best views to model from.

One more thing to point out is that the modeler should have no difficulty in modeling the Barbarian since we now have a front, side, and back view drawing of him. When drawing, it's fun to sketch the characters in cool action poses, but keep in mind that a modeler will need a front, side, and back view of the characters more often than an action pose. When you have finished the necessary sketches, then you can take the time to have fun and draw a few action poses with the character.

Sketching the face at this point is also important, because it defines the details of his scars and tattoos. The decorative circles on his head, or tattoos, a big beard, and a bald head, are a few of the tag marks that help to distinguish him from other characters. By defining these marks, you'll do a much more effective job of modeling him exactly as you want him later (See Figure 2.2).

ON THE CD

At this point, the character is basically done, but if you are interested in seeing how he would look in color, grab your markers and go to town. Make photocopies or print the picture of the Barbarian from the CD-ROM and try a handful of different color ideas; they can give you a great sense of his mood and expression. Try to picture how you would like to see him in a game. You will find that you can come up with many different looks for your Ancient Barbarian (See Figure 2.3).

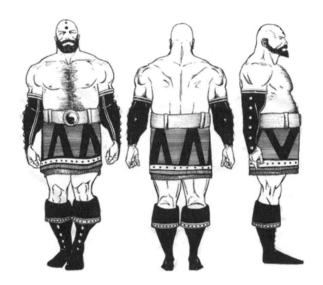

FIGURE **2.1** *Front, back, and side view sketches of the Barbarian.*

FIGURE **2.2** *Head sketch of the Barbarian.*

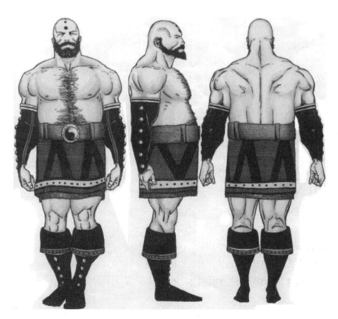

FIGURE **2.3** *Final Barbarian.*

If you've got a cool idea for a pose, go ahead and draw it now. Animators can gain a lot of insight into his character, attitude, personality, and movement by seeing your pose ideas (e.g., Is he running toward an opponent in battle with a heavy spear held high above his head, or is he slumping over a recently wounded victim?). There are many possibilities, but try at least one to give a real sense of what this character is all about. In Figure 2.4, we have an example of a generic man hunched over with clenched fists, ready to attack. The important thing to notice here is that we have a very sketchy form. This style of drawing is very useful when coming up with an action pose or any gesture in general. Be sure when you are drawing to keep your hand really loose and relaxed. There's no need to choke your pencil to death. Also, notice the small thumbnail sketches of the human poses in Figure 2.5. Drawing little sketches of your characters is a great way to start the action poses off. This gives you a starting point to go from when you draw the character larger.

The final thing we need to add to the Barbarian is the Mystic Sword of Truth. Our Barbarian never leaves his cottage without having his trusty sword at his side. Figure 2.6 shows a front-view sketch of the Mystic Sword of Truth. Notice how we have drawn in the details of the hilt and the blade in order for us to generate some good ideas for a texture map later.

Now that we have our Barbarian and his sword finished, we can work on our ideas for the Female Marine. However, if you are dying to continue working on the Ancient Barbarian, skip ahead to the next part of the book, and start modeling him. But remember, the best way to create a game is to take it one step at a time: the more organized you are, the better your game will be.

FIGURE **2.4** *Sketch of a generic man in an action pose.*

FIGURE **2.5** *Thumbnail sketches of action poses.*

FIGURE **2.6** *Sketch of the sword.*

FEMALE MARINE

Our female character will be a marine, sort of like Demi Moore in *GI Jane*. Since the Marine needs to be more feminine than Demi was, we'll keep a shoulder-length hairstyle on her and give her a curvy, athletic-looking body. Being part of the Marines, she needs to have a pair of camouflage pants and a white sleeveless t-shirt. Some black boots will complete her outfit. Keep in mind that she may be a lady, but she can be as tough and rough as a man when she's called into duty. Now, just like we did on the male figure, we are going to take the description of her and draw a picture of what we think the woman should look like. Figure 2.7 shows how we would interpret the character from words to an actual image. Remember to use the generic female from Figure 1.3 on pg. 8. Just make photocopies of it and start designing the costume.

Once again, you have to know what the character looks like from all angles. The most important sketches you can give to a modeler would be a front, side, and back view. A close-up of the face would be a great idea at this point, too, so that you can emphasize any specific facial features or markings that will be important in the final model (See Figure 2.8).

The close-up of her face helps us to define her hairstyle, and provides a better understanding of her facial structure. Besides, it's great to look at!

At this point, the Marine is done. Now, let's get the markers out and do a color guide of her. Make photocopies of the drawing and try doing a handful of different color ideas. You will find that you can come up with a lot of different

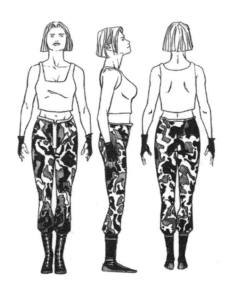

FIGURE
2.7 *Finished design for the Female Marine.*

FIGURE
2.8 *Head sketch of Marine.*

looks for the Marine. Figure 2.9 shows a good final sketch of the Marine. You can see the color version on the CD-ROM.

A few action poses or gesture sketches of the Marine can be drawn now. Other than that, the Marine is complete. Figure 2.10 is a sketch of a generic female in an action pose. At this stage in the drawing she could be anyone you want. Notice how she's drawn in the same sketchy form. Try some rough poses on your own and see what you come up with.

The last thing we need to add to the Marine is a weapon. Why don't we give her a futuristic-looking machine gun, something that would protect her from any number of enemies. Figure 2.11 shows a sketch of what we could use for her weapon and it gives us a good idea of a texture map for later. If you have another idea in mind, draw it now so that it can be her official weapon.

You should be getting the hang of the character sketches now and your artistic hands are probably all warmed up. This is a great time to do a quick sketch of a Princess, so that we can see how simple it is to change the generic female into royalty. Not all characters you create will be rough and tough. The ones that add true enjoyment to games are often the characters of noble blood. A Princess perhaps— one whose look and actions are that of the finest ladies. Since England has long line of royalty why not adorn the Princess in the costume of an English lady. She should be elegant and refined, with a gentleness that could sooth the wildest beasts. In Figure 2.12, the idea for the Princess has been

FIGURE **2.9** *Final sketch of the Marine.*

FIGURE **2.10** *Generic female action pose.*

sketched and to the side we've given her a magic wand that will protect her from any evil in the world.

ON THE CD

This is definitely a great example of how easy it is to work from the generic figures provided on the CD-ROM. Remember: you don't have to be a Leonardo daVinci to pull off a good idea. You just might need a little help.

FIGURE **2.11** *Sketch of Marine's weapon.*

FIGURE **2.12** *Princess with magic wand.*

CIVIL WAR SOLDIER

The Civil War Soldier will be the last human we sketch. Since the Civil War itself was so well-documented, we can do a little research and find details on Civil War costumes. This Soldier is going to be a typical Union infantryman from the North, so he will be wearing a blue uniform with a brownish color hat. The hat could be black (officer's hat) or even blue, but we are going to choose brown, since he may have been a farmer before he joined, and that was his favorite hat. We'll also add a pair of tan gloves to him, which were often used by the soldiers to keep their hands warm and protected. Now, just like the previous two sketches, we are going to take the description of him and draw the Soldier. Figure 2.13 shows the basic look of the infantry Soldier. Remember to use the generic male from the sketches in Chapter 1, and just make photocopies or print the images from the CD-ROM, so you can start designing the costume.

ON THE CD

The Soldier's physical proportions are going to be slightly smaller than the generic body so that you can see how simple it is to play around with the generic figure. When you are using the generic figures, be sure to use them as a basis for the character, not as the only option available.

When drawing the Soldier, make sure that the front, side, and back views are well-established, so the modeler will have a solid foundation to work with. Next, we need to create some kind of color guide. Since the Soldier is from the North, coloring him in shades of blue is essential. Take a look at Figure 2.14 to see what the final Soldier looks like. You can also see the color version on the CD-ROM. If you would like to create your own interpretations of him, go for it!

ON THE CD

The last thing we want to do with the Soldier is put him into a pose. The next style of drawing you can do is a scribble-like drawing. Take a look at the Soldier in Figure 2.15 and notice how the whole picture was drawn in a very rough, scribble-like state. This is really an enjoyable and easy method for drawing. It allows you to stay loose with the details, but still come across with a solid layout and design.

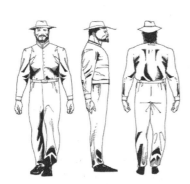

FIGURE **2.13** *Sketch of the Civil War Soldier.*

FIGURE **2.14** *Final sketch of Soldier.*

FIGURE **2.15** *Sketch of Civil War Soldier.*

CARTOON CHARACTERS

Cartoon characters are simple-shaped, outline drawings with over-exaggerated features, sometimes portraying real-life people and images. There has never been a set pattern or style for drawing cartoon characters; it is mainly up to the artist and his or her creative mind that determines the look and personality of the characters being created. Many cartoon-styled characters have made their way into video games for young and old kids alike to interact and play along with. Our goal in this chapter is to create a couple of cartoon characters, which will provide us with the practice necessary to understand what it takes to sketch believable cartoon characters. First, let's look at the underlining of cartoon characters. In Figure 2.16 we have several loosely drawn ovals. These ovals are some of the many soft cartoon shapes that go into making cartoon heads and bodies. The big gorilla-like man and bean man in Figure 2.17 show the ovals being used. This is the rough stage, right before I'd clean them up and sharpen the lines. Notice that the arms and legs look like a water hose. There is no definite shape in them and that's what gives a cartoon its cuteness and believability.

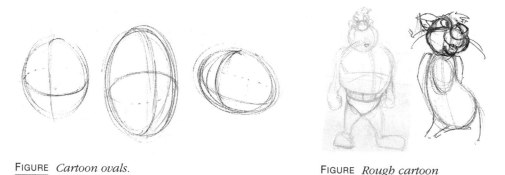

FIGURE **2.16** *Cartoon ovals.*

FIGURE **2.17** *Rough cartoon characters.*

CARTOON HERO CONCEPT SKETCH

The first cartoon character we will work on is the Hero. First, let's describe who this short-looking fellow is. The Hero is a guard from a small village in search of an emerald, which was stolen from his peoples town center. He was sent out to reclaim it, since it was his fault the emerald was stolen (he was sleeping on the job). Let's say, for his sake, that he has a lot of learning to do before he can successfully wear the name of the Hero. He will be a lot smaller than the standard male figure, standing only three heads tall. The heights for cartoon characters are not predefined nor are they set in stone, so you have the opportunity to draw them as short or as tall as you like. The Hero should have really large feet, which allow him to have a cute wobble as he walks and runs. Another distinguishing feature on the Hero is his nose, because it is rather large, just like the noses of the people from his village. This will continue to make the Hero look and feel like a cartoon character with exaggerated features. His feet and his nose both increase the detail of the profile, which is something you should keep in mind when creating a cartoon character since most of the shape found in cartoon characters is in the profile view. The Hero, is a guard so he should have a guard-like outfit. Since his people live in the forest, we should give him a pair of camouflage pants and a dark-colored t-shirt to help him blend in with the forest and look guardian-like (See Figure 2.18).

Just like with the human figures, we have included a front, side, and back sketch of the Hero. These are still the most important sketches a modeler will need. After these positions have been drawn, any other extra poses can be sketched for further examples.

Once the character has been illustrated, he needs color! The finished Hero is shown in Figure 2.19. You can see the color version on the CD-ROM. Since this is a cartoon character, we need to place solid colors on him. Keep the Hero bright and cheerful-looking so that he will stand out as a definite good guy.

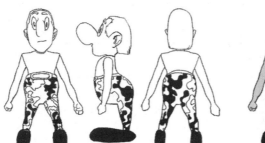

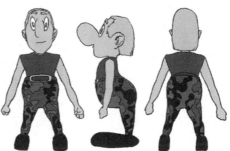

FIGURE **2.18**   *Sketch of Hero concept.*

FIGURE **2.19**   *Finished design for the Hero.*

If you would like to create a different color guide than Figure 2.19, go right ahead and do it. He might look good with brown hair and a black shirt. You never know until you try it.

NOTE

Let's take a moment to compare the Hero with other typical cartoon characters. In Figure 2.20, we have head shots of two characters. The eyes of the rabbit and the farmer are the same style as that of the Hero. They've all got those big teardrops-shaped eyes. Next, in Figure 2.21, there are a few gesture poses with cartoon bodies. Notice how the Hero's body resembles their bodies. They also have the same type of lanky arms and legs, and each of them are similar heights.

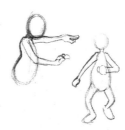

FIGURE **2.20**   *Head shots of cartoon characters.*

FIGURE **2.21**   *Gestures of cartoon characters.*

Next on the list is an evil Villain that will give the Hero a reason for having an adventure.

CARTOON VILLAIN CONCEPT SKETCH

The Villain needs to be somewhat larger and overbearing compared to the Hero. Let's make him about five heads tall and give him a really big belly. Next, give the Villain a black shirt and some bushy hair on his head. The basic idea for the Villain should look like Figure 2.22.

We have sketched a front, side, and back view of the Villain. Once again, these are always the most important sketches a modeler will need. After completing the main sketches, you can pose the character in some livelier positions to see how he might walk or fight in a game. Take your time before moving on and be sure that you have really gotten to know the character being created. You will do your best designing when you really know the character being drawn.

ON THE CD

With the Villain sketch done, we can create a color guide for him. Check out Figure 2.23 to see the final look for the Villain, and view the colored image on the CD-ROM. The Villain's camouflage pants have been colored in with darker tones than the Hero's pants. By using darker colors on the pants and a dark reddish tone for the hair, the Villain seems more wicked and evil. He kind of resembles a biker in a funny cartoon sort of way. Be sure that the side view of the Villain pushes the boundaries of size limits, as shown in Figure 2.23.

FIGURE *Sketch of Villain concept.*
2.22

FIGURE *Finished design for the Villain.*
2.23

ANIMALS

HORSE

The horse is one of the more difficult things to draw, so we need to take a moment and look at the shapes of a horse. In Figure 2.24, we have a basic drawing for a horse, or almost any four-legged animal. The body of the animal is made with the large oval in the center. On each side we have a shape that looks like the number 3, which represents the shoulder and upper leg. Below the body are box-like shapes for the lower portion of the legs, and next to the body is another oval for the head. Now in Figure 2.25, the horse's shape has been roughed in using the basic shapes shown in Figure 2.24.

Figure 2.26 shows one large circle and one small circle connected by two lines, which are the basics of an animal head. Next to that, there are two creature heads drawn (See Figure 2.27). The main thing to notice is that both of the creatures have been drawn using the same basic head, but by changing slight features, we were able to draw two very different-looking animals. Try comparing the creature heads with the horse's head in Figure 2.25, and then see if you can come up with a few different designs on your own.

Let's begin designing the Horse that we need. Our Horse is going to be a wild stallion that roams the countryside in search of adventure and the good life. A horse is usually drawn with tack, but no man has ever saddled or ridden this Horse. That's what makes him so special; he's free from the burdens of this world and the laws of man (See Figure 2.28).

FIGURE **2.24** *Basic shapes for animals.*

FIGURE **2.25** *Rough of a horse.*

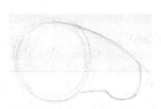

FIGURE **2.26** *Animal head basics.*

FIGURE **2.27** *Two creature heads.*

FIGURE   *Front, side, and back views of the Horse.*
2.28

Be sure that you know what the Horse looks like from all angles. This can be achieved by having the sketches of the Horse or even a toy horse found at any toy store. We will not go into the measurements of the Horse, because we could fill up a whole book with just that information. The best thing would be to be sure to print the pictures provided on the CD-ROM and draw from those. That should set you up.

ON THE CD

At this point, the Horse is ready for color. Make photocopies of the drawings or print the pictures from the CD-ROM and try doing a handful of different color ideas. Try to picture how the Horse might look in a game. Try coming up with several different versions. In Figure 2.29, we have created the final look, and on the CD-ROM you can see the color version of the Horse. If you'd like, create a black stallion, a spotted horse, or even a purple polka-dotted rabid horse. Just have fun with it.

FIGURE   *Final Horse sketch.*
2.29

Now we can move on to a creature from our history books — the stegosaurus. This dinosaur has not been used that often, but it is loads of fun to draw and model. With his huge body, scales along his back, and his tiny brain, it's no wonder why he's a hit at all the parties!

STEGOSAURUS

We are going to design a Stegosaurus. This will be a good example for illustrating the basic principles behind creating a unique character. There are a lot of toy dinosaurs on the market today for reference, so be sure and pick one up if you need to examine the creatures fully. Figure 2.30 shows a basic drawing of the Stegosaurus's underlining shapes. When you compare this with the shapes of the Horse in Figure 2.28, it's evident that both are almost the same. The Stegosaurus has a much larger oval for the body and rib cage than the Horse. Also, the legs are shorter than the Horse's legs, so that his belly nearly touches the ground. Finally, look at the Stegosaurus's head; it's very small in relation to his body, unlike the Horse's head.

In Figure 2.31, the design of the Stegosaurus has been provided for you. At this point, you can go wild with it and stick nuclear cannons on the sides and a laser beam from its head. Or maybe make it civilized and put clothes on it. It's completely up to you at this point.

When drawing an animal, dinosaur, or any creature that you have a picture of, make sure to grab it and use it as a reference. Pictures or toys can help tremendously in coming up with the look of the characters.

With the Stegosaurus basically done, we can add color to create a scary, frightening animal, or a cuddly, cute one. Make photocopies of the drawing and create a handful of different color ideas. Try to picture what the Stegosaurus

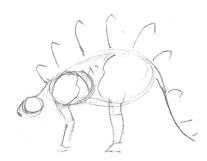

FIGURE **2.30** *Basic shapes for a stegosaurus.*

FIGURE **2.31** *Top, side, and front views of the Stegosaurus.*

would look like in a game. He might be purple, green, or even brown. Colors can give a great distinction between your dinosaur and the next guy's. You will find that it is quite easy to come up with a lot of different looks for this big fellow. Go ahead and try some. Figure 2.32 shows the final version we came up with, which can be viewed in color on the CD-ROM.

ON THE CD

We chose to make the body color of the Stegosaurus dirt brown with some pale-looking browns for the scale parts.

> *The color guides that you are creating should really be solid, broad strokes of color. We aren't trying to paint the real texture map (that's for the texture section). The main objective is to create the mood and presence the Stegosaurus will have on the screen. If you can capture that, then you will have no problem bringing to life whatever you draw.*

NOTE

The characters are all finished, but the artistic mind needs more! In Chapter 3, we will sketch some great examples of vehicles. So, sharpen those pencils and start your engines!

FIGURE *Finished design for the Stegosaurus.*
2.32

3

Sketching Vehicles

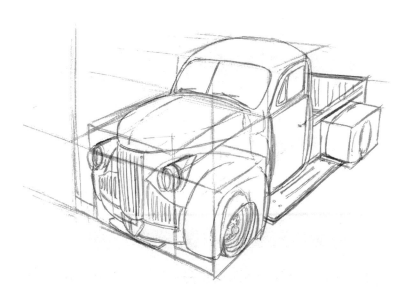

In this chapter we are going to sketch our vehicles, and the techniques used here are very similar to those used for the characters.

CAR

We will begin this section by doing a few preliminary sketches of a car. The vehicle you might have to draw could be a hover car, with tiny wings and a huge jet engine on it. Then again, you might need to come up with the next greatest racecar. Whatever the case may be, let's start off by covering the basic principles of sketching a vehicle. The most important rule of drawing is to obtain a solid foundation in normal objects, like cars and planes, before moving on to creating spaceships and hover bikes. By having this knowledge, you will be able to create futuristic vehicles and yet still keep it grounded so that the objects are realistic and recognizable. In Figure 3.1, we have drawn several shapes in perspective. These shapes are the basic building blocks for cars, ships, and even futuristic vehicles. Take a moment and sketch the shapes yourself. Make sure that you are familiar with each object before we move on to building a car.

With the shapes in Figure 3.1, let's make a vehicle. Look at Figure 3.2 to see how we apply the objects to one another to create an old-looking work truck. Notice that we have used perspective points to guide us in drawing the truck properly. This helps to make the truck more realistic and create some really interesting depth.

Now that we have an understanding of basic shapes and objects, let's design a cruising car which makes the drive into work that much more bearable. Time to go to the drawing board and see what we can come up with (See Figure 3.3).

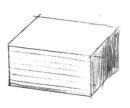

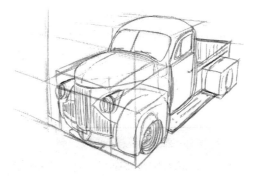

FIGURE
3.1 *Basic shapes.*

FIGURE
3.2 *Sketch of an old truck.*

FIGURE   *Multiple sketches of the Car.*
3.3

Even on a vehicle, it's a great idea to draw what it looks like from all angles. As always, the main sketch should be a solid side shot. The side view sketch for a vehicle is the one view (as we stated before) that gives the models all their shape and form.

NOTE

ON THE CD

At this point, our stylish car is ready to be colored. Make photocopies of your drawing or print the images from the CD-ROM and try doing a handful of different color ideas. Refer to Figure 3.4 in the book and in color on the CD-ROM. Try to picture how you would like to see this car racing around the corners of a game or animation. There are a variety of different paint jobs you can do for a car, and if you are having trouble coming up with some ideas, go buy a car magazine or drive to a mall and look at the parking lot filled with a wide range of colorful cars. Maybe your car is totally tricked out or has big numbers on the sides of the doors. Whatever you want, it's your world.

Our design for the Car is completed. It would be very simple to change the body of this Car into virtually any other style of vehicle, plane, or spaceship, if you wanted. So, once you get this one down really well, you can branch out to other types of cars. Let's move onto the Sci Fi Van to investigate the different details it entails.

SCI-FI VAN

The Van of the future is what some might picture when they are trying to come up with the next wave of Van designs. We need something that will conveniently haul the kids back and forth from Cyber School, and still allow us to

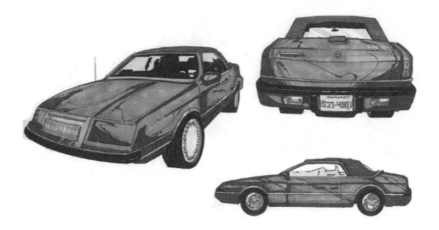

FIGURE   *Final sketch of the Car.*
3.4

enjoy flying around. So, the first thing we need to add to the Van will be rocket boosters. This will ensure that you are never late for anything again. Of course the wheels would serve us better if they provided the Van with vertical takeoff. The last thing a future Van needs is a rounder body. Try sketching your own version of a Sci Fi Van following the guidelines we've provided: be creative.

Be sure that the Van sketches include the top view as well as the front and side views. The side view sketch will provide the primary shape for the Van, but almost equally as important will be the top view sketch. This sketch will help the modeler in determining the actual distance one object is from another.

Now the Sci-Fi Van is ready to be colored. Print the images from the CD-ROM and make several photocopies of it. Try to picture how this Van might look flying around in space or landing in a parking lot. We are going to choose very soft gray tones to color the Van. If you have another idea for the Van, start coloring — your imagination is your only limitation. Check out our color solutions for

ON THE CD   Figure 3.5 on the CD-ROM.

The Van is basically finished, so let's move onto the Mech Robot.

FIGURE *Finished Van.*
3.5

MECH ROBOT

Robots can be anything from an automated butler to a fierce fighting machine. Let's take a look at the kinds of shapes that can be used to create robots and machines. In Figure 3.6, we have a cute-looking kitchen cooker. The objects next to our chef are the basic shapes that went into his design. Try drawing a few of these objects to get comfortable with robot shapes and parts. Then, using a pencil or pen, sketch a robot like the chef using the shapes shown in Figure 3.6.

ON THE CD

FIGURE *Chef and robot shapes.*
3.6

ON THE CD

The next design we need to come up with is the Mech Robot. This Robot should be slick, tough, and very fast-looking. It does most of its combat in the air but, if required, can move very well through and over rough terrain. Let's say the Robot has a cockpit for one pilot and enough guns to fight off an entire army. There are no exact measurements for robots; it's purely up to the artist's imagination and size of paper. With all this in mind, we came up with Figure 3.7.

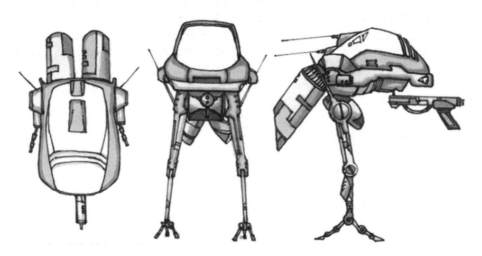

FIGURE *Finished concepts for the Mech Robot.*
3.7

As always, be sure to include all the appropriate views.

NOTE

ON THE CD

At this point, the Mech Robot is basically finished, but you can go ahead and apply your color preferences. You can see our selection on the CD-ROM.

This completes the concepts for each vehicle. If your mind is going crazy with more ideas and pictures, then grab another piece of paper and start drawing.

SUMMARY OF CONCEPT ART AND DESIGN

As you have learned from the chapters in Part 1, there are many factors involved in creating and designing a model. Imagine that what has been sketched in the previous chapters is only a tenth of what an artist may have to draw for an entire project. Many times it can require hundreds of pictures. This part of the development phase should be regarded as one of the most important phases. In doing these steps correctly, the concepts will be defined and then redefined long before a modeler begins creating a 3D model. Be sure all of your sketches have a solid front, back, side, and sometimes a top view. Action poses are fun to draw and give a good sense of character personality, but be sure to sketch these only when the initial poses have been completed. The last step in creating a sketch is to color the finished drawing. Color guides are an excellent resource for a modeler or a texture person. At this point, you should have a strong sense of what kind of concept work it takes to generate the actual models in a computer game. Using what you have learned and applying it to your next idea should allow you to dream a little bigger and create a world in which your imagination is the only limitation to how far you can go.

Let's move on to Part 2, Modeling in 3D, and put these sketches to use!

Modeling in 3D

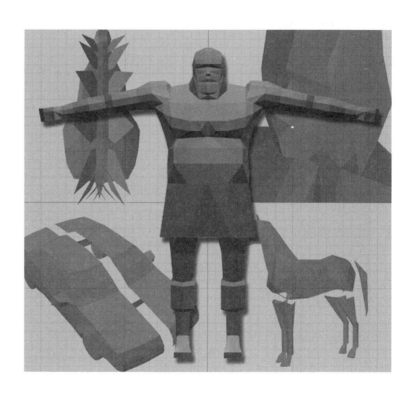

We are now entering the world of polygons, vertices, and edges. Modeling an object in 3D is much different than drawing a picture. Polygons, by their definition, are flat, finite-sized objects with a set number of at least three sides. Each side on the polygon is a vertex, or a point that defines a corner of the polygon where two or more lines meet. To create 3D models using polygons, especially ones with a low poly count, you need to understand how they work and you need the right set of tools. In this part we are going to see what kind of programs are out there, the features that we'll be using from them, and all the steps necessary to accurately model from the sketches that we have drawn. To assist you in the developing the models, all the 3D models that we will create are on the CD-ROM saved in different stages of the modeling process.

ON THE CD

4

Introduction to Low Polygon Techniques

SOFTWARE PROGRAMS

3D applications are everywhere. You can get freeware, shareware, low-cost and even high-end professional packages. Anything that allows the user to model in 3D will get the job done. Following is a list of 3D software programs that might be worth purchasing:

- Discreet *3D Studio Max*
- Alias Wavefront *Maya*
- New Tech *Lightwave*
- Maxon *Cinema 4D XL*
- Rober McNeel and Associates *Rhino*
- Eovia *Carrara*
- Caligari truespace
- Hash *Animation:Master*

These are all excellent programs to use for modeling 3D objects, and everything in this book can be created using any of these programs. 3D modeling programs all involve the use of polygons, vertices, and faces. Most of these applications also use nurbs, but for practical purposes of low poly modeling, we'll stick to using polygons. Now, there's no need to go out and break your bank account just because you don't have a certain program (but if you really want to, go ahead). Some of the software listed above can be purchased for around $200 (Animation:Master), and they can all do about the same job, although the higher end tools will have additional features. (If you are a student, most of these companies offer special student pricing or you can try purchasing through companies such as Journey Education.) The end result is that all of these programs allow you to model in 3D.

The tools that will be used are universal with almost all the programs. They might be named slightly different, but they will perform the job just the same. To make the modeling process easier, we have kept the tools used down to a minimum. Following is a list of tools that will be used throughout the entire modeling section, so if you've got these, then you should have no problem.

- **Move, Rotate, and Scale**
  These actions are used for maneuvering around the 3D model and scaling an object in size. These are also standard for any 3D application.

- **2D Line tool and 2D Shape tools (Splines)**
  The 2D tools are used for outlining and creating the basic shapes of the 3D models. It is basically like using a pencil, except that you can extrude it into a 3D form.

- **Vertices, Edge, and Face tools**
  These tools are used for selecting, creating, and deleting polygons and vertices on a 3D model. This is standard for any 3D application. They are commonly found under the Edit Mesh option.

- **Extrude**
  The extruding tool is used for creating a three-dimensional shape out of a flat two-dimensional outline. It is commonly found in most 3D applications.

- **Duplicate and Mirror**
  The duplicate tool is simply the command for copying a selected 3D object. The mirror command is used for flipping the object around so that you have an exact opposite copy of the original model. Both of these tools can be commonly found under the Edit menu button.

- **Weld**
  Welding is used for attaching two vertices together. This tool will be used quite a bit, so make sure that you know where it is. The tool can usually be found under the Vertices option menu.

- **Divide and Flip**
  The divide tool is used to create a new edge on a polygon. It is often needed when creating more of a curve to the surface of the polygons. The flip command simply turns the selected edge over to the other two vertices. Both of these tools are found under the Edge option menu.

- **Polygon Counter**
  The polygon counter keeps track of how many polygons have been created on the 3D model. This can come in handy if you have tight restrictions on how many polygons you are allowed to use.

As noted above, the tools used here are very simple and easy to understand. We are not going to use any "special features" to create the 3D models. This is what makes the process work. A good working knowledge of any 3D application is required before moving on. If you have just purchased a 3D modeling program, please take the time to read the program manual and get a firm understanding of the tools listed above.

3D MODELING MADE EASY

Now that you know which programs are available and which features you need to focus on, let's start with the modeling process. Just as in drawing, there is a pattern and method to modeling an object in 3D. Let's look at some practical ways we can create 3D objects.

We have divided the 3D modeling process into the following six major steps:

DRAW IT WITH A LINE TOOL

This step is the first and probably most important step. Here, the sketches need to be placed in the background of the view ports or under a drawing tablet. The only tools needed for this are the 2D line tool, and the 2D object tools. With the 2D line tool selected and the sketches in the background, we will outline the side view of the character. Each part of the sketch, such as the arm, leg, body, or head, is outlined separately. This step is used to get the most important features of the model. By outlining the individual pieces, you will be able to concentrate more effort in a single area rather than attempting to model the entire character at once.

EXTRUDE ALL OBJECTS

Extruding the objects is exactly what it means. Each piece that was outlined with the 2D Line tool will be extruded. Some objects will be extruded to the full width of the sketch (if they are not going to be duplicated), and the others will be extruded to half the distance of the sketch (this will be used if the object needs to be duplicated). The extruding process is helped out by having the front view of the sketch as the background image or right next to you. The front view sketch gives the width and secondary outline of the character, which is used to determine the distance to extrude the 2D line.

REFINE THE SHAPES

Refining the shapes is the first step in making each side of the character presentable. Here, we begin working each extruded object out. The front view and perspective view of the model needs a lot of attention. By taking the front and back view sketches, we correct the secondary outline shape. The secondary outline is simply the outline of the front view. This is also the stage where most of the tweaking and softening takes place.

ATTACH OBJECTS TOGETHER

This step allows us the chance to attach and weld the individual pieces together. There are three processes used in the attaching stage. One process is welding vertices together. This will create a model completely attached as one object.

The second process is used when vertices cannot be welded together; one object is placed next to another object. The last process is not attaching the objects at all. In some cases, you will be required to create a hierarchy character. A hierarchy character is made up of many separate pieces, usually requiring a boning system to animate it. Many times, a vehicle, robot, or even a person requires this system of attachment. This stage is also where the model is duplicated and mirrored.

ADD ACCESSORIES

The next process involved in modeling a character is adding the accessories. Here, we refer to the sketches and determine which objects need to be added and which objects can be pulled straight off the character. Accessories can be anything from a dress to a head of hair. This will also be an important stage for creating a real difference between models.

REDUCE THE MODEL

The final step in modeling is the reduction of polygons in a model, which is also referred to as Level of Detail (LOD). LOD is the use of lower-detail models or geometry to improve performance when a lot of objects are on the screen or an object is seen at a distance not requiring high detail. This is used primarily to reduce polygon count in a scene. When creating characters or objects in a game, you need to take into account the number of polygons that will be viewable in a scene. This is determined by the power of the 3D game engine you may be using. Say, for instance, you are making a first-person shooter game and on average can get 2,000 polygons per character. That would be the highest count and the closest character to you. As the model recedes into the background, it uses LOD testing to exchange the model with a lower-count character. Now a 1,000-count character would replace the original model. Once the character is even farther back, we could then insert a 500-polygon count character.

The human in Figure 4.1 shows how smoothly the transition can be from one model to the next. This is extremely important if you are going to use level of detail on any of your projects. Be sure that each model resembles the other so that there will be no noticeable "popping in" effects, which can happen when one model takes the place of another, causing the changeover to jump or pop in.

As a rule, always create the highest count model first. Reducing a character or object is easier than trying to add to one that doesn't have much shape. With the latest computer game technology, the reduction of a models polygon count is mainly handled by the computer or 3D game engine. In fact, many 3D applications have plug-ins for polygon reduction. One of the best programs is *Rational Reducer*, an excellent stand-alone utility that quickly and accurately reduces the number of polygons in a model, while retaining its original form. (You can

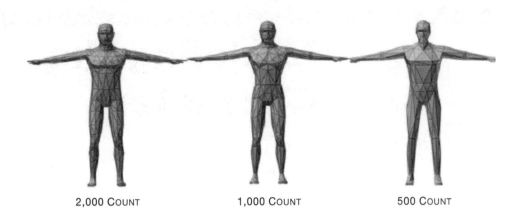

2,000 COUNT   1,000 COUNT   500 COUNT

FIGURE   *Figure 4.1 Model at different polygon counts.*
4.1

download a demo at <u>www.sim.no</u>.) These new reduction technologies mean that artists will have to do less reduction during modeling, but understanding how to manually reduce polygons is still a valuable procedure to know. If you need a character reduced, just follow the steps we mentioned for achieving a lower polygon count model.

Now that we have an idea of what we need to do, let's apply these steps to our modeling projects!

CHAPTER

Modeling the Characters

CREATING 3D MODELS FROM YOUR SKETCHES

To begin modeling any sketch, you will use the techniques detailed in Chapter 4.

The following list of steps will be the formula we use for creating our models. Remember: These are the basic principles and rules which we will follow. If you don't fully understand them, be sure to review Chapter 4, where each step is discussed in detail.

- Draw It with a Line Tool
- Extrude All Objects
- Refine the Shapes
- Attach Objects Together
- Add Accessories

HUMAN CHARACTERS

We will beging the modeling process with the human sketches.

ANCIENT BARBARIAN

ON THE CD

Let's begin modeling with the Barbarian. Go to the tutorial directory on the companion CD-ROM and open the Barbarian folder. In each folder, there are sketches, texture maps, U.V. maps, and the 3D models for you to use while you make the characters. Open your 3D application of choice and then open the Sketches folder and select the images for the Barbarian. Notice that these sketches are the ones we drew in Part 1 of this book. Next, we want to place the images into our 3D application. Most of the 3D programs are generally set up with an option to place an image into the background of your display screen.

NOTE

If you are not familiar with your 3D application, it would be a good idea to review the manuals thoroughly before continuing.

If you have options for where to place the sketches, put them in the following order:

- Side sketch of the Barbarian in the side view port.
- Front sketch of the Barbarian in the front view port.
- Back sketch in the back view port.

For those who only have one display window, make sure you put the side view sketch in that window.

TIP

By placing the sketches in the view ports, you will have an excellent guide to follow. If you are unable to put the pictures in, don't worry; just be sure that you have the pictures right next to you for reference.

Be sure to check out our Web site at www.walkerboystudio.com for all the latest models and textures created using this process. We are continually adding to our libraries and we are always available to help anyone interested in learning to develop their skills in the art of 3D modeling.

Your screen(s) should basically look like Figure 5.1.

Now we need to go to our Tools section. Get the tool that draws 2D lines. Once you have selected it, go to your side view window. In Figure 5.2, you should see a side view of the Barbarian. With the Line tool chosen, we can outline the Barbarian.

The best way to outline the character or object is to divide the drawing into sections. When doing this, you have two options. One option is to create a mesh character (first column) and the second option is to create a hierarchy character (second column).

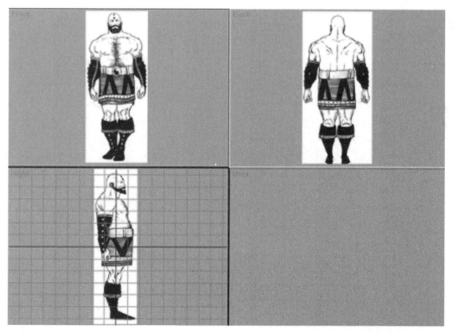

FIGURE *Side, front, and back views.*
5.1

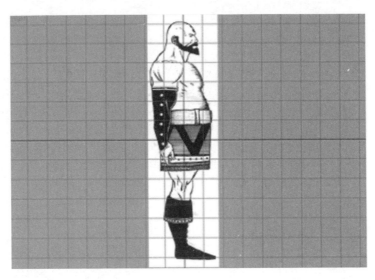

FIGURE   *Side view of the Barbarian.*
5.2

Column 1
- Head
- Body (Chest and Pelvis)
- Arm (Upper Arm, Forearm, and Hand)
- Leg (Thigh, Calf, and Foot)

Column 2
- Head
- Chest
- Pelvis
- Upper Arm
- Forearm
- Hand (Fingers)
- Thigh
- Lower Leg
- Foot

We are going to create a full-mesh character, so we will use the first column layout. If you want a hierarchy character, then separate him as shown in Column 2.

Now that we have an idea of how we are going to outline the Barbarian, it's time to begin.

ANCIENT BARBARIAN

DRAWING THE SHAPES WITH THE LINE TOOL

1. With your 2D Line tool selected, start at the top of the head and work
   around it in a clockwise direction. Be sure to leave the nose off; we will do
   it as a separate piece to be placed on the face later (See Figure 5.3). When
   using the Line tool, be sure to take into account the amount of vertices you
   click. If you want a high polygon character, then you can follow the curves
   of the Barbarian really close. If you are working on a lower count character, then try to catch just the major angles of the object while you outline
   it.

Be sure to place your points in generally the same locations, as
shown in these examples. This will make creating the Barbarian a
TIP *lot easier for you.*

2. Now that we have the side view of the head done, let's continue on with
   the body (chest and pelvis). Begin at the corner of his neck at the back.
   Work your way around in a clockwise fashion, making sure to place each
   point in its appropriate place, as shown in Figure 5.4.

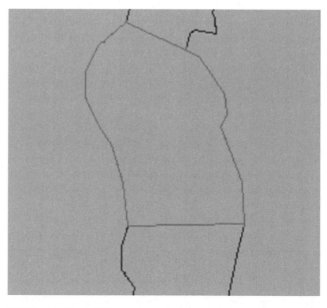

FIGURE *Outline of Barbarian*
5.3 *head.*

FIGURE *Outline of Barbarian chest.*
5.4

We are not following the skirt, but the actual body. This will give us a better model when we get done with him. Also note that the skirt is considered an accessory and will be added later when we do the accessories.

3. The arm (upper arm, forearm, and hand) can now be done. Start at the top of the shoulder and, once again, work your way around it in a clockwise direction. The sketch of the Ancient Barbarian provides a good example of a sculpted arm where the deltoid (shoulder), biceps, and triceps are well-defined. This will transition well into the 3D model if it is outlined properly, so be sure to take your time. If you get it wrong the first time, that's okay; just start over and try it again (See Figure 5.5).

 The hands that we outlined for the Ancient Barbarian are simple block- shape hands. We will use this type of hand first, and then later replace them with real hands.

4. The last object on our list is the leg (thigh, calf, and foot). Begin outlining the shape, starting at the top and working your way around, as shown in Figure 5.6.

Once you have outlined these shapes, your screen should look like Figure 5.7.

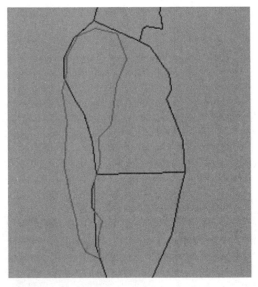

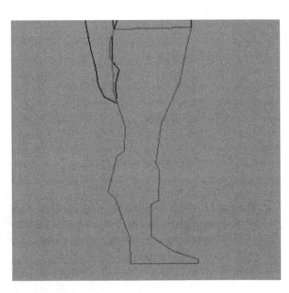

FIGURE *Outline of Barbarian arm.*
5.5

FIGURE *Outline of*
5.6 *Barbarian leg.*

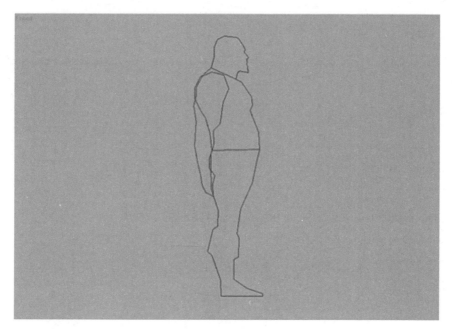

FIGURE   *Finished outline of Barbarian.*
5.7

EXTRUDING ALL YOUR SHAPES

Extruding our shapes into 3D forms is our next task at hand. The Extrude tool is a common tool in 3D programs. We will use it to add depth to the lines we have just created. The first thing to do is to find it, then select the Head Line. Now go to either your perspective view or your front view.

For those working on a single window layout, you should change your side picture to the front picture of the Barbarian.

NOTE

Use the Extrude tool to turn the 2D shapes into 3D objects.

1. We will only be working with half the head width, so extrude the head until it is the width of half the head in the front view (See Figures 5.8 and 5.9). We are going to make a copy of these shapes and mirror them to be used for the other half. When modeling forms and shapes, it's best to create and finish one-half of the object and simply duplicate it, making the other half an exact match. This may feel weird at first, but once you do it a few times you should begin to see the simplicity in all of it.

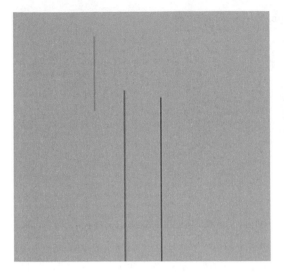

FIGURE **5.8** *Front view, head selected.*

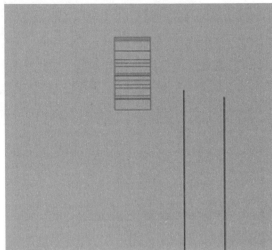

FIGURE **5.9** *Front view, head extruded.*

This process will continue with the rest of the shapes. If you feel like you know how to do it, then go for it! For the rest of us, let's continue.

2. Select the Body (chest and pelvis) Line. Use the Extrude tool to extrude your Body Line out, so that it goes to the center of the body sketch in the front view. Then divide the chest piece in half with another edge (SeeFigures 5.10 and 5.11).

3. Select the Arm (upper arm, forearm, and hand) Line. Using the Extrude tool, pull it out to match the width of the whole arm in the front view of the character sketch (See Figures 5.12 and 5.13).

4. Now select the Leg (thigh, calf, and foot) Line. Use the Extrude tool to pull it out to the width of the whole leg in the front view character sketch. Then divide the leg in half as shown In Figures 5.14 and 5.15.

The front view or perspective view should now look something like Figure 5.16.

With all of the major shapes created, we will proceed to sculpt the figure, just like a sculptor would do with a lump of clay. We need to begin refining the pieces so that they can start to take more shape.

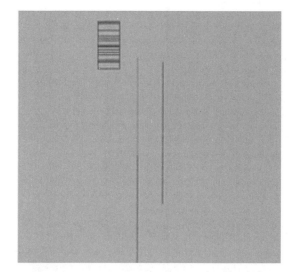

FIGURE
5.10   *Front view, body selected.*

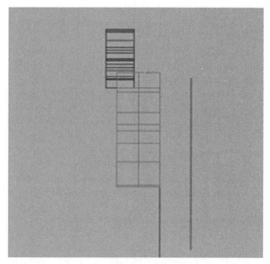

FIGURE
5.11   *Front view, body extruded.*

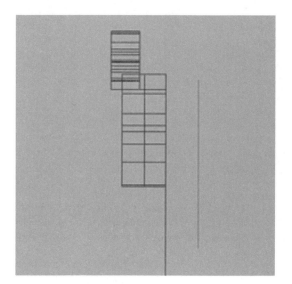

FIGURE
5.12   *Front view, arm selected.*

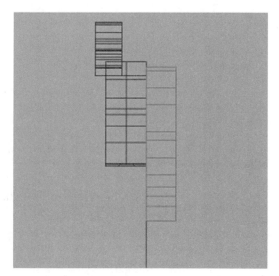

FIGURE
5.13   *Front view, arm extruded.*

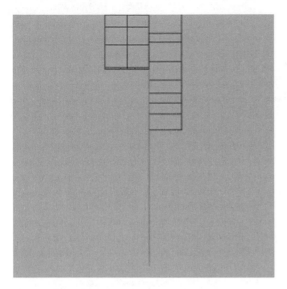

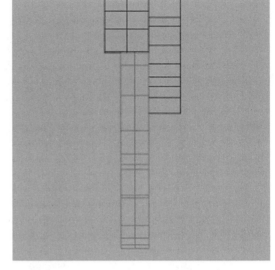

FIGURE
5.14 *Front view, leg selected.*

FIGURE
5.15 *Front view, leg extruded.*

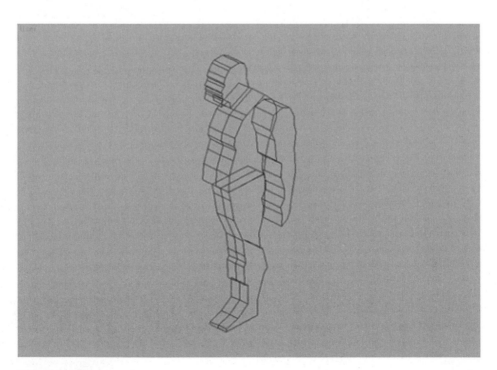

FIGURE *Perspective view.*
5.16

REFINING THE OBJECTS

Each shape that you have outlined and extruded looks really good on a side view. We need to start correcting the front view and three-quarter view. In order for us to fix these views, we will need to use the front, perspective, and possibly the side view ports.

For those with one window, keep it in the perspective view port for most of the time.

When refining the objects, you will need the vertices, polygon, and face tools. Each of these tools will be used for moving, adjusting, and creating a more defined look for the character. There are many "feature tools" in 3D applications, but the vertices, polygon, and edge tools are the true core set of tools used in this modeling process. We will be using the vertices select tool for most of the work that is about to be done.

1. In the perspective view port, select the head object. Remember: This is just half of the head. Next, select the vertices highlighted in Figure 5.17. Now scale all the vertices inward so that you line them up with the profile of the face sketch. Then select and divide two edges on the inside of the head. Next, use the Divide tool to divide the side of the head through the center, as shown in Figure 5.18 below. With the Edge tool selected, flip the edge directions to mimic the edges highlighted. Be sure to line them up in the

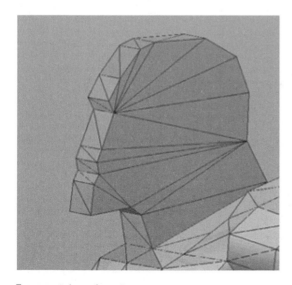

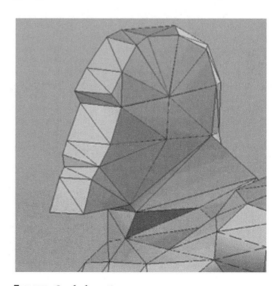

FIGURE *Selected vertices.*
5.17

FIGURE *Scaled vertices.*
5.18

center, as shown in Figure 5.18. This will allow the face a more realistic and rounder appearance in a front view. One of the secrets to creating a good low polygon head is to make sure that the polygons are used to sculpt the major features such as the brow ridge, cheekbones, and the mouth and chin box. Using your polygons wisely will help you to better model a well-defined low polygon character.

2. Go to a side view and select the vertices shown in Figure 5.19. Shrink them just a little bit to create a nice angle. This angle is also the side plane of the face where, basically, your head begins to recede back. Also, the way you shape this line will either strengthen or hinder the general shape of the face from a quarter view to a seven-eighths view, so make sure that you take your time with it and shape it properly (See Figure 5.20).

3. With the face being constructed, this would be a good time to model the nose. Just outline the side view of the nose sketch and then simply extrude it to the full width of the nose, as shown in Figure 5.21.

For now, just keep the nose off to the side. We will be using it shortly.

4. The next shapes to refine will be the chest box and the leg. We can do both together as a matter of convenience for our Barbarian. In Figure 5.22, we have selected the outside vertices of the body, which are highlighted.

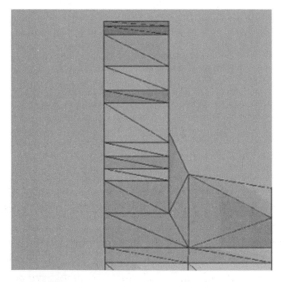

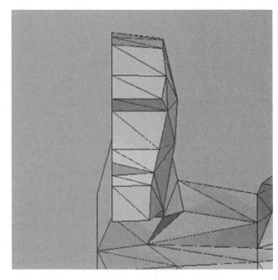

FIGURE *Front view with vertices selected.*
5.19

FIGURE *Front view with vertices moved to create*
5.20 *profile.*

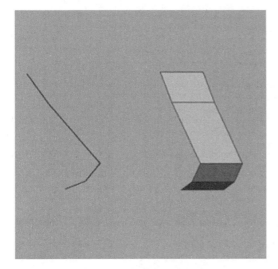

FIGURE   *Nose.*
5.21

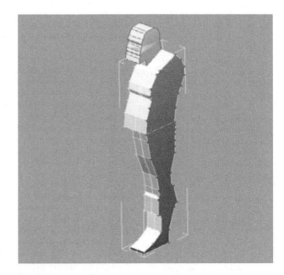

FIGURE   *Outer body and leg vertices selected.*
5.22

If you have a Scale tool, lock it on one axis so that when it is scaled down, you can shrink it inward only or simply select each vertex and move them in to the appropriate place. Notice in Figure 5.23 you have created a smoother side plane for the upper body and the legs.

You can move each vertex by itself if you want. Some models may call for you to move certain vertices in very different directions. Be sure that the inward curve is great enough that you can really feel the softness between the front plane and the side plane.

5. We are now going to pull the side of the body out some more to create thickness. Rotate the view port to the front view of the model, as shown in Figure 5.24. Next, pull the vertices in and out to match the model shown in Figure 5.25.

6. Select the vertices of the leg on the inside. Scale them down to about the same width as you did the outside of the leg (See Figure 5.26). Next, we have to fill in the inside of our leg, so move the model around in the perspective view until you can see the inside portion of his leg. Now, get your tool that makes faces. It is usually called a Face tool. Build the new faces to close in the leg, as shown in Figure 5.27.

7. The next step is to shape the arm. Just like with the leg and chest, we need to give the arm a sense of roundness. Rotate the arm until it looks like Figure 5.28. Select the outside vertices and just scale them in until the arm looks like Figure 5.29. Next, we want to do the same steps, but on the underside of the arm.

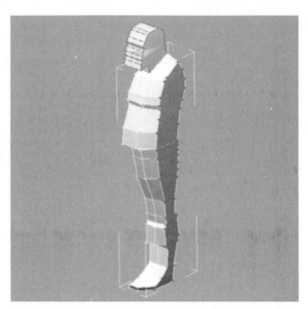

FIGURE   *Outer body and leg vertices scaled in.*
5.23

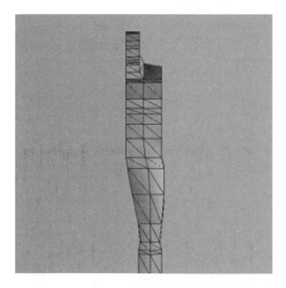

FIGURE   *Front view of the Barbarian.*
5.24

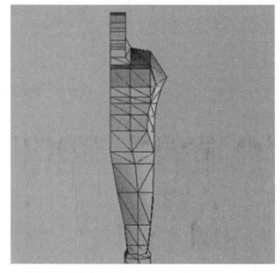

FIGURE   *Front view of the Barbarian with pulled*
5.25   *vertices.*

The arm has a lot of shape because of the muscles involved, so be sure to use the sketches when you refine the shapes, and pay close attention to how the muscles curve and flow. Try to give your model that same feeling and look.

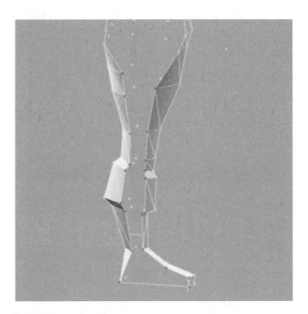

FIGURE   *Inside of leg.*
5.26

FIGURE   *Faces built inside of leg.*
5.27

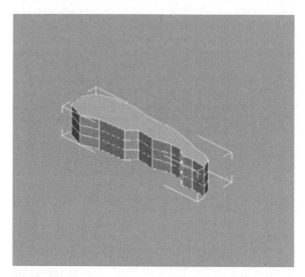

FIGURE *Barbarian arm with vertices selected.*
5.28

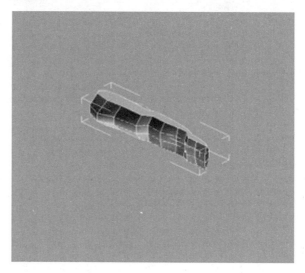

FIGURE *Barbarian arm with vertices scaled.*
5.29

We now have all the pieces of our model extruded and refined, and you should have something that looks like Figure 5.30.

 The arm has been raised up so that it is now perpendicular to the body. Be sure to do this before proceeding to the next part. Simply rotate the arm in the side view port until you get what you see here.

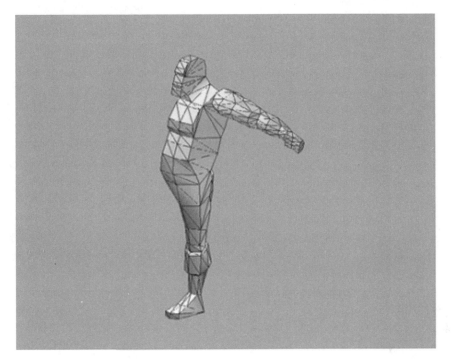

FIGURE   *Barbarian refined.*
5.30

ATTACHING THE OBJECTS TOGETHER

Since we are creating a full-mesh character, we will need to attach all the individual parts. Let's start by attaching all of our objects (if they are not already) and then getting our **Welding tool** that we'll use to pull our object all together. This is a very common tool in 3D applications, so be sure to take a moment to find it and become familiar with it, if you aren't already.

Our main objective is to make sure that when the pieces are welded together, they look "pretty and smooth." Oftentimes, when objects get attached, they stiffen up and begin getting sharp and create hard angles across the surface. The next set of steps should guide you carefully through this process and give you a clear understanding of how to attach objects while keeping the overall shape smooth and realistic.

1. Let's start off with the simplest welding parts — the neck and the waist. In Figure 5.31, notice how we find the closest vertices together and use them to connect the body with the head. The body and the waist (leg) are almost completely in the same places. Be sure to weld your vertices in the same location as highlighted in Figure 5.32.

FIGURE
5.31   *Welding the head and body together.*

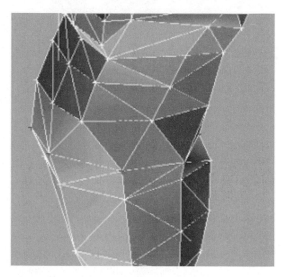

FIGURE
5.32   *Welding the body and legs together.*

2. The arm may be a little bit more difficult your first time around, so pay close attention to what we are about to do. Be sure that the arm is perpendicular to the body, as shown in Figure 5.33. Now, using the top view port, put the arm right next to the body. Line the vertices of the arm with the nearest vertices of the body, so that when we weld them together, neither side has to suffer much change. Next, we want to start filling in the

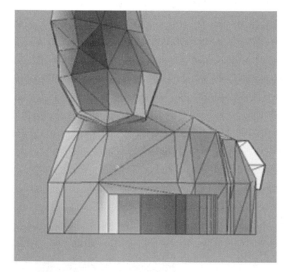

FIGURE
5.33   *Top view, arm connection.*

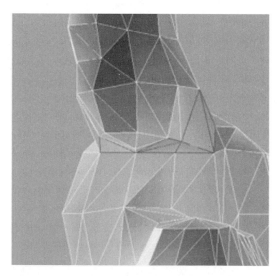

FIGURE
5.34   *Top view, building faces.*

gaps to connect the arm and the body. Get your Face tool and start build-ing faces in between, as indicated in Figure 5.34.

3. Once you have the top faces built, go to the back view. Rotate the model until your character looks something like Figure 5.35. Now, finish building the rest of the faces between the arm and the body. Notice the highlighted faces under the arm; they close in the rest of the spacing (See Figure 5.36).

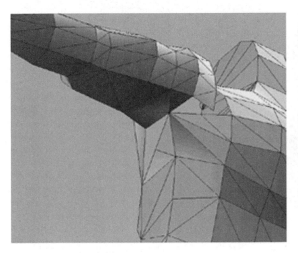

FIGURE *Underside of arm.*
5.35

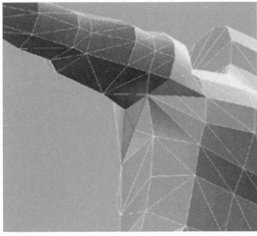

FIGURE *Underside of arm with built*
5.36 *faces.*

4. Just to be sure that you have the same connection as this model, here are a few more views of the arm. Be sure that most of your vertices line up in the same places (See Figures 5.37 – 5.40). If you are having difficulty seeing everything properly, try using the wireframe mode to view your objects. This may help you see the faces and vertices better.

Congratulations!! You have completed half of your model! The next thing we want to do is create the other side of the Ancient Barbarian. So let's get going!

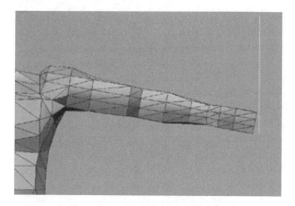

FIGURE
5.37　*Front view of Barbarian arm.*

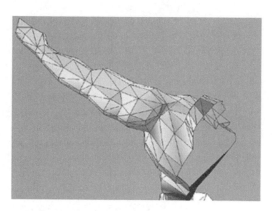

FIGURE
5.38　*Top view of Barbarian arm.*

FIGURE
5.39　*Shoulder connection.*

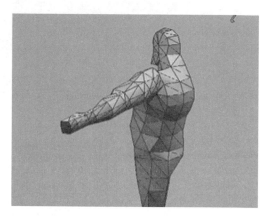

FIGURE
5.40　*Back view of shoulder connection.*

5. Start by duplicating/copying the figure. Almost all programs have some type of 3D duplicator tool, so select the figure and make a copy of it (See Figure 5.41). Now choose the Mirror option, which will allow the model to flip over as shown in Figure 5.42. We now have a perfect mirrored copy for the other side. See how easy it was to make the other side of the Barbarian.

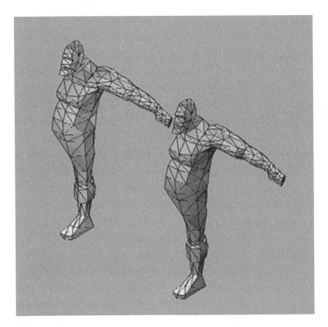

FIGURE   *Copy of Barbarian.*
5.41

6. Bring the two pieces of the Barbarian together and line the vertices of each side as close as you can (See Figure 5.43). Be sure that you are looking at it from the front view port. Our objective here is to weld the vertices that are similar and to build faces that are in the open areas without having to distort or change the placement of the current vertices. Figure 5.44 shows a close-up shot of the Barbarian. Weld the highlighted vertices together.

7. In Figure 5.45, we have filled in the empty spaces with new faces. These faces will give the Barbarian a much more developed chest by having an in and out fill. In some cases, we can just weld the head together; but to give us a more rounded, shaped head, we are going to build a whole new row of faces (See Figure 5.46).

TIP

It is very important to weld the top of the brow together, as shown in Figure 5.46. This will create a triangle-looking shape, in which to place our nose. At the bottom of the chin, be sure to weld those vertices together as well.

FIGURE
5.42
Mirrored copy of Barbarian.

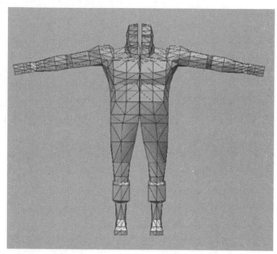

FIGURE
5.43
Barbarian pieces.

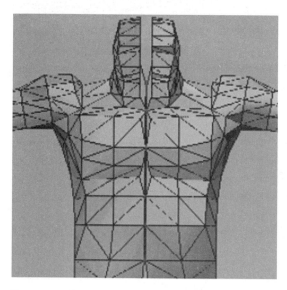

FIGURE
5.44
Barbarian with welded vertices.

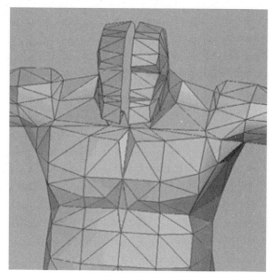

FIGURE
5.45
Chest faces built.

8. Once the face is welded together, we can go ahead and stick the nose in its proper place. Take the nosepiece that you have modeled and position it in the open place of the head. The nosepiece was a rectangle-looking shape, but what you need to do is collapse the top of it together and weld it in the center of the brow ridge, as shown in Figure 5.47. Also, weld the two ends of the nostril to each side of the lower polygons, respectively. Now select your Face tool and close in each side of the nose by building polygons, as they appear in Figure 5.48.

Be sure to close off both sides of the nose, and make sure that all the polygons are welded together.

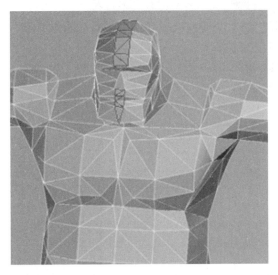

FIGURE *Built faces around the head.*
5.46

FIGURE *Close-up of nose.*
5.47

FIGURE *Nose faces built.*
5.48

9. Rotate the model to the back view so we can begin welding the vertices there. Fortunately, the back is relatively simple. All we have to do is select adjacent vertices and weld them together (See Figure 5.49). The last thing we want to do is select all the centerline vertices, as shown in Figure 5.50. Move them in toward the chest just slightly, enough to give the back a sense of volume and structure.

We've finished refining the shapes and attaching the Ancient Barbarian all together. Now we need to give him a costume to wear.

ADDING ACCESSORIES

Adding accessories deals with what the character is wearing, holding, using — anything else that, in some form or fashion, he has with him. For the Ancient Barbarian, we will look to the sketch to see what needs to be added to him. We discover that he needs a skirt and a mystic sword. The skirt is going to be a simple object that comes directly off of him, but the sword will be an object all to itself, which means we will have several steps involved in creating it. So without further ado, let's jump to it.

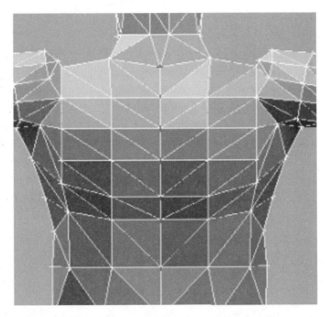

FIGURE *Back view of Barbarian.*
5.49

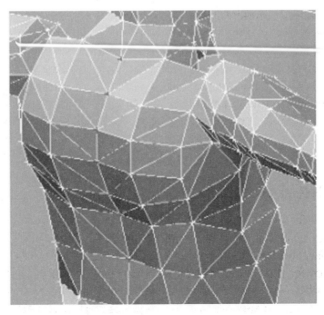

FIGURE *Vertices on spine pulled in.*
5.50

1. In order to put a skirt on the Barbarian, we need to select the edges around his waist. (See Figures 5.51 and 5.52).

2. After you have selected the edges, choose the Extrude tool. With the edges still selected, extrude the highlighted area. The result should look something like Figure 5.53. Notice how we have created a new set of polygons that go completely around the character.

We are not going to delete the upper legs, but to conserve polygons and keep the figure count as low as possible, you can delete some of the faces that are not going to be visible once the skirt is finished. Remember, though, if the skirt goes flying up or he falls over dead, we definitely want to have some legs under that skirt, just in case.

3. We need to pull it down so that it will look more like a skirt on him. By selecting the bottom skirt vertices and pulling them in toward the body, you will create a very pleasing outfit (See Figure 5.54)! If you want to give the skirt more fluff, you could add more polygons around the skirt, in order to apply more motion to it.

4. Use the sketch of the Barbarian's sword that we did in Part 1. Place it in the background of your side view port and select the 2D Drawing tool. Now outline the entire sword (See Figure 5.55). Next, extrude the sword until it looks wide enough for his hands to properly hold it, as shown in Figure 5.56.

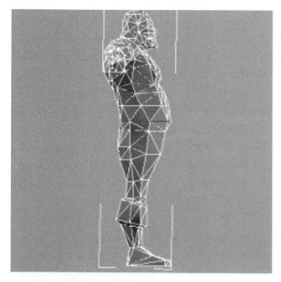

FIGURE
5.51
Waistline selected.

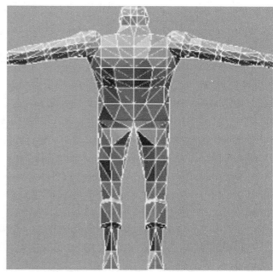

FIGURE
5.52
Waistline selected.

FIGURE   *Barbarian skirt extruded.*
5.53

FIGURE   *Barbarian with skirt pulled down.*
5.54

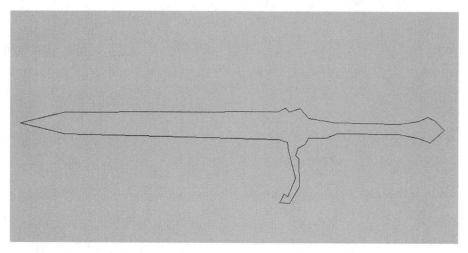

FIGURE *Outline of the sword.*
5.55

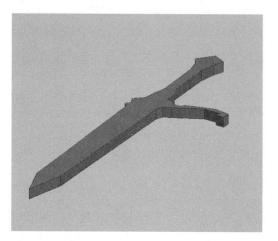

FIGURE *Sword extruded.*
5.56

5. We need to have a few extra polygons down the center of the blade so that we can collapse the outside vertices together. In Figure 5.57, the blade has been divided using the Edge tool. This will allow us to give the mystic sword more depth and realism. Be sure that the new edge you divided is straight down the center of the blade.

6. With the sword extruded, we need to work on refining the blade to make it appear sharp and dangerous. Right now the blade looks like a pointed box. Go ahead and select the outside vertices and weld each set of vertices with its appropriate point. In Figure 5.58, the vertices are welded together,

creating a thin, sharp edge along the perimeter of the sword. The handle doesn't need to be refined unless you want a lot of detail added, like a six or eight-sided curved handle. Since the Ancient Barbarian will be holding the sword, there's no reason to increase the polygon count with more poly's, so we will keep it low and simple.

Let's take a look at the Ancient Barbarian at this stage (See Figure 5.59).

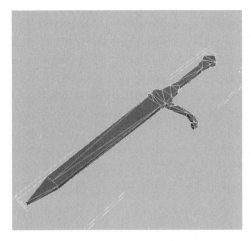

FIGURE **5.57** *New edge going through the center of the blade.*

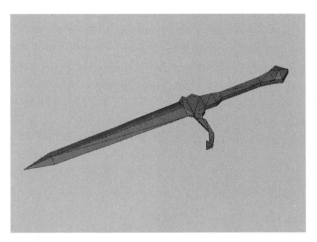

FIGURE **5.58** *Barbarian's sword refined.*

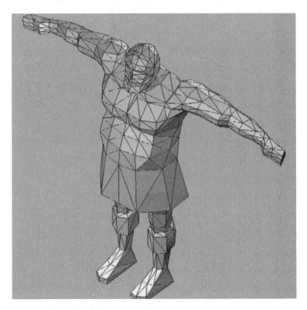

FIGURE **5.59** *Finished Barbarian.*

Don't forget to go back and look at him from all angles. Tweak whatever you feel is necessary and add to him whatever else you would like.

ON THE CD

The last thing we need to do is replace the stand-in hands. They are really good for low polygon characters, but by adding just a few more polygons we would be able to give him fingers and an opposable thumb. This way, when your characters want to point somewhere or grab hold of a mystical sword, they can use their fingers. We have not sketched the hand, but we have provided pictures on the CD-ROM as well as the finished model of the hand. The hand is created separately so that you can attach it to any character you want. This is one feature of the body that doesn't need to be remodeled over and over again, unless you are simply trying to perfect it for your own artistic purposes.

DRAWING THE SHAPES WITH THE LINE TOOL

ON THE CD

All right, let's start off by selecting our Line tool. Be sure that the top view hand photo is placed into the top view port. Also, place the side view photo in the side view port. Both of these images are available on the CD-ROM under the Hand folder.

Once you have the view port prepared, select the top view port. This will be the biggest difference for modeling the hand. The top view instead of the side view has the most important shape and features for the hand, which means we will be using the top view to outline our hand. If you do not quite understand why we are doing it this way, try a quick illustration. Take your right hand and hold it in front of you. Stare at the top flat portion of your hand with your fingers stretched out. Now, turn it side ways so that you can only see the side of your hand. Notice how much shape you lost and how many fingers disappeared when you turned your hand to a side view. This is why we are changing over to the top view for the outlining shape.

Choose the Line tool and begin outlining the top of the hand. Start by the wrist and work around it in a clockwise direction (See Figure 5.60). When outlining the fingers, only put points where you want the knuckles to go. This will help keep the polygon count down to a minimum and allow for good bending points when animating.

You'll only have to model it once. Be sure to save the hand model as a separate file so that you can reuse it over and over again. This way, when you do your next character, you can import this cool hand into your file and weld the hands onto the end of your character's arms.

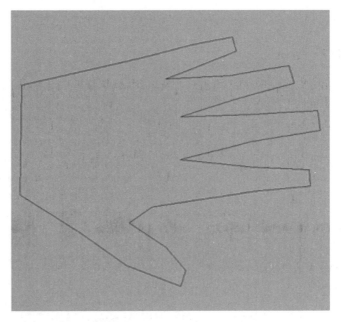

FIGURE   *Outline of hand.*
5.60

That's all there is to it. You now have a hand! Let's go ahead and extrude our new object.

EXTRUDING THE HAND

By now you should have a pretty good idea of the tool locations. Before you extrude the line, however, make sure you look at the width of the side view sketch of the hand. This will help you determine the distance to pull it out. Basically, we want to extrude it the width of the mid-section of the hand.

Go to either your perspective view or your side view port. Select the Extrude tool and select the hand, as shown in Figure 5.61. Pull the Hand Line up until it looks like Figure 5.62.

FIGURE **5.61**   *Hand selected.*

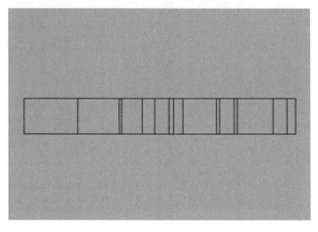

FIGURE **5.62**   *Hand extruded.*

 You are creating the whole model this time — not just half of it — so be sure to keep that in mind.

The hand extruded should now look like Figure 5.63.

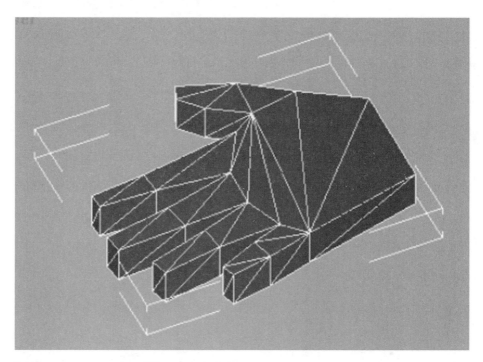

FIGURE   *Perspective view of hand extruded.*
5.63

REFINING THE HAND

As you can tell, the hand is currently very blocky-looking. We need to go in and move a few vertices and change a few edges, so that the hand will have a refined and realistic appearance.

Now for a quick recap: the tools you will be using here are the vertices, edge, and face tools. If you are comfortable using them, that's excellent. If you're still a little unsure of working with them, that's okay. By the end of this book, you'll be a professional low polygon modeler.

1. Select the vertices highlighted at the back of the hand, by the wrists (See Figures 5.64 and 5.65).
2. With the vertices selected, move them apart as shown in Figures 5.66 and 5.67. You can use the Scale tool to pull them outward at the same time, if you want.

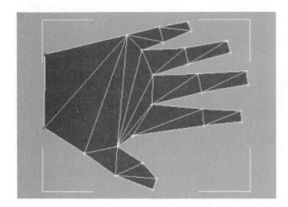

FIGURE
5.64   *Vertices selected.*

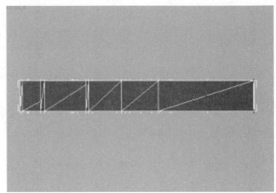

FIGURE
5.65   *Vertices selected.*

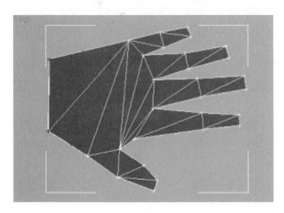

FIGURE
5.66   *Vertices scaled outward.*

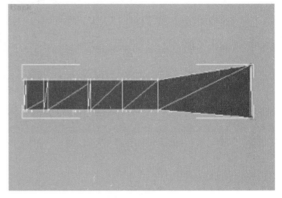

FIGURE
5.67   *Vertices scaled.*

We are going to start defining the palm edges. If you have questions about how it really looks, use your hand as an example.

3. With the Vertices tool chosen, select the tips of the fingers (See Figure 5.68). Now scale them in together until they look like Figure 5.69. If you don't wish to scale them, just select each vertex and move them in until you have something that looks like Figure 5.69.

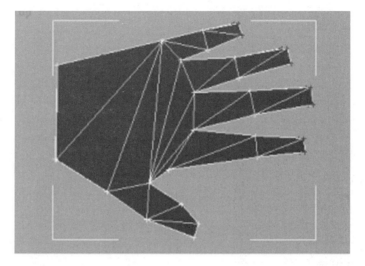

FIGURE   *Vertices selected.*
5.68

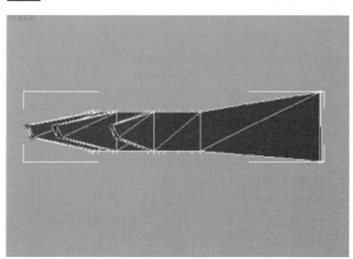

FIGURE   *Vertices adjusted.*
5.69

4. Now select the mid-knuckles of the hand, as shown in Figure 5.70. Scale them in toward each other (if you don't know how to scale them, just move each set of vertices in together) (See Figure 5.71).

We only have one set of knuckles instead of two, which allows for movement, but at the same time keeps its poly count low. If you feel that you need the full set, it's best you add them when outlining the hand.

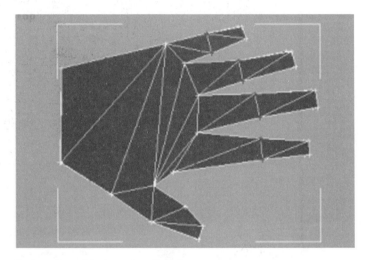

FIGURE **5.70** *Knuckle vertices selected.*

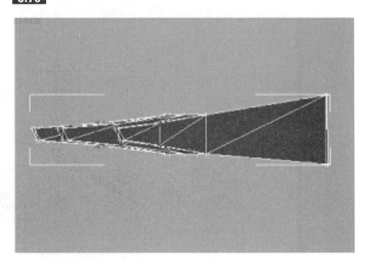

FIGURE **5.71** *Vertices scaled in.*

5. Rotate the hand around to where you can get at the palm of the hand (See Figure 5.72). Select the Edge tool and begin turning the edges highlighted. Each edge should look something like Figure 5.73. Notice that we have flipped them around the other direction, as well as divided them twice by the thumb.

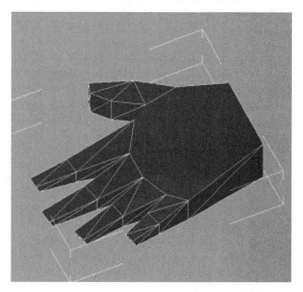

FIGURE *Edges selected.*
5.72

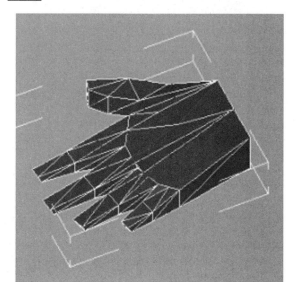

FIGURE *Edges divided.*
5.73

6. With the edges turned around, we can now move the vertices into their places. In Figure 5.74, the vertices highlighted are the ones that will be moved around. Move the vertices of the knuckles and the tips of the fingers in together, as shown in Figure 5.75. Now move the vertices at the edge of the palm wedge up just a little. This will help to create a soft curve between the fingers.

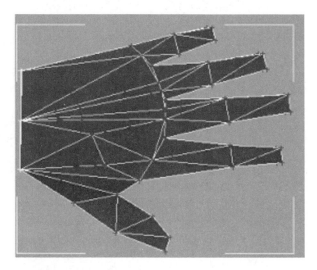

FIGURE *Vertices selected.*
5.74

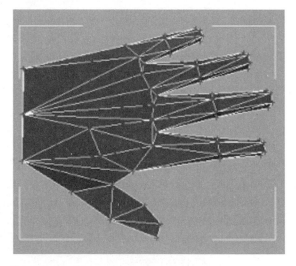

FIGURE *Vertices corrected.*
5.75

7. Rotate the hand around until you are looking at it from the front of the hand. Select the vertices shown in Figure 5.76. Now move the selected vertices down until they look like Figure 5.77.

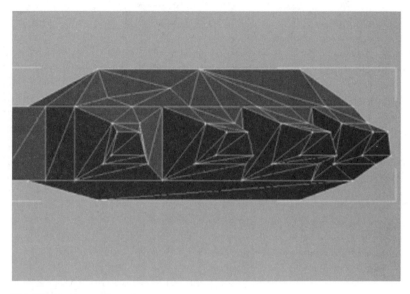

FIGURE *Vertices selected.*

5.76

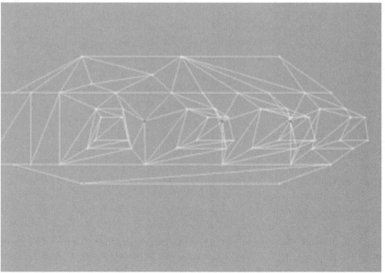

FIGURE *Vertices adjusted.*
5.77

8. Now let's clean, up the top of the hand just a little more. Select the highlighted vertices in Figure 5.78. Move it to the vertex at the center of the wrist and weld them together with the Welding tool, as shown in Figure 5.79.

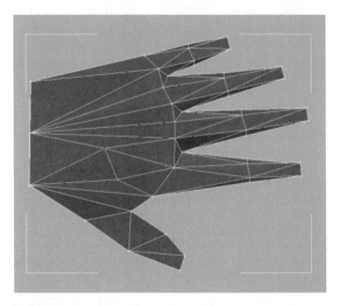

FIGURE *Vertices selected.*
5.78

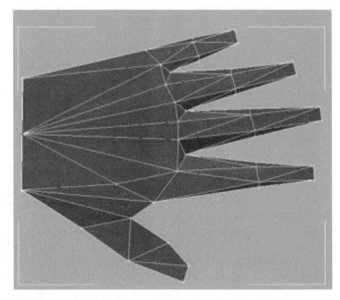

FIGURE *Vertices welded.*
5.79

9. Rotate the hand to the underside, (See Figure 5.80). Select the Edge tool and flip the highlighted edges around so that they look like Figure 5.81.

 With the edges turned like Figure 5.81, we will be able to curve the hand and animate it without any discrepancies to the model.

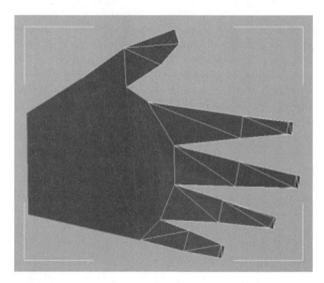

FIGURE *Underside of hand.*
5.80

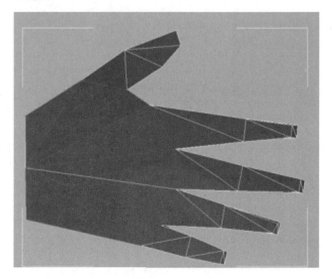

FIGURE *Edges flipped.*
5.81

10. Next, we need to refine the thumb. In Figure 5.82, we have provided multiple views of the vertices selected around the thumb, as indicated.
11. Move the vertices of the inside portion of the thumb in just a little. Also, move the hand down at about a 15-degree angle from the palm wedge (See Figure 5.83).

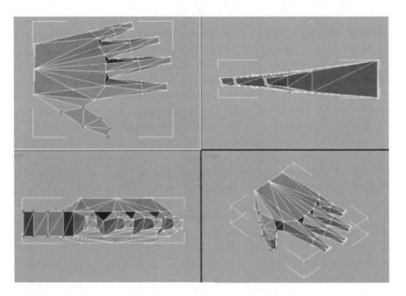

FIGURE *Multiple views of vertices selected.*
5.82

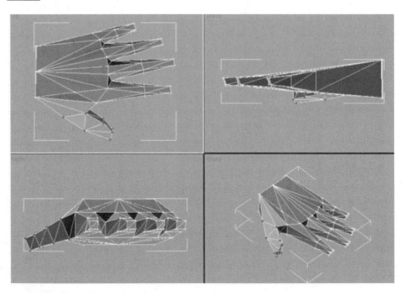

FIGURE *Thumb angled down.*
5.83

12. Rotate your hand around to the back. Select the center vertices of the wrist and scale them away from each other (See Figure 5.84).

13. Now choose the Face tool and select the faces of the wrist, as shown in Figure 5.85. Then just hit the Delete key to remove them from the model. Since the hand will be attached to another character, it doesn't need to have any back faces (See Figure 5.86).

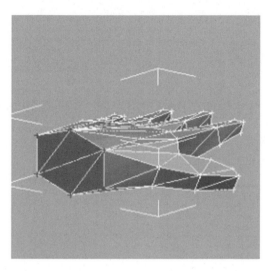

FIGURE *Back view of hand with selected vertices.*
5.84

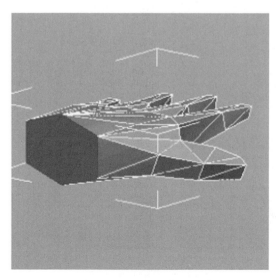

FIGURE *Faces selected.*
5.85

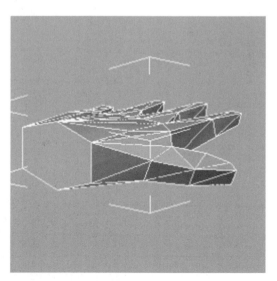

FIGURE *Faces deleted.*
5.86

14. Jump back to the front view of our hand once again. Select the two vertices shown in Figure 5.87. Move them in toward each other (See Figure 5.88).

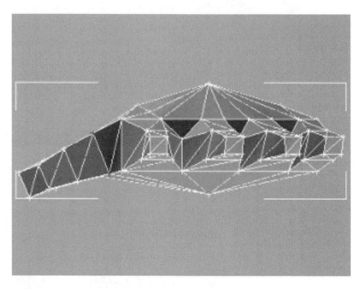

FIGURE *Front view with vertices selected.*
5.87

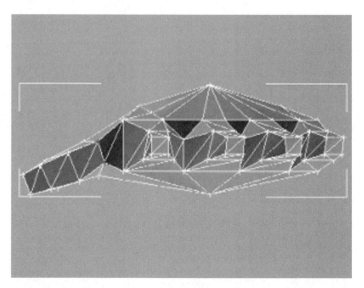

FIGURE *Thumb vertices scaled inward.*
5.88

15. Next, we want to select the top and bottom edges shown in Figures 5.89 and 5.90.

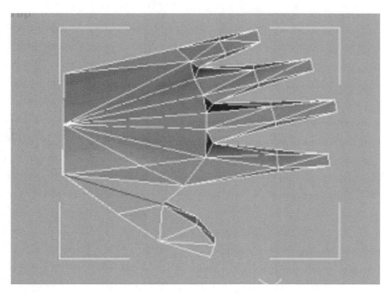

FIGURE *Top edge selected.*
5.89

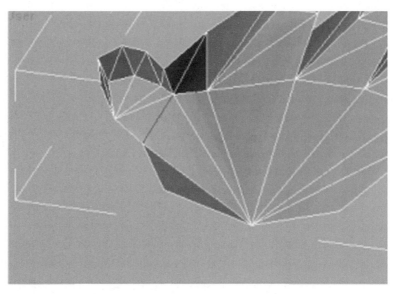

FIGURE *Bottom edge selected.*
5.90

16. With the edges selected, use your flip option to turn the edges around, as shown in Figures 5.91 and 5.92. As you can see, we are trying to move our edges into the best possible places for optimal movement.

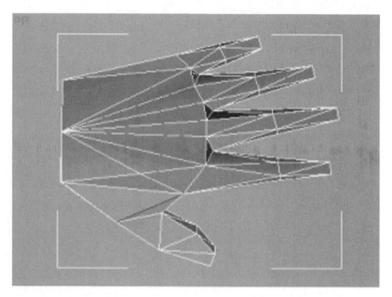

FIGURE   *Edges flipped.*
5.91

FIGURE   *Edges flipped.*
5.92

17. Let's go ahead and get rid of the vertex shown in Figure 5.93. Move it to the end of the hand at the edge, as shown in Figure 5.94. Now weld them together. This cleans our hands up, so that they look nice and smooth.

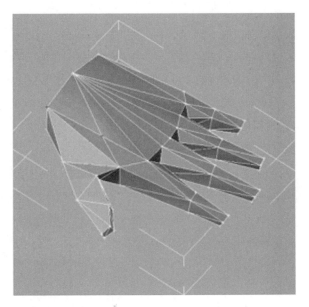

FIGURE *Vertex selected.*
5.93

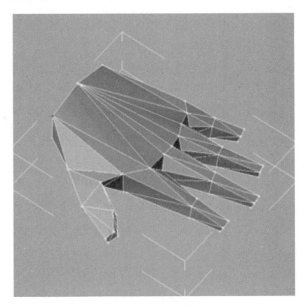

FIGURE *Vertices welded at corner.*
5.94

18. Now let's squeeze the front side of the palm wedge in just a little. Select the vertices highlighted in Figure 5.95. Then pull the vertices in together, shown in Figure 5.96.

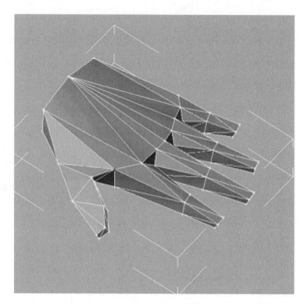

FIGURE *Vertices selected.*
5.95

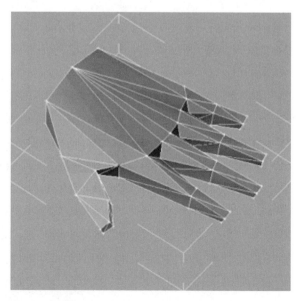

FIGURE *Vertices scaled inward.*
5.96

19. Rotate the hand over to the pinkie side of the hand. Select the vertices on the side of the hand (See Figure 5.97). Move them in toward each other, as shown in Figure 5.98.

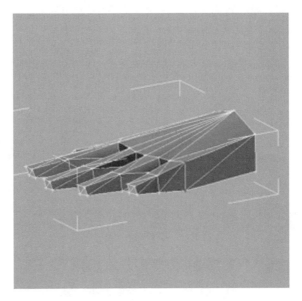

FIGURE *Vertices selected.*

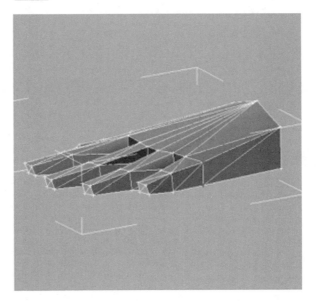

FIGURE *Vertices scaled inward.*
5.98

Your hand is now finished and should look like Figure 5.99.

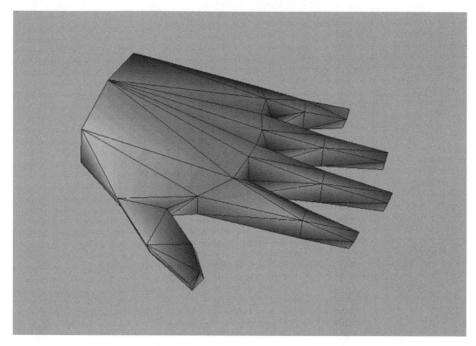

FIGURE *Barbarian hand Finished.*
5.99

Now that the hand is complete, we need to attach it to the Barbarian's fore-arm. The block-like hand that is currently on the character is okay to use, but giving him a real set of hands raises the professional appeal of the character that much more.

ATTACHING THE HAND

1. With the Barbarian model in the view port, move the hand down to the side of the Barbarian, as shown in Figure 5.100.

Make sure that the hand and Barbarian are scaled in relation to each other. You don't want a five-foot-tall hand.

TIP

2. Select the Ancient Barbarian and close in on his hand (See Figure 5.101).
   Next, select the faces of the hand and then press Delete to erase the
   polygons. This will prepare him for the new hand (See Figure 5.102).

FIGURE   *Side view of Barbarian and hand.*
5.100

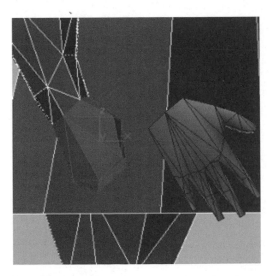

FIGURE   *Faces selected.*
5.101

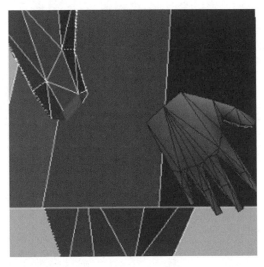

FIGURE   *Faces deleted.*
5.102

3. Now select the hand and move it where the old hand was before. Be sure to get the hand as close to the matching vertices as you can (See Figure 5.103). Some programs require you to use the Attach button before you can work with two objects together. Go ahead and attach the objects together, if you have to. This should make the hand turn the same color as the Barbarian (See Figure 5.104).

4. Rotate the model around to the front view. Next, select the vertices around the Barbarian's wrist (See Figure 5.105). Pull the vertices in using the Scale tool or just by moving each vertex to its proper place, as shown in Figure 5.106. Make sure to position the arm vertices right next to the hand vertices, then weld them together.

The finished hand should look like Figures 5.107 and 5.108.

The last step in the process is to repeat the same steps for the other side of the hand. When you finish it up, the Barbarian should have two hands and resemble Figure 5.109.

Congratulations! The Ancient Barbarian is completely modeled! Now let's try some techniques that can be applied to other types of models.

FIGURE
5.103
Hand moved.

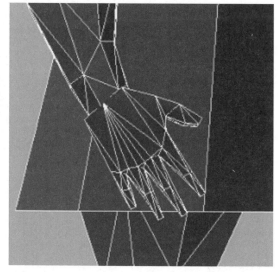

FIGURE
5.104
Hand attached to Barbarian.

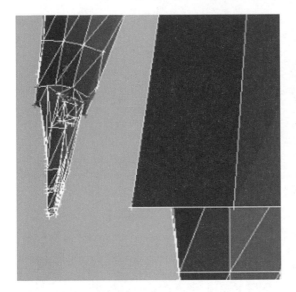

FIGURE
5.105 *Wrist vertices selected.*

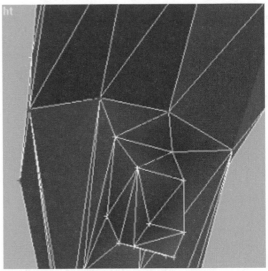

FIGURE
5.106 *Vertices adjusted.*

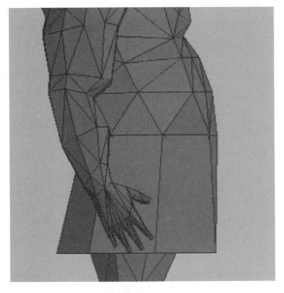

FIGURE
5.107 *Side view of the hand attached.*

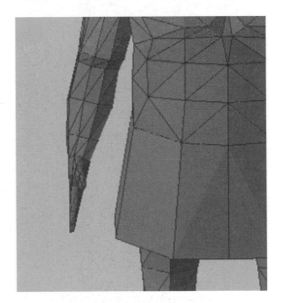

FIGURE
5.108 *Front view of the hand attached.*

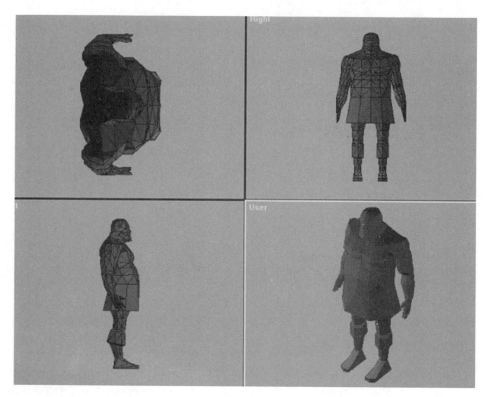

FIGURE **5.109** *Barbarian with both hands finished.*

VARIATIONS

The Ancient Barbarian is an excellent example of how to create a male figure and any other character that stands on two legs and walks around. There are, however, variations that could be applied to this form of construction. We are going to take a moment and illustrate the major differences that may come up when modeling female characters, lower- count polygon characters, and even cartoon characters, so that you will have a better understanding of how subtle changes can create new and exciting models.

Since we have already gone over the steps for creating a human character, the next examples only include the steps needed to illustrate the major points of character differences. To begin a new model, you will use the same procedure outlined for the Barbarian and just apply the necessary variations according to your needs. Let's begin by showing the distinctions needed when creating the Female Marine.

Each of the characters will have the same initial set-up and will follow the same five-step list that we discussed at the beginning of this chapter.

FEMALE MARINE

ON THE CD

The makeup of a female character is quite similar to that of a male, but there are some differences that need to be addressed. To begin, go to the Tutorial directory on the CD-ROM and use the sketches of the Female Marine for the background images or use the pictures in the book and set them next to you for reference.

DRAWING THE SHAPES WITH THE LINE TOOL

Once the images have been placed properly into the view ports, go ahead and outline the side view of the Marine using the Line tool. The outlining shapes should look something like Figure 5.110. The immediate difference that you've probably already noticed is the outlining shape. The Barbarian is a large, hefty fellow, while the Marine is slender and less muscular. Also, be sure to outline the pants of the Marine just the way they have been drawn. In the side view, it is clearly visible that the pants poof out right by the boots where they are tucked in. If you keep that true to form, you'll have an easier time creating wrinkle-like clothes for her.

EXTRUDING ALL THE SHAPES

Use the Extrude tool to make the shapes into 3D objects, as we did for the Ancient Barbarian. Make sure that you keep the sketch of the Marine in the background or next to you because the width you extrude the model will differ greatly compared to the Barbarian, since the Marine is a female.

The objects should look like Figure 5.111 after the shapes have been extruded.

With all of the major objects created on our heroine, we will now refine the figure.

REFINING THE OBJECTS

The Marine is different enough from the Barbarian that we should take the time to go over how to refine the model. This will be a good chance to figure out how to make a character soft and slender, unlike the Barbarian who was big and hefty. Let's go over the refining elements of the Marine, which makes her the lady that she is.

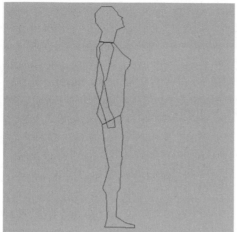

FIGURE **5.110** *Finished outline of Marine.*

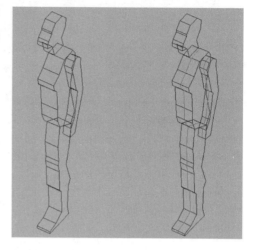

FIGURE **5.111** *Extruded Female Marine.*

1. In the front view port, select the head object. Remember this is just half of the head. What we want to do is begin rounding it out to give it a more head-like appearance. Start by selecting the Vertices tool. Once you have it, go ahead and select the vertices on the side of the head, as shown in Figure 5.112. Now use the Scale tool and shrink all the vertices in toward each other like Figure 5.113. If you want to, you can pull the vertices in manually. It doesn't really matter.

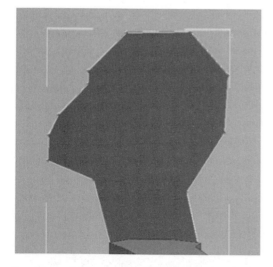

FIGURE **5.112** *Side view of Marine with vertices selected.*

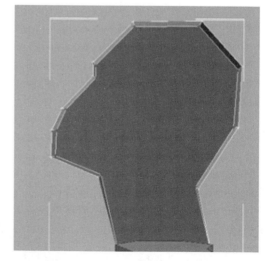

FIGURE **5.113** *Side view of Marine with vertices pulled in.*

2. Next we want to rotate the head just slightly until it looks like Figure 5.114. Now select your Edge tool, divide the center of the head, and begin changing the edges so that they come from the center of the head, as shown in Figure 5.115.

We have increased the poly count on the head by adding more edges. Also, be sure that your new polys and vertices line up with the ones shown here.

NOTE

3. From here, we are going to define the side view line. Go to the front view and select each vertex highlighted (See Figure 5.116). One at a time, move the vertices in toward the center of the face until your front face looks like Figure 5.117. Take into account that we are dividing the front plane of the face and the side plane of the face. This gives us a smoother, less ridged head, which is more appropriate for our female character.

That's all we need to do for the head right now.

4. If you like, go ahead and draw the nose and extrude the form. We won't be attaching it yet, so just set it out of the way until we are ready to use it (See Figure 5.118).

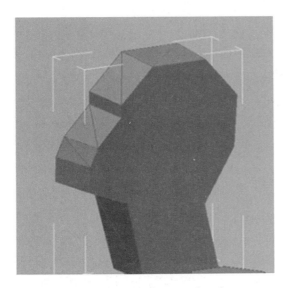

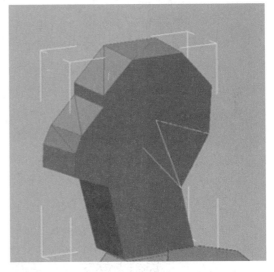

FIGURE *Perspective view of Marine head.*
5.114

FIGURE *Head divided through center.*
5.115

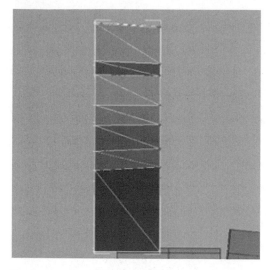

FIGURE **5.116** *Front view of Marine.*

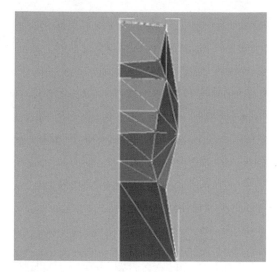

FIGURE **5.117** *Front view with vertices pulled in.*

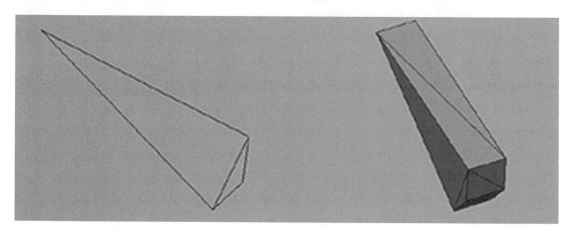

FIGURE **5.118** *Nose.*

This is a different type of nose than we created for the Barbarian. It's actually going to be a lower-count model, so we are showing you a few different ways to do things. For one thing the nose is slightly less detailed, yet will still bring about a very convincing profile.

5. We will now refine the chest and the hip. Since this model is a female, a little bit more attention will be used to create a more feminine feel to the character. To give our Marine more shape, we first need to divide her down the side (See Figures 5.119 and 5.120).

6. Next, straighten the new edges up so that they go smoothly down the center of our model, as shown in Figure 5.121. This allows us to curve the body of our model and provide a softer more realistic appearance.

FIGURE
5.119
Outside edge of Marine body.

FIGURE
5.120
Outside edge divided.

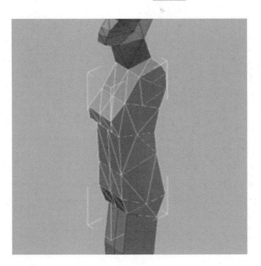

FIGURE
5.121
Edge line straightened up.

7. Select the outside vertices shown in Figure 5.122. Move each vertex in to its proper place, as shown in Figure 5.123. Notice that we have also moved the inside center line of the body inward above the chest and hip section, and we moved the shoulder region out a little and the outside hip in a little. Most of these pulls are very subtle, but remember, if you keep the front view sketch of her on your screen, it will be a lot easier lining up the character's major curve points.

8. Next, with a front view of our model, we want to straighten up the waist-line. By correcting our geometry here, we will be able to place texture maps on our character with ease. Select the vertices one at a time, as shown in Figure 5.124. Move them up until they form a straight line across, as shown in Figure 5.125.

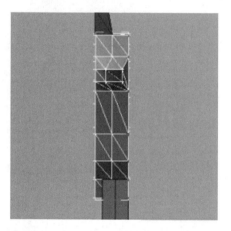

FIGURE
5.122 *Front view of Marine.*

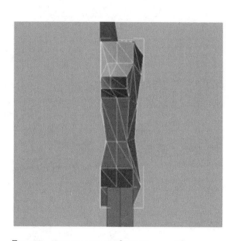

FIGURE
5.123 *Front view of Marine with vertices moved.*

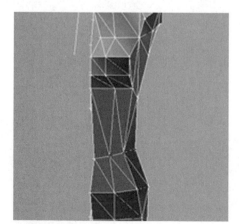

FIGURE
5.124 *Waist vertices selected.*

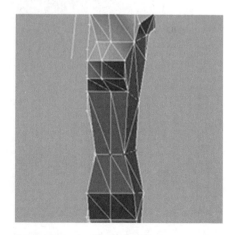

FIGURE
5.125 *Waist vertices moved up.*

9. Our next step is to refine the leg. Move the leg around the outside view of the leg is shown on your screen. Select the vertices that are highlighted in Figure 5.126. Now, either move them in separately, or scale them down until the leg vertices move in, as shown in Figure 5.127.

10. Next, we are going to do the inside of the leg. Move your model around until you see the inside view of the leg. Select the outlining vertices, as shown in Figure 5.128. With the vertices selected, go ahead and scale the leg in toward the center until it looks like Figure 5.129. After that, pull the two vertices on the outside of the foot in towards the heel.

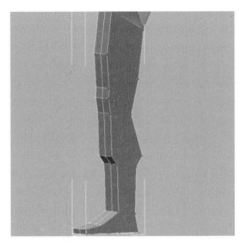

FIGURE 5.126   *Outside of leg.*

FIGURE 5.127   *Vertices moved inward.*

FIGURE 5.128   *Inside of Marine leg.*

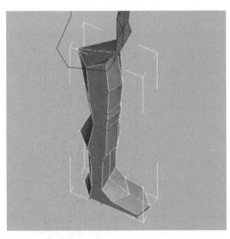

FIGURE 5.129   *Vertices pulled in.*

11. Change your view to the front view of the leg. In Figure 5.130, we see that the leg in a front view is still lifeless and dull. So we need to give it some shape. Select the vertices at the knee and scale them down, or just move each one in toward the center of the leg until it looks like Figure 5.131. Then select the vertices of the boot and scale them down as well. If you want to be more precise, just move each vertex one at a time. This will create the feel of pants above the boot. You can also pull the top of the boots out just a hair to give it more shape as well.

When creating legs, be sure to keep the legs going in and out. Don't leave straight lines down the body. We are trying to create organic shapes with only a few polys, so the more ins and outs we give them, the better off our model will look.

12. Next, we want to increase the width of the upper leg so that it fits in with the pelvis region better. To do this, we need to select the top vertices of the leg, as shown in Figure 5.132. Then simply scale the vertices until you have reached the outside points of the pelvis. This will fill out the top part of the leg very nicely.

13. The last step is to increase the width of the foot just a little. You can select the front vertices, as shown in Figure 5.133, and then scale them out just a bit. This way, when you are looking down on your feet, they won't look like square boxes.

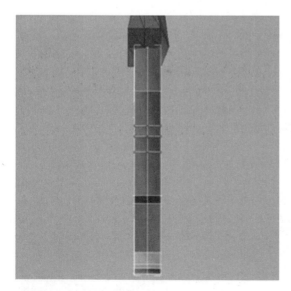

FIGURE
5.130
Front view of Marine leg.

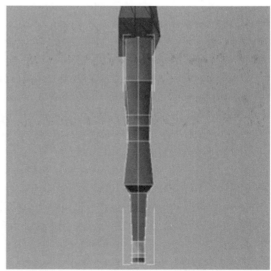

FIGURE
5.131
Front view, vertices corrected.

You should now have a leg that looks something like Figure 5.134.

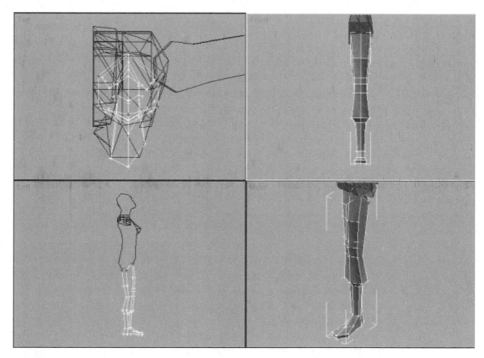

FIGURE   *Multiple shots of Marine upper leg.*
5.132

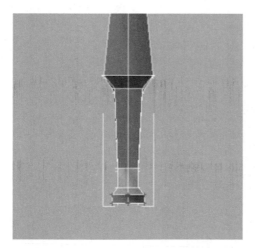

FIGURE   *Front view of Marine foot.*
5.133

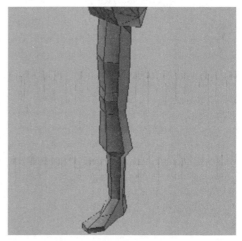

FIGURE   *Finished Marine leg.*
5.134

The arm is the last thing we need to refine. So select the extruded arm and lets start working on it.

14. Rotate the arm up until it is perpendicular to the body as shown in Figures 5.135 and 5.136. We do this for two main reasons — because it is easier to attach it to the body and it makes it easier to attach a skeletal system for animating our character later.

15. Once the arm has been moved up, select the vertices on the top of the arm (See Figure 5.137). Next, we use our Scale tool and shrink the arm in towards the body. Notice that we are only shrinking them up along one axis so that they move toward the centerline of the arm (See Figure 5.138).

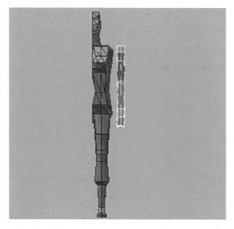

FIGURE **5.135** *Marine front view, arm down.*

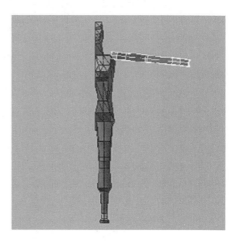

FIGURE **5.136** *Marine front view, arm up.*

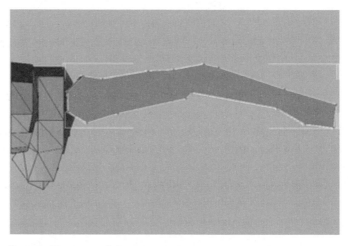

FIGURE **5.137** *Top view of Marine arm.*

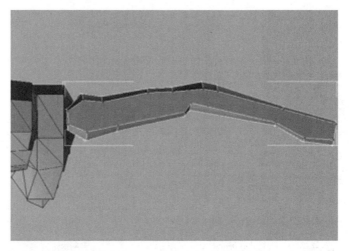

FIGURE   *Top view of Marine arm, vertices pulled inward.*
5.138

NOTE

Remember that you can move each vertex in until you get exactly what you want.

16. Now rotate your model until you get the underside of the arm, as shown in Figure 5.139. Select the vertices along the outside of the under portion of the arm. Scale them in toward each other, just like you did on the top part of the arm (See Figure 5.140).

TIP

When modeling any part of the character, it is always important to make every part of it as "round-looking" as possible.

17. The last thing we want to do is refine the front view of the arm. So go to the front view of the arm, select the vertices at the wrist, and move them in toward each other. Next, pull the forearm out just a hair. It should look something like Figure 5.141, which should wrap up the arm for us. Great job!

The Female Marine should now look something like Figure 5.142.

FIGURE *Underside of Marine arm.*
5.139

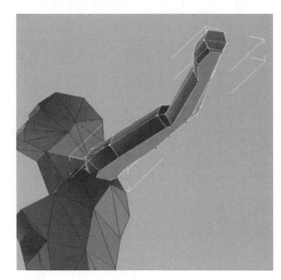

FIGURE *Vertices pulled in.*
5.140

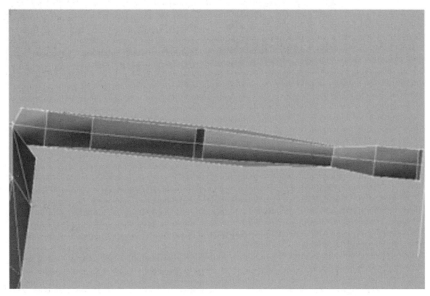

FIGURE *Front view of Marine arm with corrected vertices.*
5.141

FIGURE   *Refined Female Marine.*
5.142

ATTACHING THE OBJECTS TOGETHER

Attaching objects together can get kind of complicated, so we are going to show you the steps involved for the Female Marine. The reason for this is because, when dealing with two separate objects, the main points/vertices may not all be located in the same place from one object to the next. In most cases, you will have to move vertices around and even create new faces to fill in the gaps where parts of the objects may not come close to each other. Make sure you pay close attention to where and how we connect the vertices, so that you can use these techniques for the rest of your models.

Our main objective is to make sure that when the pieces are welded together, they look "pretty and smooth." We don't want these attached objects to look angular or, for that matter, look as though they are not attached at all. The point is to make sure that, as a whole, the objects feel as though they belong together.

1. Let's start off with the simplest welding part the neck. Rotate the figure until you see the front of the neck, as shown in Figure 5.143. Notice how we find the closest vertices together and use them to connect the body with the head. Be sure to weld your vertices in the same location as shown Figure 5.144.

We selected the vertices closest to one another. This makes it easier to weld your shapes together and still keep the same form that you started with. Also notice how we used the wire frame mode to make it easier to select all the vertices. Be sure to do it whichever way you are most comfortable.

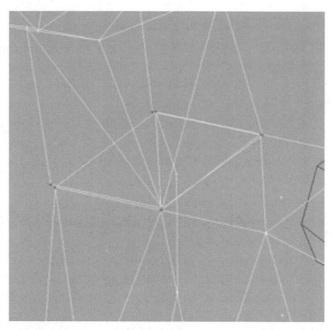

FIGURE
5.143   *Front neck view of Marine.*

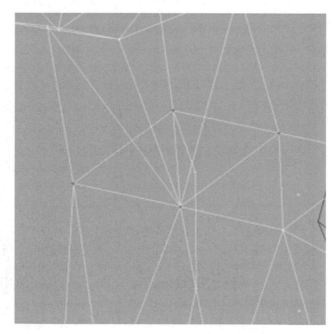

FIGURE
5.144   *Head and body vertices welded together.*

2. Now move down to the midsection of the body (See Figure 5.145). In this front view, the body and leg are almost in the same places. We need to move the vertices of the leg up and over to their appropriate places (See Figure 5.146).

FIGURE
5.145   *Front view of Marine waist and leg.*

FIGURE
5.146   *Waist and leg welded.*

3. Now rotate the model to the back view so that you see the leg and bottom, as shown in Figure 5.147. Attach the highlighted vertices to their proper places as indicated (See Figure 5.148).

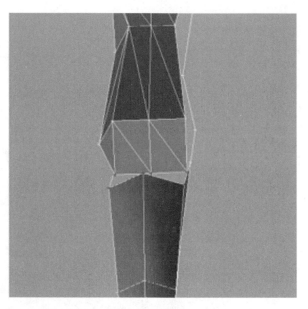

FIGURE *Back view of Marine waist and leg.*
5.147

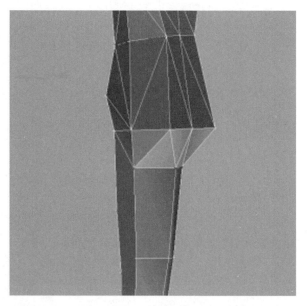

FIGURE *Back leg and lower waist welded.*
5.148

4. The arm is the last thing we are going to attach. Following are several shots around the arm before it's attached. Be sure that your arm is placed close to the body, as shown in Figure 5.149.
5. Grab the highlighted front and back vertices of the body and attach them to the mid edge on the arm (See Figure 5.150). Be sure that the chest vertices are pulled in to the shoulder.

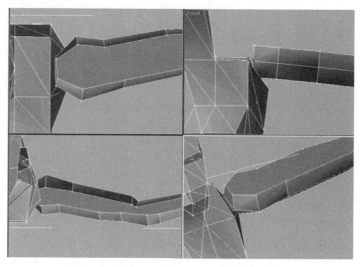

FIGURE *Multiple shots of Marine arm before attaching.*
5.149

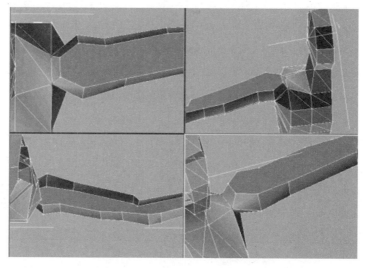

FIGURE *Multiple shots of Marine shoulder attached to body.*
5.150

6. Now change the view until you can see the front arm and the underside, as shown in Figure 5.151. Select the vertex at the bottom edge and attach the vertex to the inside portion of the chest (See Figure 5.152).

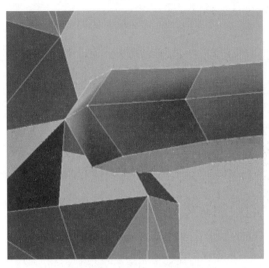

FIGURE *Front view of Marine arm.*
5.151

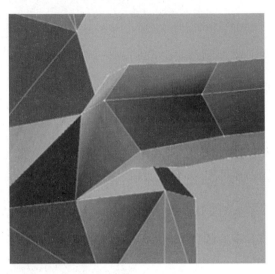

FIGURE *Attached vertice from arm to chest.*
5.152

7. Next, select the other vertex on the arm and pull it down. Weld the two together, as shown in Figure 5.153.

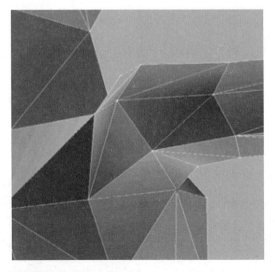

FIGURE *Vertices welded.*
5.153

8. Next, rotate the model until it looks like Figure 5.154. With these back vertices welded, we need to turn them around so that their bends will be in the right places (See Figure 5.155). If you have the Flip tool for the edges, then use it. But if not, then just delete the highlighted faces and build three new ones to match Figure 5.155.

FIGURE *Back view of Marine shoulder.*
5.154

FIGURE *Edges in red flipped.*
5.155

Following are a few shots around the arm just to be sure you have it connected the same way (See Figure 5.156).

The arm is welded, but our job is not done.

9. We have one final open area to close in, on the chest. Move the model until it looks like Figure 5.157. Select your Face tool and build a new face in the highlighted area shown in Figure 5.158.

10. Once you have created the new face, use your Edge tool to divide the two faces into four (See Figure 5.159). After that, use the Vertices tool to select the center vertex of the new faces and move it upward to match Figure 5.160. This will allow for a smoother inward and outward pull when the Marine is animated.

By dividing the polygons, we not only helped the effectiveness of the eventual animation, but we also continued to create a smoother more feminine look.

NOTE

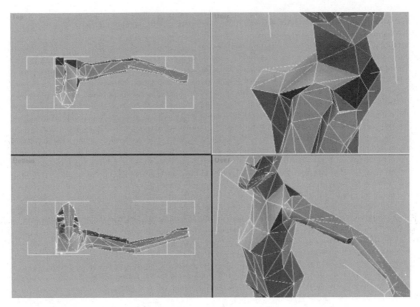

FIGURE *Multiple views of Marine arm attached.*
5.156

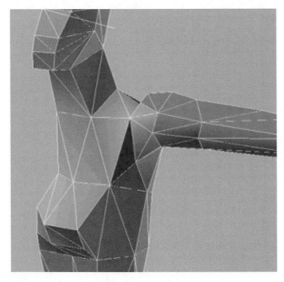

FIGURE *Front view of Marine chest.*
5.157

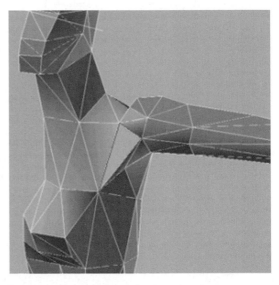

FIGURE *Chest with built face.*
5.158

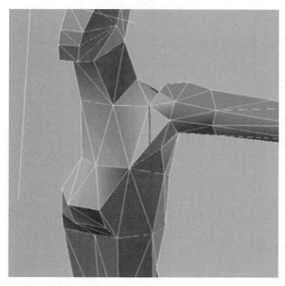

FIGURE *Face divided.*
5.159

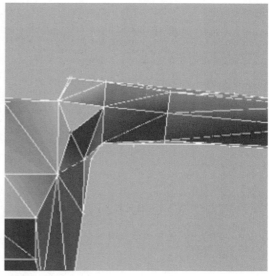

FIGURE *Vertex corrected.*
5.160

Your attached character should now look something like Figure 5.161.

FIGURE *Marine attached.*
5.161

11. Now that we have a refined-looking half model, it's time to duplicate it. So select the figure (See Figure 5.162). Make a copy of it, as shown in Figure 5.163.

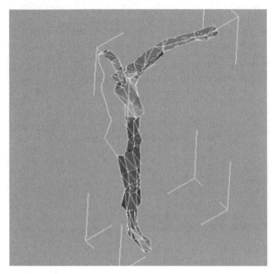

FIGURE *Marine half selected.*
5.162

FIGURE *Marine duplicated.*
5.163

12. Next, select the duplicated image. Choose the Mirror option. This will allow the model to flip over, as shown in Figure 5.164. Now you have a perfect copy for the other side. Move the mirrored model right next to the original piece. This will allow us to start welding the two pieces together (See Figure 5.165).

13. In Figure 5.166, pay close attention to the vertices that we are selecting to actually weld. Be sure that these are the only ones that you weld (See Figure 5.167). We will build faces into the other open areas.

14. Now rotate the model slightly to the side. Select your Face tool and build the new faces where they are highlighted. These will close in the front areas of the body (See Figure 5.168).

15. Since we are on the front view, it would be a good time to attach the nose to the face. Bring the nose over to the center of the face, as shown in Figure 5.169. Use a side view, if necessary, to line the nose up (See Figure 5.170).

FIGURE
5.164
Marine copy mirrored.

FIGURE
5.165
Marine pieces moved in together.

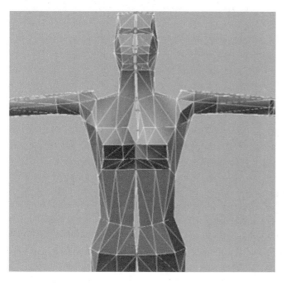

FIGURE
5.166
Front view of Marine with vertices selected.

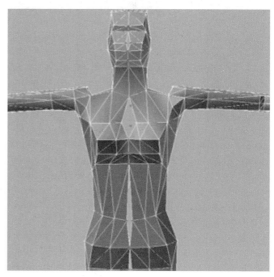

FIGURE
5.167
Vertices welded.

FIGURE *Built faces on front view of Marine.*
5.168

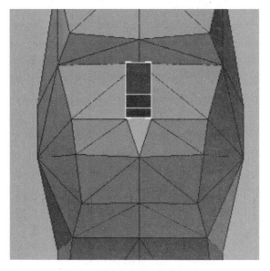

FIGURE *Close-up of face with nose.*
5.169

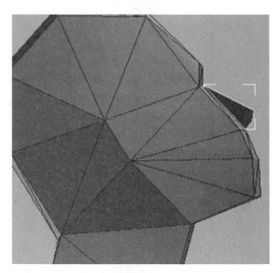

FIGURE *Close-up of side view with nose.*
5.170

16. Next, we want to attach it to the face. Use the Vertices tool to collapse the top of the nose in together. Then weld it to the face, as shown in Figure 5.171. Also, weld the two vertices at each corner of the nose. Now get your Face tool and build one face below the nose, as shown in Figure 5.172. This will finish off the features of the head.

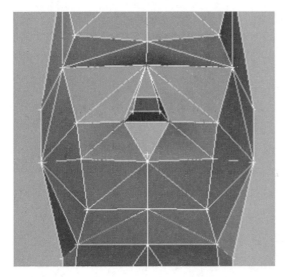

FIGURE   *Nose correction and attachment.*
5.171

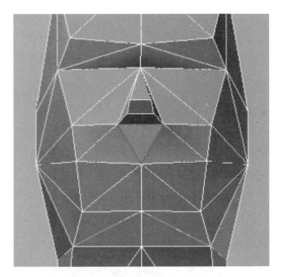

FIGURE   *Building face under nose.*
5.172

17. Let's go to the back of the body and weld it together. In Figure 5.173, select the vertices highlighted and weld them together. Weld the last vertices in the back to close it off (See Figure 5.174).

 If you want to create more of an indention on her lower back and bottom, you can add two more polys to the back instead of closing the vertices as shown in Figure 5.174.

TIP

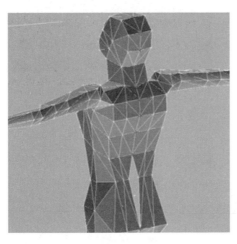

FIGURE   *Weld vertices on back.*
5.173

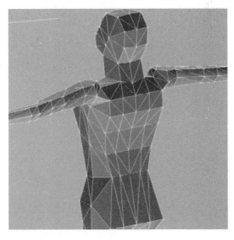

FIGURE   *Weld last vertices together.*
5.174

18. Now we need to close off the under-side of the pelvis and legs. Rotate your model until you can see something like Figure 5.175. Select your Face tool and build the faces shown in Figure 5.176. This will complete the legs and pelvis.

Now that our Female Marine is all welded together, she should look like Figure 5.177.

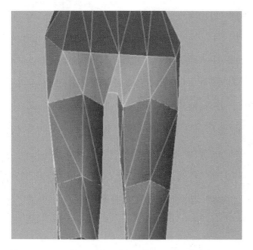

FIGURE **5.175** *Back underside of Marine body.*

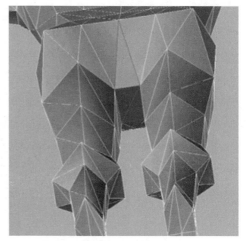

FIGURE **5.176** *Built faces for the underside of the Marine body.*

FIGURE **5.177** *Female Marine attached.*

She is still a little rough around the edges, so lets go back and smooth her out some more.

19. Let's start with the shoulders and work our way around her. First, let's make the shoulder softer. Right now, it's too angular (See Figure 5.178). Use your Vertices tool to select the center vertex and pull it down, as shown in Figure 5.179. This will greatly soften the angular look of her shoulders.

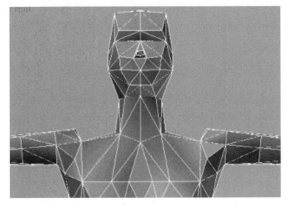

FIGURE *Front view of Marine.*
5.178

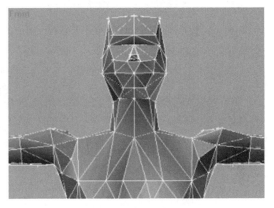

FIGURE *Shoulder vertice corrections.*
5.179

20. Our next step is to better define the chest. Right now, the front of the chest is too angular and flat. By moving the vertices in and back a little, we can soften those edges (See Figure 5.180).

21. Next, we'll want to flip some edges to bring out the side of the chest. If you flip the three inside edges around, you should be able to see the difference that were mentioned before (See Figure 5.181).

22. Rotate your Marine so that you can see the back, as shown in Figure 5.182. Using your Vertices tool, select the center vertices. Pull them in towards the center of the body. Next, select the outside vertices, as shown in Figure 5.183. Pull them out just slightly to help round out the back some more.

23. The last thing we are going to soften up is the bottom. Move your model around until you get a view like Figure 5.184. Select the edges and flip them around, as shown in Figure 5.185. With these vertices welded together, we have two edges that look a lot softer.

The Female Marine has now been refined, attached, and smoothed out! Great job everyone! Let's hope it looks something like Figure 5.186.

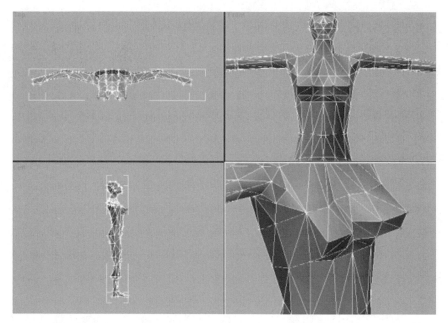

FIGURE *Multiple views, chest correction.*
5.180

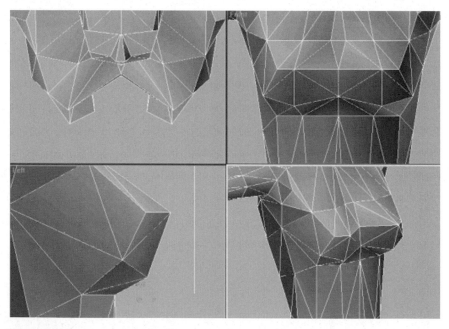

FIGURE *Multiple views of edge flipping on the chest.*
5.181

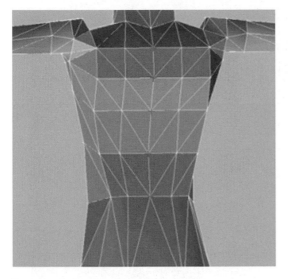

FIGURE **5.182** *Back view of Marine, vertices pulled in.*

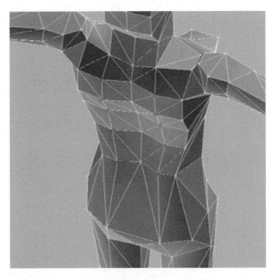

FIGURE **5.183** *Outer vertices selected and pulled out.*

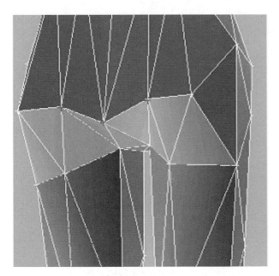

FIGURE **5.184** *Back view of lower pelvis.*

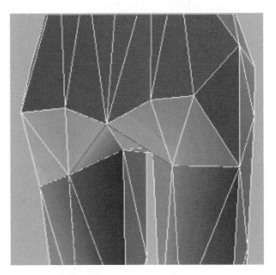

FIGURE **5.185** *Flipped edges.*

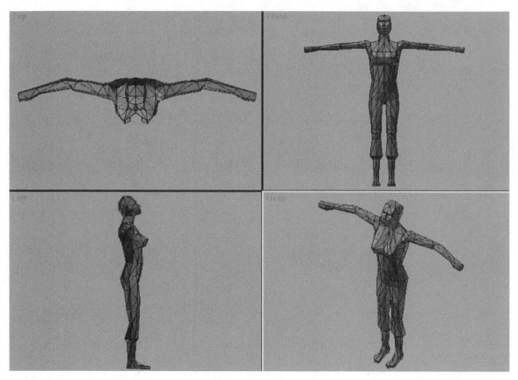

FIGURE   *Multiple views of refined Female Marine.*
5.186

ADDING ACCESSORIES

The only accessories the Marine has are her hair and weapon. Both of these are new to our list, so let's go over them in detail.

1. The first step in adding hair is to use the Edge tool to select all the edges highlighted below. Notice that you only want to select the sides and the back; there is no need to select the front edges unless you want to create some bangs for her (See Figure 5.187).
2. The next step in creating a nice head of hair is to pull the hair down. Use your Edge tool to extrude the hair down, as shown in Figure 5.188.
3. Select the vertices shown in Figure 5.189. Pull them out as shown to make the hair feel like it has volume and thickness. This is the cornerstone behind creating hair for any type of figure or creature. Also, if you feel the need for more movement in the hair, continue to add extra polygons until you get what you want.

The next accessory for the Marine is the weapon that we drew earlier in Part 1. In Figure 5.190, we have the outlining shape of the weapon. Be sure to have

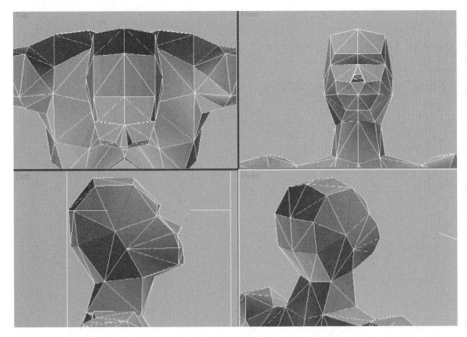

FIGURE *Multiple views of hair selection.*
5.187

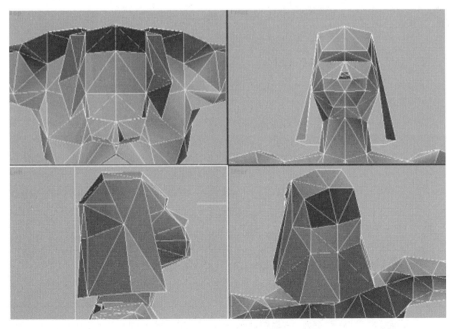

FIGURE *Multiple views of hair extruded down.*
5.188

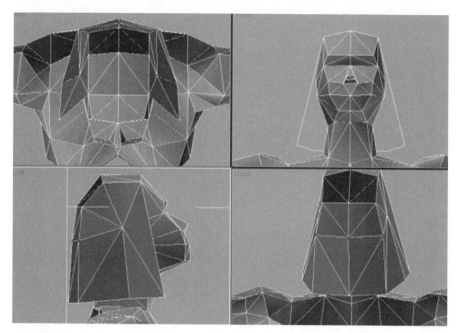

FIGURE   *Vertices pulled out.*
5.189

ON THE CD

the sketches from the CD-ROM loaded into the background or at least next to you for reference before you start creating the gun.

Each shape of the weapon has been outlined separately so that they can have their own individual widths, which allows the gun to have more shape and look highly detailed. Make sure to outline each shape the way we've done it.

First, we need to extrude each shape to its appropriate width so that the gun can begin looking three-dimensional. In Figure 5.191, we have each object extruded to their full extent.

Now that each shape is extruded, it's time to rotate around the model and get a feel for what it is looking like. At present, the model's shape has a lot of definition, but still needs to be tweaked here and there to make it just right.

1. Rotate the weapon so that the barrels can be seen, as shown in Figure 5.192. Next, select the top barrel and add a line segment down the center of it. Also, do the same with the bottom barrel (See Figure 5.193). This will allow us to round the barrels out.

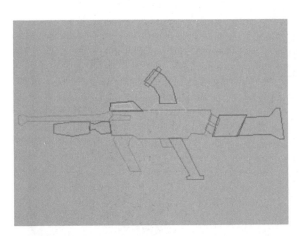

FIGURE
5.190 *Weapon outline.*

FIGURE
5.191 *Weapon extruded.*

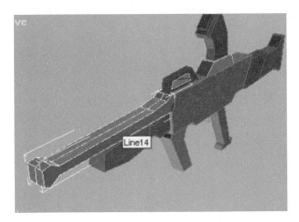

FIGURE
5.192 *Barrel top divided.*

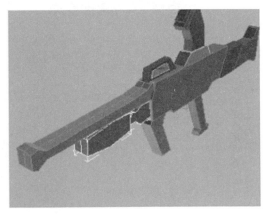

FIGURE
5.193 *Barrel bottom divided.*

2. Select the outside vertices of the top barrel (See Figures 5.194 and 5.195). With the vertices selected, use the Scale tool to scale it down, as shown in Figure 5.196, or simply move each set of vertices until they look like the image below.

3. Select the vertices highlighted in Figure 5.197. Scale the vertices in until you get a slender-looking barrel, as shown in Figure 5.198.

You should be able to tell just with scaling the barrel down, how much of a difference it made.

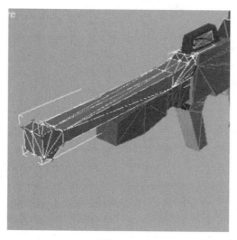

FIGURE *Vertices selected.*
5.194

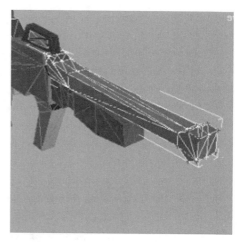

FIGURE *Vertices selected.*
5.195

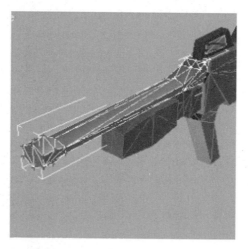

FIGURE *Vertices scaled in.*
5.196

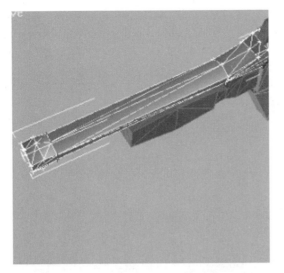

FIGURE *Vertices selected.*
5.197

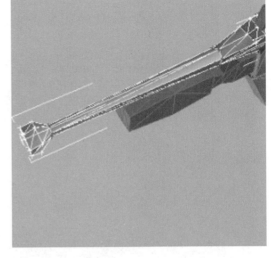

FIGURE *Vertices scaled.*
5.198

4. Rotate the model toward the end of the barrel (See Figure 5.199). Select the three vertices highlighted in Figure 5.200 and scale (or move) them in toward each other.

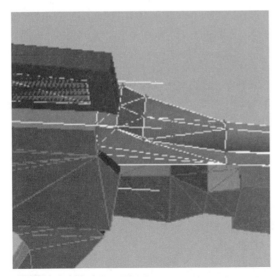

FIGURE *Back end of barrel.*
5.199

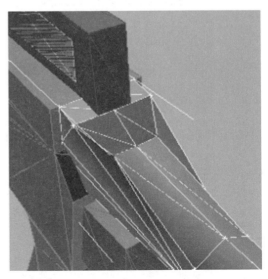

FIGURE *Vertices selected and moved in.*
5.200

5. Use the Edge tool to select the two edges indicated in Figure 5.201. Then flip them around, as shown in Figure 5.202.

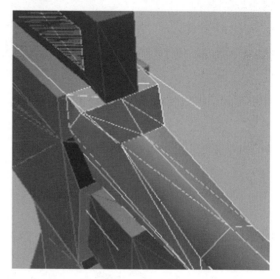

FIGURE **5.201** *Edges selected.*

FIGURE **5.202** *Edges flipped.*

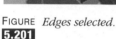

We flipped these edges so that the barrel would be better defined.

6. Drop down to the bottom barrel now. Select the vertices along the outside edges, as shown in Figure 5.203. Then scale the sides down until it looks like Figure 5.204. Make sure that you do not select the inside vertices. We only want the outside ones.

7. Next, we want to shape the top handle of the weapon. Select the handle, as shown in Figure 5.205. We are going to do a Boolean operation. This is where we subtract the inside object from the outer object. In Figure 5.206, we have the finished shape.

We used the Boolean operation to speed up the process. If you would like to model the piece, you can, but Boolean is definitely a quicker, easier way to model complex shapes.

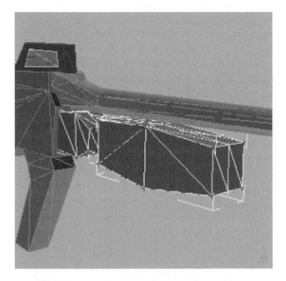

FIGURE *Vertices selected.*
5.203

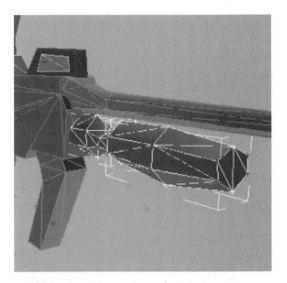

FIGURE *Vertices scaled inward.*
5.204

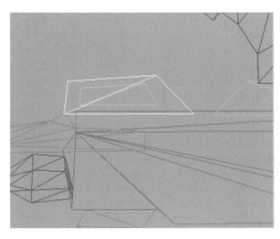

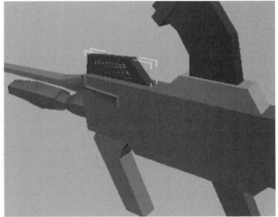

FIGURE *Side and perspective view of top handle.*
5.205

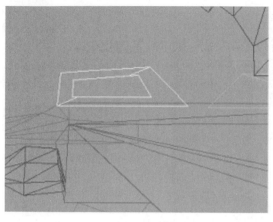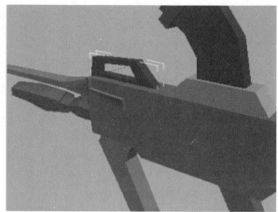

FIGURE
5.206 *Side and perspective view of top handle with Boolean completed.*

8. Create a box, as shown in Figure 5.207. We are going to do one last Boolean operation. Make sure that the box extends past both sides of the butt of the gun. Then subtract the box from the gun, and presto! You now have a cool-looking end to the gun (See Figure 5.208).
9. Select the vertices highlighted in Figure 5.209. Scale them in as shown in Figure 5.210. Make sure to keep the butt of the gun big.
10. Jump back over to the front end of the gun right by the top handle (See Figure 5.211). We need to move two vertices in a little more. Select the vertices shown in Figure 5.212 and move them in toward the center of the gun.

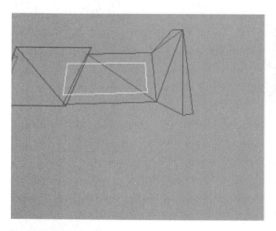

FIGURE
5.207 *Side and perspective view of box created and set in place.*

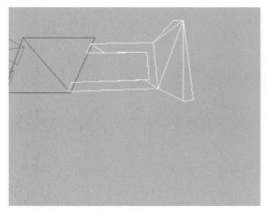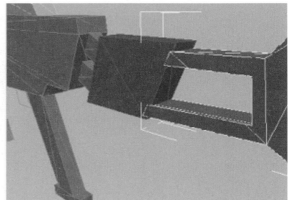

FIGURE   *Boolean the box and the gun.*
5.208

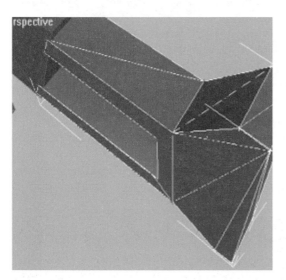

FIGURE   *Vertices selected.*
5.209

FIGURE   *Vertices scaled inward.*
5.210

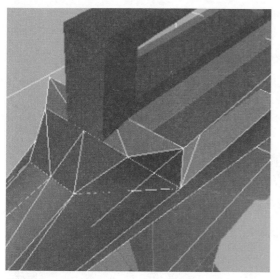

FIGURE **5.211** *Perspective view of gun barrel.*

FIGURE **5.212** *Vertices selected and moved in.*

11. Let's add two extra pieces onto the weapon. After rotating the gun, we need a piece on the top of the gun. Draw the shape with the Line tool, as shown in Figure 5.213. Then extrude it out so that it looks like Figure 5.214.

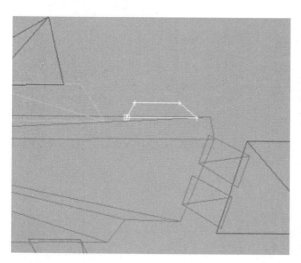

FIGURE **5.213** *Side view with new shape drawn.*

FIGURE **5.214** *Object extruded.*

12. Move the model down to the bottom hand, as shown in Figure 5.215, and with the Line tool, draw the shape shown. Next, select the Extrude tool and extrude the new shape out to the distance shown in Figure 5.216.

These last two steps were to show you that shapes could be added on a whim. If you see something that needs to be added or taken away during any part of the operation, then go ahead and do it. Sometimes you have to vary from the structured atmosphere and be a little artistic.

This should finish up the basic look of the weapon. Here's one final look at our Marine with all of her accessories (See Figure 5.217).

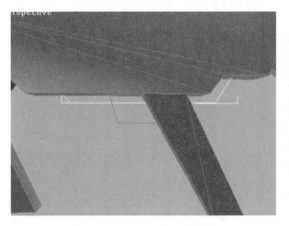

FIGURE *Side view with new shape outlined.*
5.215

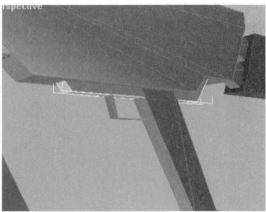

FIGURE *Shape extruded.*
5.216

FIGURE *Finished Female Marine.*
5.217

PRINCESS

The Princess is slightly different from the Marine because of the costume she wears. Her weight and size are about the same, but she is a few years older. In Figure 5.218, we have a shot of her in a very princess-like outfit, which we designed in Part 1 of this book.

Using the Marine that you've just modeled, let's create the Princess. Figure 5.219 shows a close-up shot of the Marine's head. We need to select the vertices around the head and pull them up, as shown in Figure 5.220. Then collapse the top vertices or simply move them toward the center and weld them together. This will create the hat she is wearing.

FIGURE **5.218**   *Shot of the Princess.*

Now we need to add two skirts to the Princess. In Figure 5.221, the vertices around the waist have been selected and pulled out twice. Finally, pull the skirts down and in, so that the two skirts create the dress shown in Figure 5.222.

The last thing we need to do is expand the sleeves of her costume, as shown in Figure 5.223. This should finish off the Princess, originally known as the Marine.

FIGURE
5.219
Marine head shot.

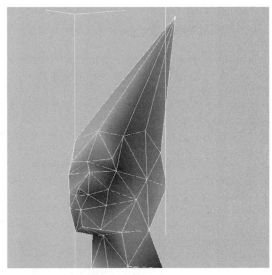

FIGURE
5.220
Hat created.

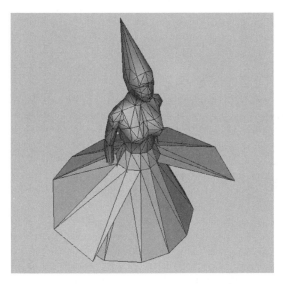

FIGURE
5.221
Vertices for the dress are pulled out.

FIGURE
5.222
Skirts are finished off.

FIGURE   *Sleeves of the Princess.*
5.223

Now let's give her a magic wand. With the picture of the wand set into the front view port, use your 2D Line tool to outline the wand, as shown in Figure 5.224.

The rest should be pretty simple. Extrude the shape and then refine the wand by making the handle and the top piece round-looking (See Figure 5.225).

That should about do it for the Princess. If you want to take this further or feel the need to tweak parts here and there, go for it.

Both the Princess and the Marine are shown in Figure 5.226 to illustrate how simple and effective it is to create different characters using preexisting models.

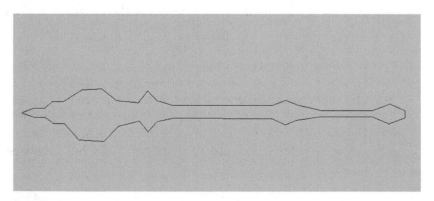

FIGURE   *Outline of the Princess's wand.*
5.224

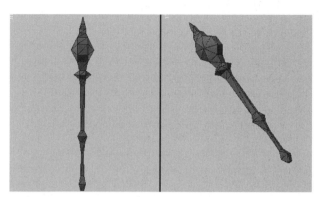

FIGURE *Refined wand.*
5.225

FIGURE *Princess and Marine compared.*
5.226

Notice that both characters were derived from the female model, but yet they look completely different. One advantage of using this type of process is that you can create a perfect male and female character which you can use as the basic model set for all other characters. This is very useful if you are on a deadline or time limit of some sort.

The last human figure we want to look at is the Civil War Soldier, who is generated with a very low polygon frame.

CIVIL WAR SOLDIER

This Civil War Soldier is currently in use in a PC game entitled *Civil War: War Between the States™* being developed by Walker Boys Studio and will be slightly lower than the other models since he is used for a Real Time Strategy style game. Another reason for its apparent lower poly count is because of the way the game plays out. The camera angle used in *Civil War: War Between the States™* is from slightly above and allows for a limited zoom distance between the user and the characters, which means the amount of detail seen will not be as predominate as it would be if you were right next to the character. The setup and directions for the Soldier are the same as the Ancient Barbarian and the two female models, since they are all in the form of a human shape. The one point we want to touch on is the outlining shape and the lack of detail that comes from it.

DRAWING THE SHAPES WITH THE LINE TOOL

In Figure 5.227, the Civil War Soldier has been outlined with a minimum amount of vertices so that the final character will have very few polygons.

Notice how the points plotted are at the major angles of the body. There's no room for extra vertices when you are trying to create a very low polygon character, so be sure to follow the same lines that we have here. Also, the face is straight, allowing no angles for the nose, brow ridge, or the chin box. Just think simple and you should do fine.

Once each shape has been outlined, you can go ahead and extrude the parts just as you have done with the Ancient Barbarian. In Figure 5.228, we have the Soldier extruded and ready to be refined. Notice that the figure has only four sides to his arms and legs. We are not going to be dividing the parts down the center with new edges because we are trying to create it with the least amount of polygons as possible.

After you are finished refining and attaching the Soldier together using the steps and techniques we have talked about, we'll need to make a hat for him.

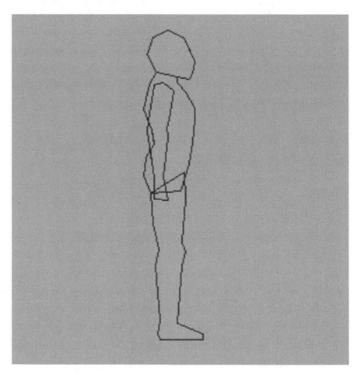

FIGURE   *Finished outline of Soldier.*
5.227

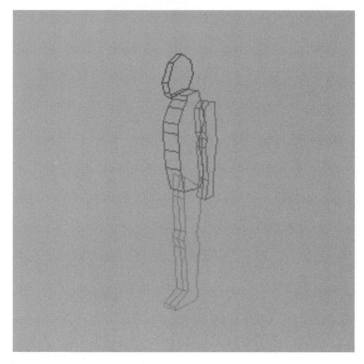

FIGURE   *Soldier extruded.*
5.228

The first step in adding a hat to the Soldier is to select a 2D drawing tool from your 3D application. Use either the Line tool or the Rectangle tool. Now, with your tool selected, go ahead and draw a rectangle on the ground in front of the soldier (See Figure 5.229). Once you have drawn the rectangle, move it up to the top of his head. Be sure that it's set down just a little below the top (See Figure 5.230).

Here's one final look at our Civil War Soldier. For being a very low polygon character, he looks pretty good. (See Figure 5.231).

Now it is time for us to move into the wonderful world of cartoons. You've learned how to model people, and to change them, but there are still a few things left to learn, especially when it comes to creating cartoon characters.

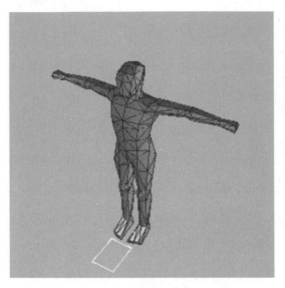

FIGURE
5.229
Rectangle drawn in front of Soldier.

FIGURE
5.230
Hat now on top of head.

FIGURE
5.231
Finished Civil War Soldier.

CARTOON CHARACTERS

CARTOON HERO AND VILLAIN

Both of the cartoon characters that we sketched in Part 1 of this book are outlined below. In Figure 5.232, we have the outline of the Hero, who in all respects does not resemble the shape of a person. The same can be said of the Villain, with his small head and oversized belly (See Figure 5.233). This is the part where things become a little different. With humans, you had an anatomy, which you could stick to, and use as a guide for sculpting the figure. But with cartoon characters, it's closer to the other side of the spectrum. A cartoon character will usually have a very simple body (arms and legs that look like water hoses), so the need for keeping these shapes very round is quite important. The structures of our cartoon characters are spherical and cylindrical, with a tad bit of shape thrown in there. Each of the cartoon characters varies from three to five heads tall, and just as these characters demonstrate, their features are sometimes a bit exaggerated.

Since both cartoon characters are basically identical in their construction, we'll go over just the Villain model.

The extruding process is still the same as the Barbarian, so you can go ahead and do that part. Just make sure that you either have the sketches in the background of your 3D application or next to you for reference.

FIGURE
5.232   *Hero outline.*

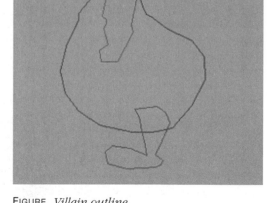

FIGURE
5.233   *Villain outline.*

Once you get done extruding the shapes into three-dimensional objects, we'll go over a few pieces that need to be studied. The first shape that's constructed differently is the head.

1. As in Figure 5.234, select the outside vertices of the head. Then scale all the vertices inward so that you line them up as shown in Figure 5.235. This will help to make our front view of the head rounder and more believable. We have two line segments that we are scaling down in size, so be sure that the first one you scale down is farther than the second one.

2. Select the edges highlighted around the head, as shown in Figure 5.236. With the Divide tool chosen, divide both edges so that you get two new edges, as shown in Figure 5.237.

3. We need to divide one more edge. Notice the divided edge at the bottom of the jawline in Figure 5.238. This should be enough to give some good shape to the overall look of the Villain.

   If you would like to add a few more edges to the head, feel free to do that now.

4. Next, select the middle set of vertices shown in Figure 5.239. We need to move these vertices down just a little more. With the vertices selected, go ahead and scale that segment in just slightly. Once you have moved it in, take the vertices of the cheek and pull them out to match the front view in Figure 5.240.

FIGURE
5.234 *Select vertices.*

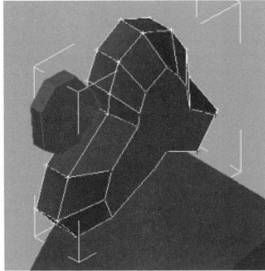

FIGURE
5.235 *Scaled vertices.*

FIGURE
5.236   *Edges selected.*

FIGURE
5.237   *Edges divided.*

FIGURE
5.238   *Edge divided by jaw.*

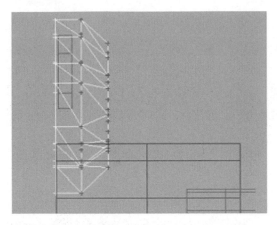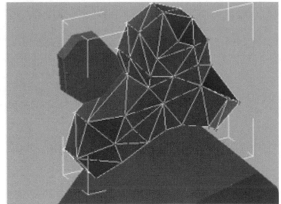

FIGURE *Front and perspective view of vertices on head selected.*
5.239

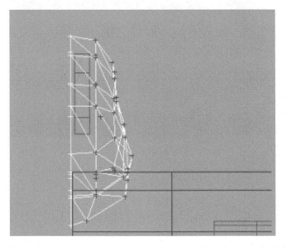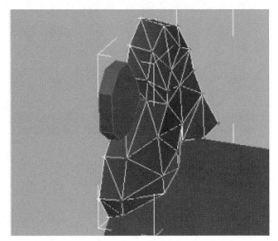

FIGURE *Front and perspective view of vertices scaled in and cheek pulled out.*
5.240

5. All right, let's work the nose over. Select the vertices on the outer rim of the nose (See Figure 5.241). Scale them down or move each one separately until it looks like Figure 5.242.

6. Our next shape to refine is going to be the chest box. In Figure 5.243, we have selected the outside vertices of the body. Use the Scale tool to scale the selected vertices in toward the center of the model (See Figure 5.244). Select the top vertices of that row and move them in toward the body just a little.

FIGURE *Nose vertices selected.*
5.241

FIGURE *Nose vertices scaled down.*
5.242

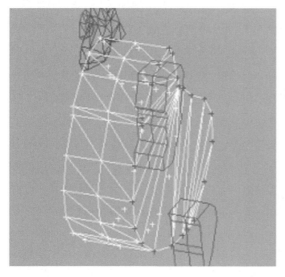

FIGURE *Villain body.*
5.243

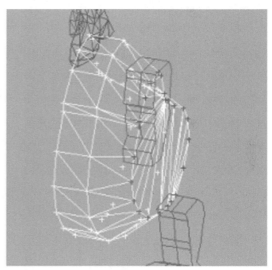

FIGURE *Outer vertices scaled in.*
5.244

7. Select the next row of vertices, as shown in Figure 5.245. Select the Scale tool and move the vertices in just a hair. In order to keep the Villain looking like a cartoon character, we don't want to have a straight line going across him, move the vertices over just enough to make it feel like it's curving downward slightly (See Figure 5.246).

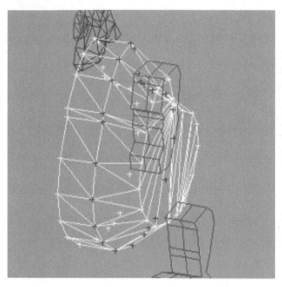

FIGURE **5.245** *Vertices selected.*

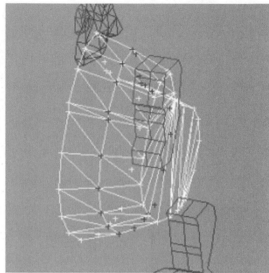

FIGURE **5.246** *Vertices scaled in just slightly.*

8. Rotate the model so the side can be visible (See Figure 5.247). Use the Divide tool to divide the center of the edges highlighted, as shown in Figure 5.248. Be sure that the new edges created are lined up with the direction of the edges that were on the object to begin with (See Figure 5.249).

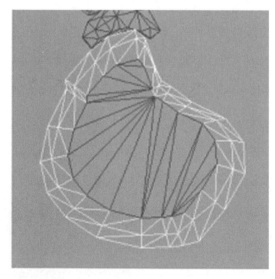

FIGURE **5.247** *Side view of Villain.*

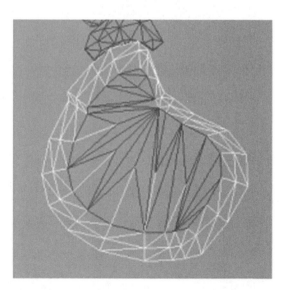

FIGURE **5.248** *Edges divided.*

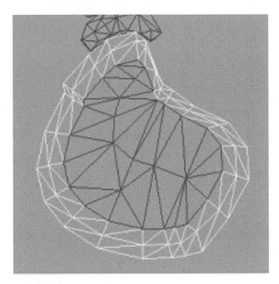

FIGURE *Edges straightened.*
5.249

9. Rotate the model back to a perspective view or front view, as shown in Figure 5.250. Select the vertices of the centerline and move them in and out until the chest and pelvis areas look similar to Figure 5.251.

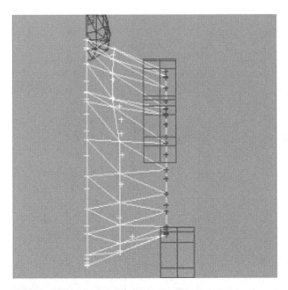

FIGURE *Front view of Villain body.*
5.250

FIGURE *Vertices adjusted for outside line.*
5.251

10. Next, we need to start moving a lot of vertices around. In Figure 5.252, we have a top and front view showing some of the vertices that need adjusted. Notice in Figure 5.253, we are basically moving the vertices in an outward direction. On the back, we have moved some of the vertices in. If you look at the top view differences, you will notice that the body has become very round-looking.

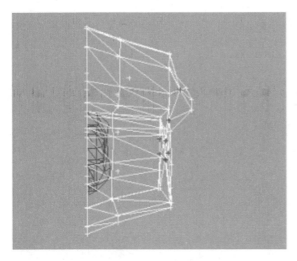
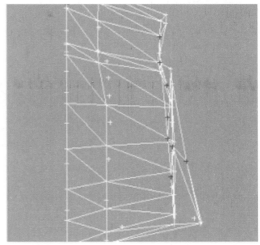

FIGURE **5.252** *Top and front view of the Villain.*

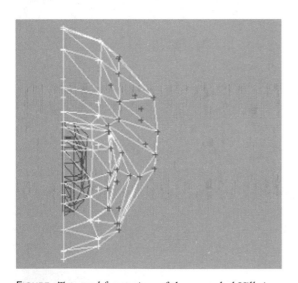
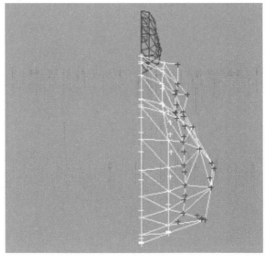

FIGURE **5.253** *Top and front view of the rounded Villain.*

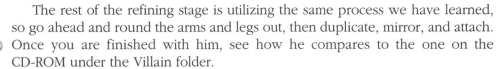

11. With a few more minor vertex movements your Villain's body should look like Figure 5.254. Be sure to "keep it round."

The rest of the refining stage is utilizing the same process we have learned, so go ahead and round the arms and legs out, then duplicate, mirror, and attach. Once you are finished with him, see how he compares to the one on the CD-ROM under the Villain folder.

ON THE CD

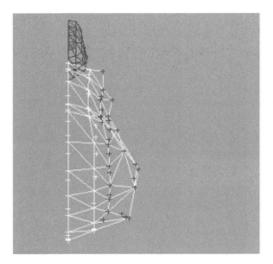
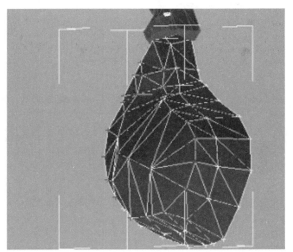

FIGURE   *Front and perspective view of Villain with rounded body.*
5.254

ANIMALS

Modeling animals is very similar to what we have covered so far, but we'll investigate the variations and differences in this section.

HORSE

Here we are going to model an animal, a horse, to be specific. An animal or creature is very simple to create if we use the side view, which is definitely the most important feature in creating any animal. This will give us the outlining shape that we need for capturing the major look and appearance of the Horse. For the most part, the Horse is similar in some respects to that of the human figures, which we have already modeled. The legs and arms do look different, but they are modeled and placed in approximately the same places as on a human. Just pretend that you are looking at a person who is hunched over on all fours and that's what a horse is.

It is assumed you have already placed the sketches of the Horse in their proper view ports, like you did with the Barbarian, and that you are ready to outline him.

Select the 2D Line tool and go to the side view port. Start at the top of the head and work around it in a clockwise direction until you have outlined the head and body of the Horse. Now outline the front and back legs, each as separate shapes. Make sure to outline the ears and tail of the Horse individually, also (See Figure 5.255).

The legs of the Horse were not completely outlined because half of the leg muscle is going to be modeled with the body. This will make it easier for us to attach the legs onto the Horse later. Be sure to place your points in generally the same locations as shown in these examples. If you decide to place more points along the legs, make sure that one set of your points matches the ones shown, so that when we attach the legs you'll have the same vertices to deal with.

Once you have the outlining shapes completed, go ahead and extrude each shape to its approximate width, as we have done in Figure 5.256. Be sure to divide all of the objects that you have extruded with a new line segment, as shown. We will use these lines to help us create a smoother, more believable horse.

Refining the Objects

The Horse objects that we have created are slightly different and therefore require a full and somewhat special look into how we will refine it. The refining

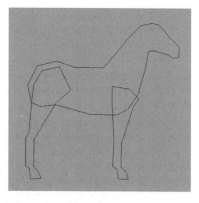

FIGURE *Horse outline finished.*
5.255

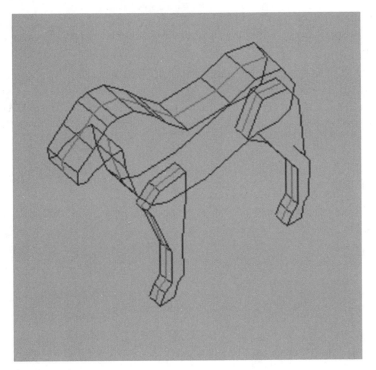

FIGURE *Horse extruded and all parts divided.*
5.256

process on the Horse will be divided into body parts. For this to work properly, we need to move the legs away from the Horse or hide them, so that the body is by itself.

1. In the perspective view, select the body-extruded object. Remember: this is just half of the body. We want to select the outside edges of the Horse, as shown in Figure 5.257. These are the vertices that we are going to weld together to create a side for the Horse. Be sure to connect the vertices in their correct places (See Figure 5.258).

ON THE CD   *NOTE*

The Horse will have a lot of small corrections and pulls during its modeling phase, so pay close attention to what we are doing. If you need to see the color images of the Horse, they are available on the companion CD-ROM.

A side view of the vertices welded and the direction of the polygons are shown in Figure 5.259.

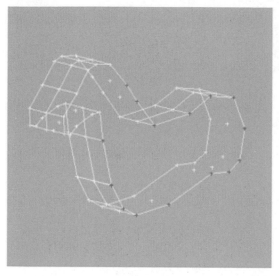

FIGURE *Perspective view with vertices*
5.257 *selected.*

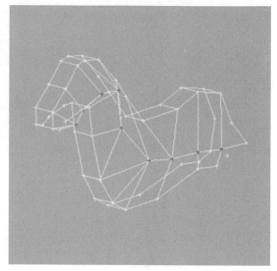

FIGURE *Vertices moved.*
5.258

FIGURE *Vertices welded.*
5.259

2. The next step in modeling a Horse is to change to the top view or rotate your model in the perspective view until you see something like Figure 5.260. Next, get your Vertices tool and select the vertices indicated, and move each one into its current location shown in Figure 5.261. What we are trying to achieve in the top view is to get our basic in's and out's of the Horse. Pull the hind leg form and the front of the shoulder outward.

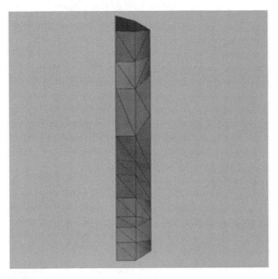

FIGURE *Top view of Horse.*
5.260

FIGURE *Vertices adjusted.*
5.261

3. Now we need to define the front shoulder and the stomach region of the Horse. Select each of the vertices indicated below, and move them until they line up with the picture below. Now you should have a stomach barrel and a front shoulder modeled (See Figure 5.262).

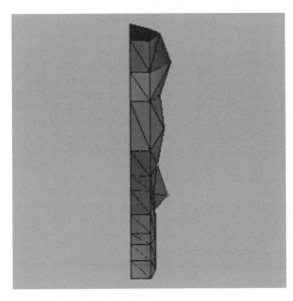

FIGURE *Shoulder defined.*
5.262

Be sure to follow along with the sketch; it will really help keep your model proportioned correctly.

TIP

Just to keep you updated, the Horse should be looking like Figure 5.263. Currently, we have the basic shape of the Horse, but we are a good ways from having him completed.

4. In Figure 5.264, select the middle line of vertices highlighted. Next, choose the Scale tool or move each vertex in toward the center of the body (See Figure 5.265). Notice how everything is beginning to round out.

   This side view of the Horse shows the center line scaled in. The highlighted vertices show how much we moved the lines in, so be sure to pay close attention to the distance in Figure 5.266.

5. With the side view selected, we need to clean up and define some more of our polygons. Select the vertices highlighted with the Vertices tool Figure 5.267). Now select the Welding tool and weld the vertices to their respective places, as shown in Figure 5.268.

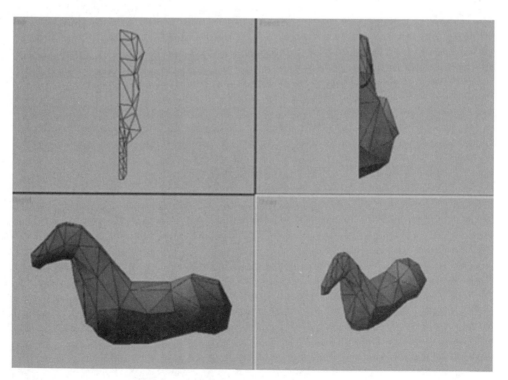

FIGURE *Multiple views of Horse's body.*
5.263

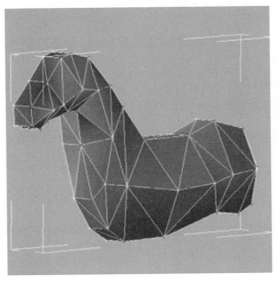

FIGURE *Vertices selected.*
5.264

FIGURE *Vertices scaled inward.*
5.265

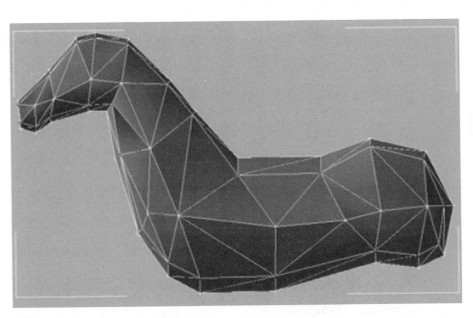

FIGURE *Side view of corrected vertices.*
5.266

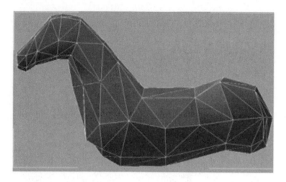

FIGURE **5.267** *Side view with vertices selected.*

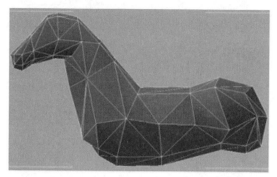

FIGURE **5.268** *Vertices welded.*

Now select the vertex and move it over to the center of the neck, as Figure 5.269 illustrates. Then select the Edge tool and select the edge shown in Figure 5.270.

7. With the edge selected, flip them so that the Horse looks like Figure 5.271. Also, select the edge on the center of the body, as shown in Figure 5.271. Using your Divide tool, divide it to get the two extra polygons shown in Figure 5.272. Then select the new vertex and move it over until it looks like Figure 5.272.

8. Next, we want to flip some of our Edges. Select your edge tool and select the edges shown in Figure 5.273. With the Flip command, turn your edges the other direction (See Figure 5.274). This will allow us to smooth the Horse out and keep the geometry isometric. Most programs have a way of turning the edges the other direction, but if your program doesn't, then you can simply delete these edges and rebuild the faces going in the other direction

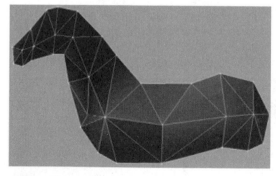

FIGURE **5.269** *Vertices moved.*

FIGURE **5.270** *Edge selected.*

FIGURE **5.271** *Edge flipped.*

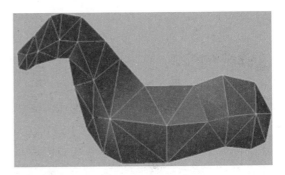

FIGURE **5.272** *Edges divided.*

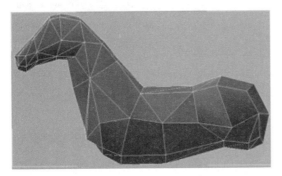

FIGURE **5.273** *Edges selected.*

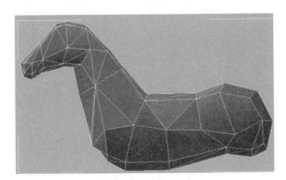

FIGURE **5.274** *Edges flipped.*

9. We need to divide the lower part of the shoulder once more. Use your Edge tool and select the two lower edges highlighted (See Figure 5.275). Now divide them in two so that it will look like Figure 5.276.

10. Rotate the view until you can see the bottom of the Horse. This view is the front part of the Horse, at the neck. Once you have it, select the edge that is highlighted in Figure 5.277. Now, as shown in Figure 5.278, flip the edge the other way.

11. Take your model and rotate it until you see the whole underside of the Horse. In Figure 5.279, the vertices you are going to move have been highlighted. Take your Vertices tool and move each vertex to its appropriate position, as shown in Figure 5.280. The vertices do not have to be moved a great distance, we are just moving them enough to further define and round the Horse's body. This will also allow us to attach the legs to the Horse without having to distort the look of our Horse's body

Let's jump to the face and fix it all up.

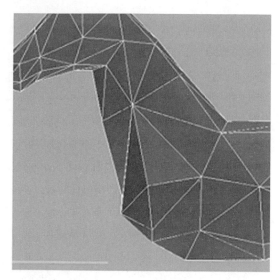

FIGURE
5.275 *Edges selected.*

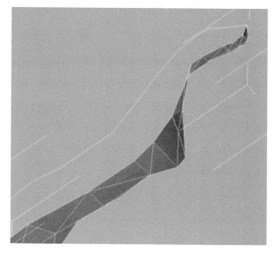

FIGURE
5.276 *Edges divided.*

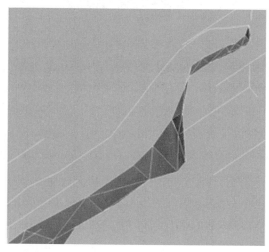

FIGURE
5.277 *Edge selected.*

FIGURE
5.278 *Edge flipped on underside.*

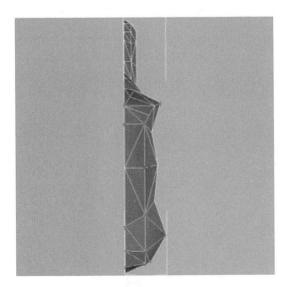

FIGURE *Vertices selected.*
5.279

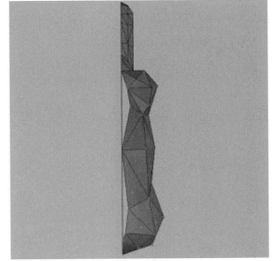

FIGURE *Vertices adjusted.*
5.280

12. Choose the front view port and close in on the head, or just rotate the model until you get something like Figure 5.281. The selected vertices are the ones that need moving. Starting at the top of the head, move those two vertices up together and out, creating a skull base for the Horse. The vertices in the middle of the head just need to be moved inward and up a little. This will help us to define the ridgeline and the jawline. The lower vertices are going to sculpt out our nose for the Horse. Move those vertices inward so that the nose is a realistic size. This should give you enough detail in the Horse's head to create the illusion of a Horse (See Figure 5.282).

Figure 5.283 illustrates what the Horse looks like currently.

The body of the Horse is now complete. If you have moved the legs off or hidden them, go ahead and bring them back into their original positions.

13. Figure 5.284 shows the legs back where they were.

14. The Horse's legs are going to need a few faces deleted. The lines that are above the highlighted edge are used as extras and won't be needed anymore, so delete them as shown in Figure 5.285.

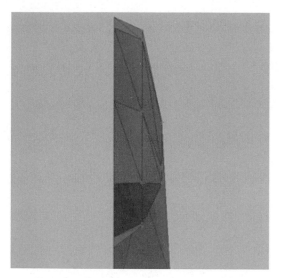

FIGURE *Vertices to be selected.*
5.281

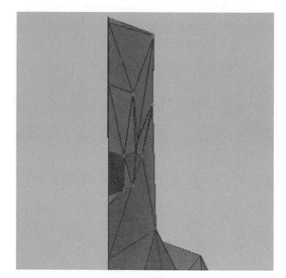

FIGURE *Vertices corrected.*
5.282

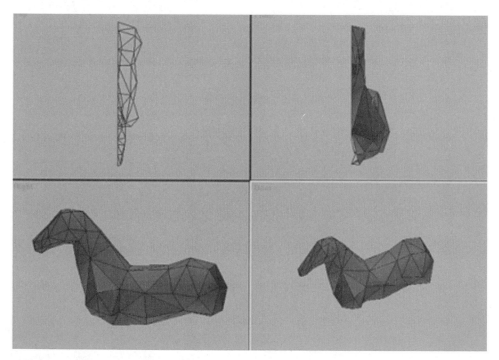

FIGURE *Multiple views of the Horse.*
5.283

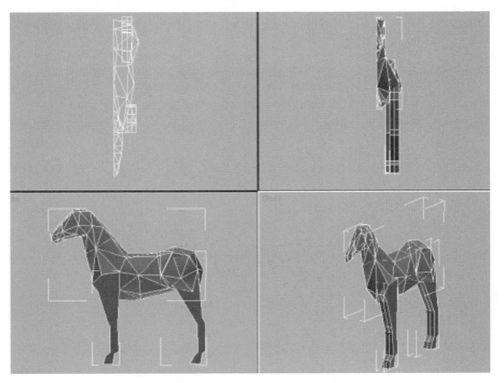

FIGURE   *Multiple views showing the legs.*
5.284

FIGURE   *Side view of legs.*
5.285

15. Now that the legs are cropped down, we need to go ahead and set them in to the body (See Figure 5.286).

Let's go ahead and refine the legs before we connect them.

16. In Figure 5.287, we have selected the vertices that you will pull in toward each other. Be sure to select each one of the vertices and move them into their appropriate positions, as shown in Figure 5.288.

FIGURE *Faces deleted.*
5.286

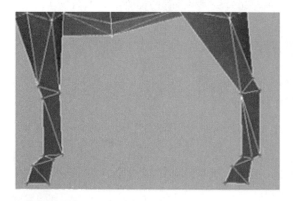

FIGURE *Vertices selected.*
5.287

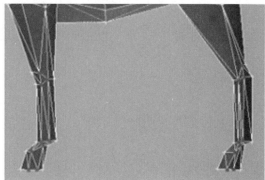

FIGURE *Vertices pulled in.*
5.288

17. Now rotate the model to the other side so that you are looking at the other side of the front leg. In Figure 5.289, we have selected the vertices around the leg, which are the same ones we had selected in the other view. So, just like you did in Figure 5.288, move those vertices in toward the center, as shown in Figure 5.290. When doing this, pay attention to how the leg is being rounded out by very simple and subtle changes in the vertices.

18. Now move the model down to the hind leg and perform the same steps as we did on the front leg (See Figure 5.291).

    Remember to keep it simple. We are doing a low polygon Horse, so all we need to achieve is a look and feel of smoothness and roundness.

19. We have the side views finished. Now we just need to give some shape to the front views. Rotate your model until you are able to see both legs in a front view. First, select the front leg, vertices as shown in Figure 5.292. Move them in toward each other so that the leg is given more shape. Be sure to keep the hoof broader at the base. Now select the hind leg vertices (See Figure 5.293).

20. Move the vertices of the hind leg in toward each other, just like you did on the front leg. This is the last step in refining the legs (See Figure 5.294). If you feel as though you need to tweak them some more to fit your Horse, then go for it!

The refined Horse should resemble Figure 5.295.

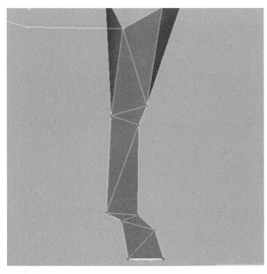

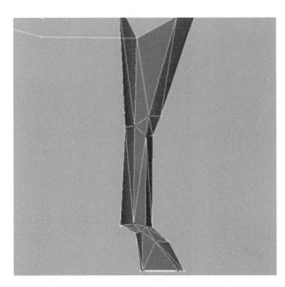

FIGURE *Vertices selected.*
5.289

FIGURE *Vertices pulled in.*
5.290

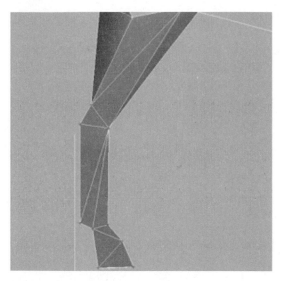

FIGURE
5.291   *Vertices adjusted.*

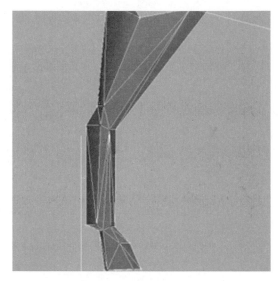

FIGURE
5.292   *Perspective of legs with vertices selected.*

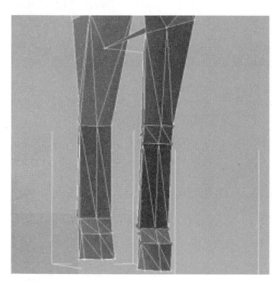

FIGURE
5.293   *Vertices selected and moved inward.*

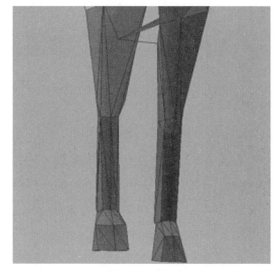

FIGURE
5.294   *Vertices moved in on hind leg.*

FIGURE   *Horse refined.*
5.295

Attaching the Objects Together

Since we are creating a full mesh character, we will need to attach all the individual parts. If you have done the human models, then you should have a pretty good idea of what is going on. If this is the first model you are doing, you should go back through the other models, because attaching these legs can be difficult without having tried the previous characters.

Our main objective is to make sure that the pieces look natural when they are welded together. If you have followed all the steps before this, then welding the legs on will be very easy!

1. First, rotate your model so that you are looking at the side view. Figures 5.296, 5.297, and 5.298 all show the front leg. Select the vertex of the shoulder and pull it over, as shown in Figure 5.297. Next, select the front vertex of the leg and weld the two together (See Figure 5.298).

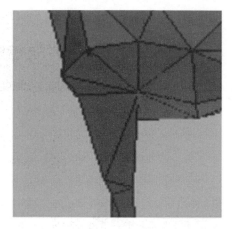

FIGURE *Side view.*
5.296

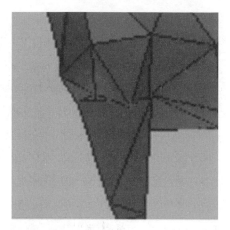

FIGURE *Vertex adjusted.*
5.297

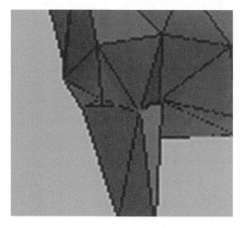

FIGURE *Vertices welded.*
5.298

2. Select the leg vertex that is in the body of the Horse (See Figure 5.299). Pull it out and weld it to the shoulder vertex of the Horse, as shown in Figure 5.300.
3. Next, go to the inside of the leg again (See Figure 5.301). We need to connect the front side of the leg vertex to the highlighted vertex on the body. Weld the two together, as shown in Figure 5.302.
4. Now slightly rotate the model until you can see the underside of the front of the leg (See Figure 5.303). We need to connect the three vertices that are hanging loose. In Figure 5.304, we pulled the vertices of the leg to the closest vertices of the body and then welded them together.

FIGURE
5.299
Vertex selected.

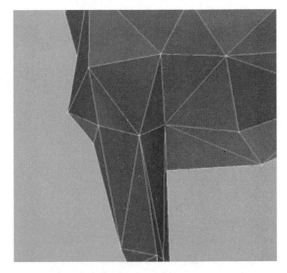

FIGURE
5.300
Vertices welded.

FIGURE
5.301
Vertices selected.

FIGURE
5.302
Vertices welded.

If you are having a hard time finding your vertices, then switch to a wireframe mode. This should help you find and select your vertices easier.

TIP

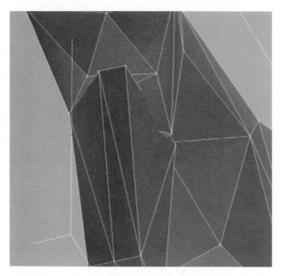

FIGURE
5.303
Underside of leg.

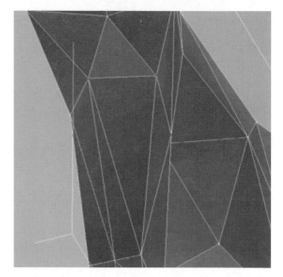

FIGURE
5.304
Closest vertices welded.

5. We need to weld the hind leg to the body now. Rotate the model until you see the inside of the hind leg. We are going to connect the bottom and the hind leg together. The two vertices selected on the left side of Figure 5.305 should be welded together. With the vertex on the right selected, you will need to pull the leg vertex over to it and weld them together (See Figure 5.306).

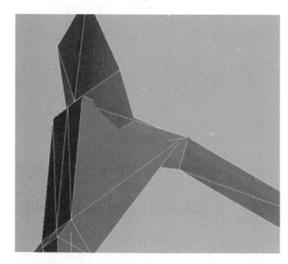

FIGURE
5.305
Vertices selected.

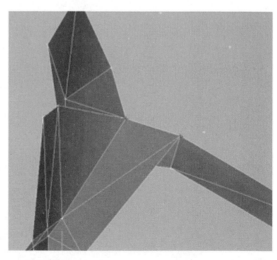

FIGURE
5.306
Vertices welded.

6. Now select the two vertices highlighted in Figure 5.307. Pull the leg vertex up to the body vertex and weld them together (See Figure 5.308).

7. Go to the side view of the hind leg. Select the two vertices shown in Figure 5.309. Now move the leg vertex over to the body vertex and weld the two together (See Figure 5.310).

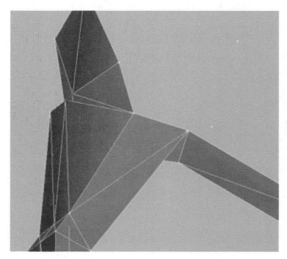

FIGURE **5.307**   *Vertices selected.*

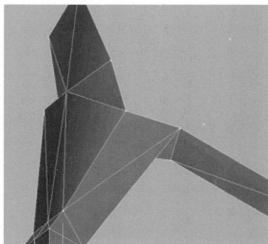

FIGURE **5.308**   *Vertices welded.*

FIGURE **5.309**   *Side view of vertices selected.*

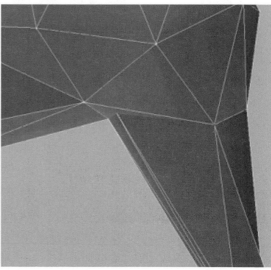

FIGURE **5.310**   *Vertices welded.*

8. The last vertex needing welding is the front of the hind leg (See Figure 5.311). Now, as shown in Figure 5.312, move the vertex to the body vertex and weld them together.

FIGURE *Underside of Horse.*
5.311

FIGURE *Vertices welded.*
5.312

Your Horse should now be completely attached and welded. It should look something like Figure 5.313.

FIGURE   *Multiple views of attached Horse.*
5.313

9. Go to the front view of the Horse's head. We need to outline the ear and place it on him. Select your Line tool and outline the sketch of the Horse's ear (See Figure 5.314). You can either extrude the bottom end of the ear out or leave it flat since it is just an ear. In Figure 5.315, we have extruded it so that we might have a little bit more depth. There is no need to weld it; all you should do is place the ear right on top (and a little under) the head.

10. Select the Horse, as shown in Figure 5.316. Choose Duplicate and move it over, next to the original model (See Figure 5.317).

11. With the duplicated model selected, choose the Mirror tool. Mirror the Horse so that it is now an exact opposite copy of the original model (See Figure 5.318).

Be sure to move the duplicated model as close to the original Horse as you can. This will make it easier to weld the two pieces together.

FIGURE 5.314 *Outline of ear.*

FIGURE 5.315 *Multiple views of ear.*

FIGURE   *Horse selected.*
5.316

FIGURE   *Horse duplicated.*
5.317

FIGURE   *Horse copy mirrored.*
5.318

12. Select the vertices shown in Figure 5.319. Notice we have provided four views to make sure that you can see each group of vertices that are to be welded. Now weld the vertices together.

13. Next, rotate the Horse until you can see its underbelly. We need to fill in a few polys here (See Figure 5.320). Select your Face tool and build four new faces on the lower end of our Horse, as shown in Figure 5.321.

14. With the Face tool still selected, finish filling in the open polys (See the faces highlighted in Figure 5.322).

15. The last thing we need to add to our Horse is the tail. Change your view so that you are looking directly at the back of the Horse (See Figure 5.323). Once you have it, draw the shape of the tail with the Line tool. Be sure to use the sketch of the Horse for the actual look of the tail. It can remain flat; there is no reason to extrude it (See Figure 5.324).

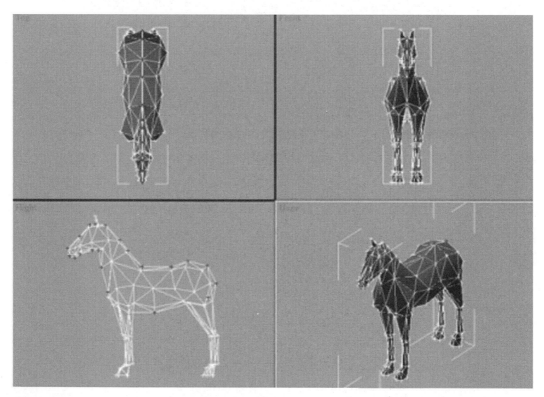

FIGURE
5.319   *Vertices selected and welded together.*

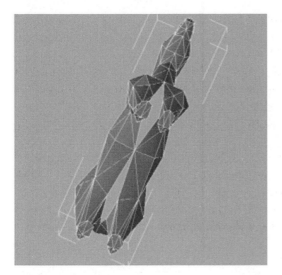

FIGURE *Bottom view of Horse.*
5.320

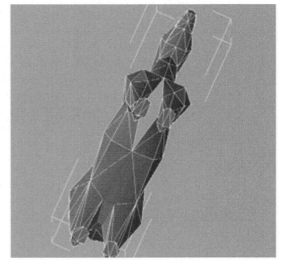

FIGURE *Faces built.*
5.321

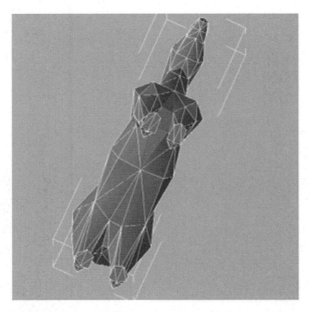

FIGURE *Faces built.*
5.322

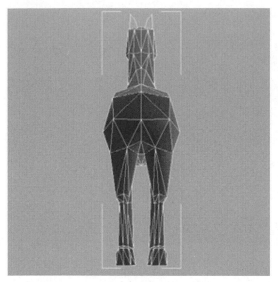

FIGURE **5.323** *Back view of Horse.*

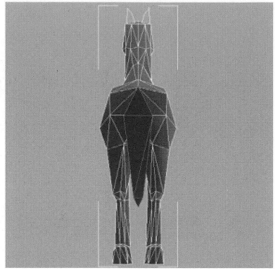

FIGURE **5.324** *Tail outlined.*

16. Using your Vertice tool, select the highlighted tail vertex (See Figure 5.325). Now move it over to the back end of the Horse and weld the two vertices together, as shown in Figure 5.326.

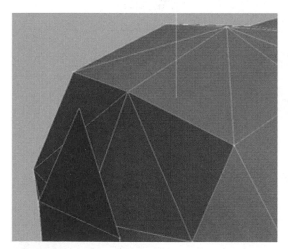

FIGURE **5.325** *Vertex selected.*

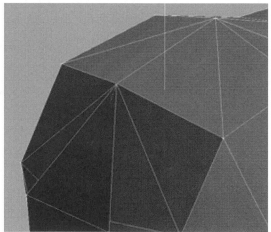

FIGURE **5.326** *Vertex moved and welded.*

The finished Horse looks pretty good! Check out Figure 5.327.

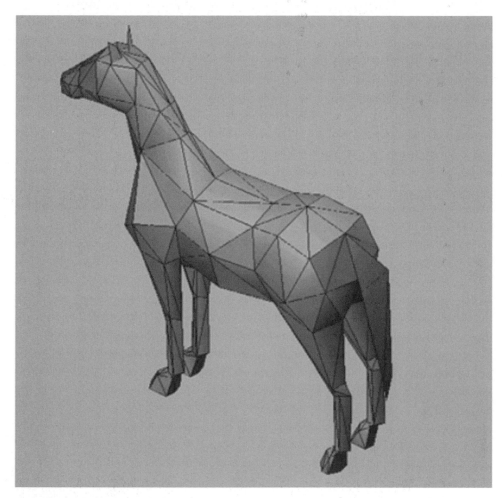

FIGURE *Finished Horse.*
5.327

Stegosaurus

The Stegosaurus is very similar to the Horse, in that it stands on all fours and has the basic shape of any animal. What we need to look at, though, is the difference between the two in weight. If you look at the two animal sketches provided on the CD-ROM, you can see how similar the side view pictures are. Imagine if the Horse started eating a ton of food everyday and his head became too heavy for him to hold up and his belly continued to grow. The Stegosaurus is nearly what he might wind up resembling. In Figure 5.328, we show the Stegosaurus outline created with the 2-D Line tool. Go ahead and outline the side view sketch of the dinosaur, dividing it into the proper pieces as shown.

Once the Stegosaurus is outlined, we can move on to extruding each shape. You've had a lot of practice at this, so we'll just show you what the finished shape should look like (See Figure 5.329).

The scales of the Stegosaurus are single polygons, which help to keep the polygon count low while still retaining the look of complex shapes. Also, make sure that you divide the edges of all the objects, as they appear in Figure 5.330, so that when you begin refining the objects, you will have a sufficient amount of polygons to play with. The head of the Stegosaurus is very similar to that of the Horse, which means all you have to do is apply the identical steps we used for the Horse to the dinosaur. If you start getting lost, you may be thinking into it too much. Keep it simple and you shouldn't have any problems.

FIGURE *Outline of Stegosaurus.*
5.328

The final version of the Stegosaurus should look like Figure 5.331. Notice how much smoother and refined the dinosaur looks once you move the vertices around a little. This method of constructing an animal, or even a human, is extremely simple and straightforward. We refined and attached the legs of the Stegosaurus in the very same manner as the Horse, so this shouldn't be anything new to you. The only difference you may come across is the width of the legs for the Stegosaurus compared to the Horse's legs. They are much wider and meatier than the slender legs of a Horse.

That's it! We've wrapped up the lessons on modeling characters. With this newfound knowledge, modeling any form of human or creature should be relatively simple. In Chapter 6, we will switch gears and begin modeling vehicles and robots! See you there.

FIGURE   *Stegosaurus extruded.*
5.329

FIGURE *Objects divided.*
5.330

FIGURE *Multiple views of finished Stegosaurus.*
5.331

CHAPTER
6
Modeling Vehicles

In Chapter 6, we will demonstrate the ease of turning your Vehicle sketches into fun, realistic 3D models. If you are a beginner at modeling, then these should be a good challenge to get you on the road to modeling. Our basic approach to modeling vehicles will be similar to the human figures, with the exception of one thing — they're two completely different-looking objects. So, hang on tight. We're about to throw it into high gear, and model a Sci-Fi Van, a Car, and a very creative Mech Robot!

SCI-FI VAN

The Sci-Fi Van will be a good starting point for how to create any type of normal everyday or futuristic vehicle. Here, we'll be able to transform a sketchy drawing into a refined, slick-looking Sci-Fi Van. All right, let's get to it.

Getting to know the CD-ROM that comes with this book can be a very good thing. Let's take a moment to go to the Tutorial directory on the CD-ROM and click the Van folder. In each folder, there are sketches, texture maps, U.V. maps, and the 3D models for you to use while you make the characters that are in this book. If you have trouble with any portion of these chapters, or if you need to view an image in color, all the pictures and files are available on the CD-ROM for you to use. Be sure to explore the CD-ROM and remember to have fun!

Let's start by making sure the sketches of the Van are placed into the proper view ports.

- Side sketch of the Van in the side view port
- Front sketch of the Van in the front view port
- Top sketch of the Van in the top view port

For those who only have one display window, make sure you put the side view sketch in the window to use for now.

NOTE

DRAWING THE SHAPES WITH THE LINE TOOL

1. Select the 2D Line tool and go to the side view port. Outline the body of your Van, as shown in Figure 6.1.
2. Next, you can outline your tires with the Line tool or use the Cylinder tool to create a ten-sided circle (See Figure 6.2).

If you would like to have a higher polygon tire than the one we are doing, just increase the sides of the wheels.

TIP

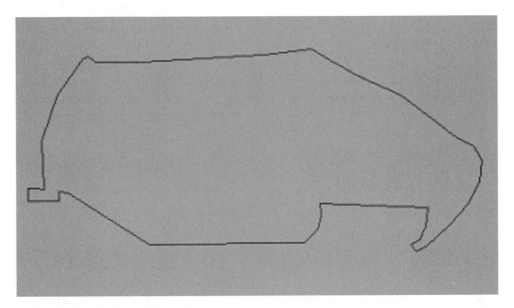

FIGURE *Outline of Van body.*
6.1

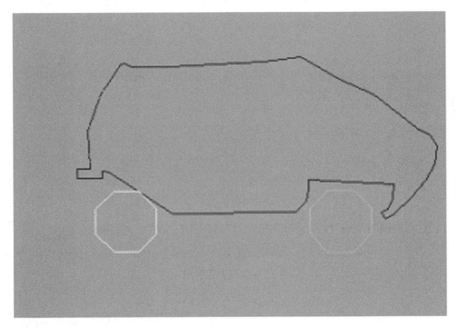

FIGURE *Outline of Van wheels.*
6.2

3. Next, go to the front view and create a seven-sided cylinder. This will be the rocket booster on the Van (See Figures 6.3 and 6.4). Since the rocket booster is on the side of the Van, place the rocket outline on the side of the Van, as shown.

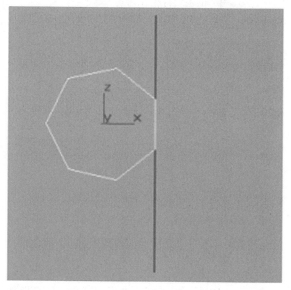

FIGURE   *Front view of Van and rocket booster.*
6.3

FIGURE   *Side view of Rocket booster.*
6.4

4. Let's draw in one more shape, which looks similar to the rocket. Notice in Figure 6.5 and 6.6, the end booster is smaller in size and placed on the back end of the Van.

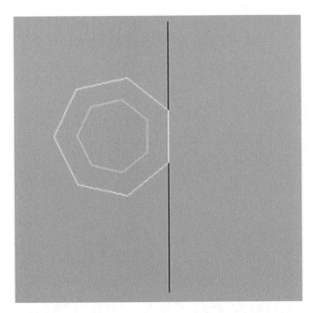

FIGURE *Front view of end booster outline.*
6.5

FIGURE *Side view of end booster outline.*
6.6

EXTRUDING ALL THE SHAPES

Now that the sketch has been outlined, we need to transform the 2D lines and shapes into 3D objects. By using the Extrude tool, you'll be able to turn your shapes into 3-dimensional objects that we can work from.

1. Go to your front view or your perspective view port (See Figure 6.7). Choose the Extrude tool and extrude the wheel of your Van, as shown in Figure 6.8.

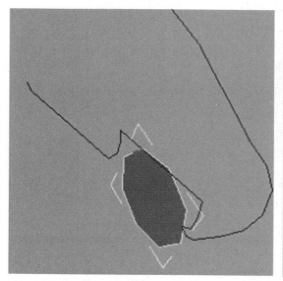

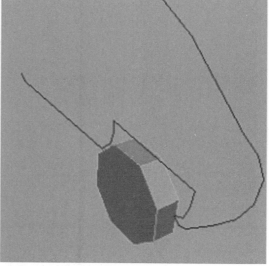

FIGURE **6.7** *Perspective view of wheels selected.*

FIGURE **6.8** *Wheels extruded.*

Be sure to pull it to the approximate width of the Van tire, as shown in the sketch.

NOTE

2. Now select the Van frame (See Figure 6.9). Use the Extrude tool to extrude the Van line to half the width of the actual Van (See Figure 6.10).

3. Select the booster end, as shown in Figure 6.11. With the booster selected, extrude the booster end to where it is just touching the main booster (See Figure 6.12). We have been using different views to extrude the objects. Make sure to get the best angle possible when extruding a line That way, you know exactly how long you have extruded it.

FIGURE   *Side view with main booster selected.*
6.9

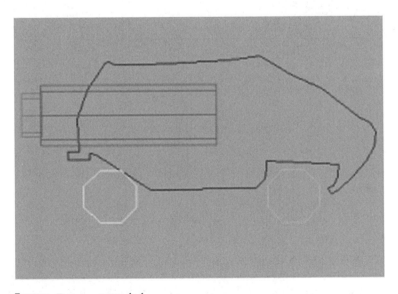

FIGURE   *Booster extruded.*
6.10

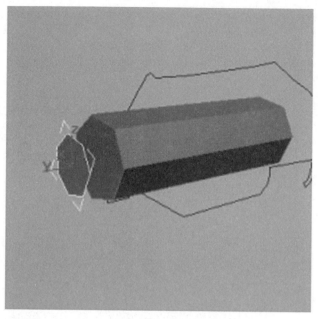

FIGURE   *Perspective view of booster end.*
6.11

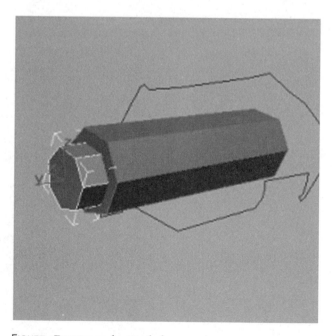

FIGURE   *Booster end extruded.*
6.12

4. The last thing to extrude is the Van body (See Figure 6.13). With the Extrude tool chosen, go ahead and extrude the body out half the distance of the actual Van width (See Figure 6.14).

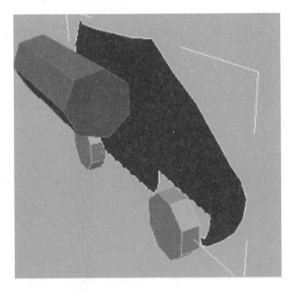

FIGURE *Van body selected.*
6.13

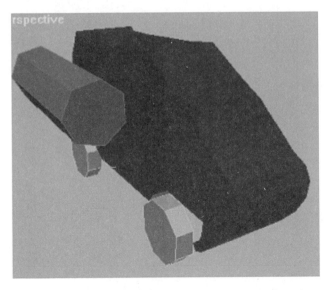

FIGURE *Van body extruded.*
6.14

5. With the body still selected, add an extra line segment down the center of it, as shown in Figure 6.15, so that we will have more polygons to play with later.

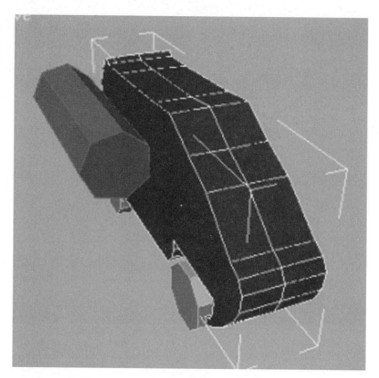

FIGURE *New line down the center.*
6.15

REFINING THE OBJECTS

With all the objects extruded, it's time to start refining each piece. When refining the objects, you will need the Vertices, Polygon, and Face Tools. You should have become very familiar with using them from the previous chapter, so we will not go into detail about them. If you need to find out what they are, go back to Chapter 5 for review of each tool used.

1. Rotate the model around so you can see the inside portion of the Van, as shown in Figure 6.16. If you have any extra polygons on the inside, then select all of them using the Face Tool, and delete the extras by pressing the Delete key (See Figure 6.17). Be sure that you have not deleted any of the other faces in the model

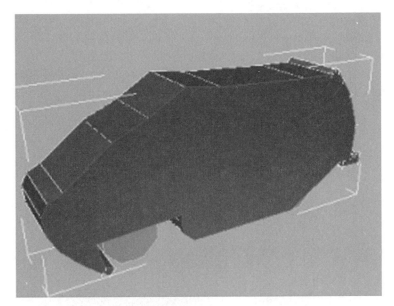

FIGURE   *Inside of Van with faces selected.*
6.16

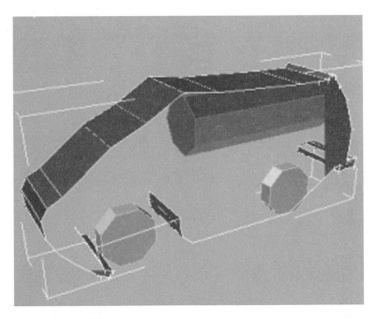

FIGURE   *Faces deleted.*
6.17

2. In Figure 6.18, select the tires and booster. Now hide them or move the parts away from the main body of the Van so that we can work on it with nothing in the way.

3. Go to the front view of the Van (See Figure 6.19). With the vertices selected, pull both sides in together, as shown in Figure 6.20.

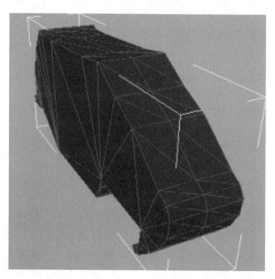

FIGURE *Tires and booster moved away.*
6.18

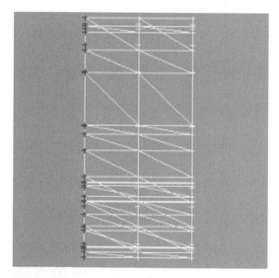

FIGURE *Front view with vertices selected.*
6.19

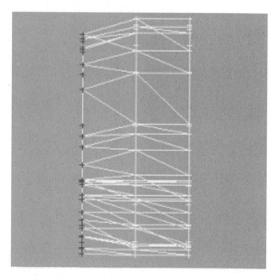

FIGURE *Vertices pulled in.*
6.20

4. In Figure 6.21, we have selected the inside vertices. Pull the vertices up, as shown in Figure 6.22, to create the back end of the Van.

 You do not have to select all the vertices at once. Just select each vertex, one at a time, and move it to the proper position.

5. Change the view to the front view port. Select the Vertices tool. In Figure 6.23, we have highlighted the vertices on the top that you will need to move around. Next, pull the vertices up, as shown in Figure 6.24.

6. Rotate the model so that you can see the back end, as shown in Figure 6.25. Select the center vertices with the Vertices tool. Pull the vertices outward to match the distance shown in Figure 6.26.

7. Now change to the top view and select the vertices shown in Figure 6.27. These are the vertices at the front of the Van. Pull them down until it looks like Figure 6.28.

8. Select the inside vertices of the Van (See Figure 6.29). Once the vertices are selected, pull them to the front of the Van, as shown in Figure 6.30.

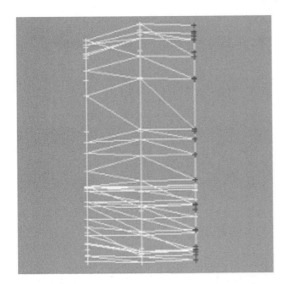

FIGURE *Vertices selected.*
6.21

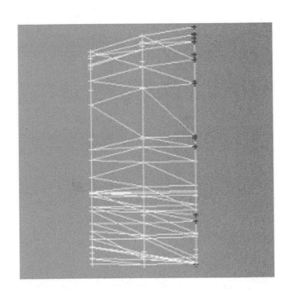

FIGURE *Vertices moved up.*
6.22

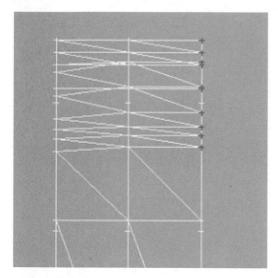

FIGURE *Front view.*
6.23

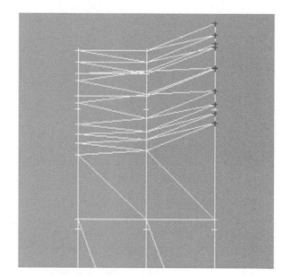

FIGURE *Vertices moved.*
6.24

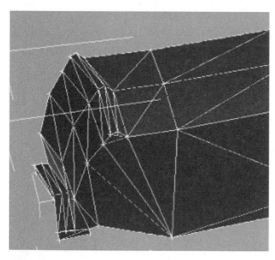

FIGURE *Perspective view with vertices selected.*
6.25

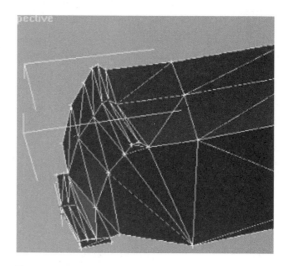

FIGURE *Center vertices pulled out.*
6.26

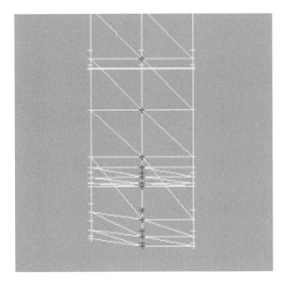

FIGURE   *Top view.*
6.27

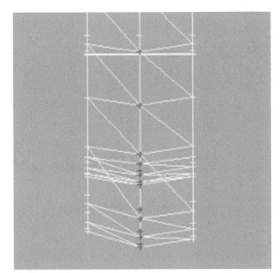

FIGURE   *Vertices moved down.*
6.28

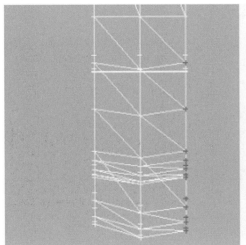

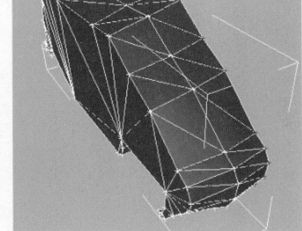

FIGURE   *Front and perspective views of vertices selected.*
6.29

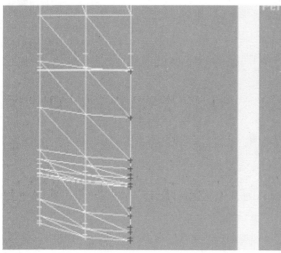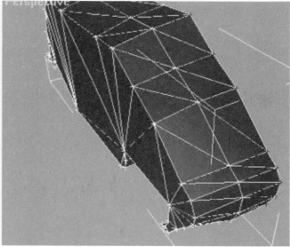

FIGURE *Vertices pulled to the front of the Van.*
6.30

9. Rotate the model around to the side view (See Figure 6.31). The highlighted edges need to be divided in order to create a more believable side
   view of the Van, so select the Divide tool and divide the edges once, as
   shown in Figure 6.32.

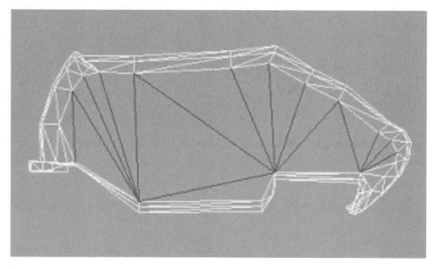

FIGURE *Side view of Van.*
6.31

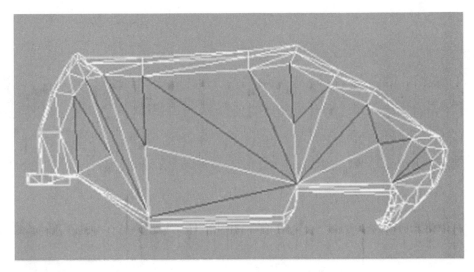

FIGURE   *Edges divided.*
6.32

10. Now flip the highlighted edges so that the Van looks like Figure 6.33.

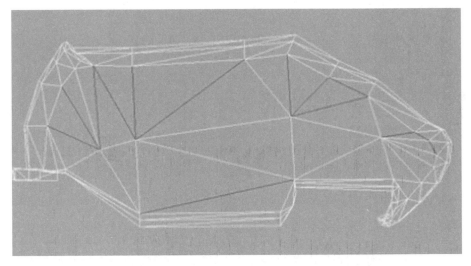

FIGURE   *Vertices flipped.*
6.33

11. Select the Vertices tool and choose the vertices shown in Figure 6.34. Straighten them up so that there is a centerline, as shown in Figure 6.35.

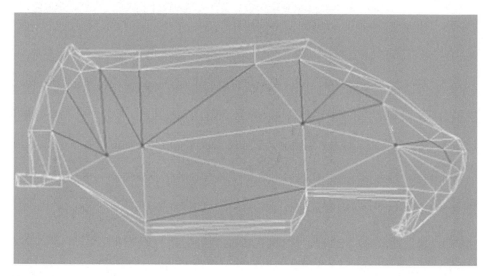

FIGURE   *Vertices selected.*
6.34

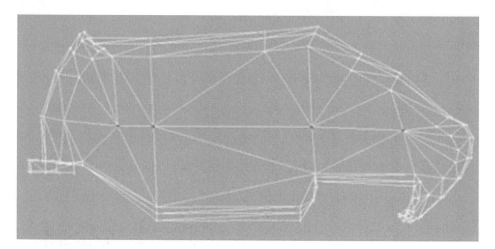

FIGURE   *Vertices corrected.*
6.35

12. Rotate the model so that the side is visible (See Figure 6.36). With the vertices still selected from Step 11, pull them out, as shown in Figure 6.37.

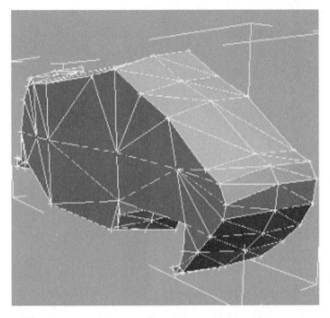

FIGURE *Perspective view with vertices selected.*
6.36

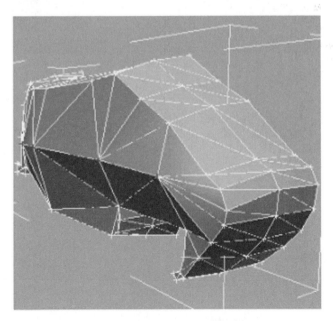

FIGURE *Vertices pulled out.*
6.37

13. We are going to need a few more edges to play with, so go back to the side view and divide the highlighted edges. It should look like Figure 6.38 when you get the edges divided.

If you have difficulty seeing the images in the book, refer to the ones found on the CD-ROM in color.

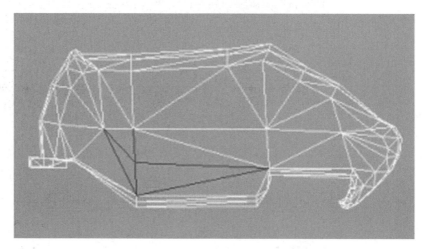

FIGURE *Edges divided.*
6.38

14. Next, flip the new edge so that its appearance is like Figure 6.39.

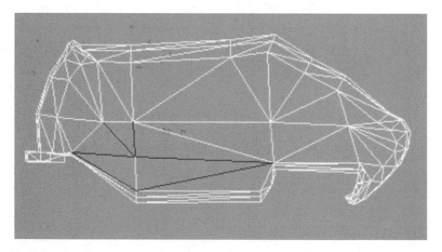

FIGURE *Edge flipped.*
6.39

15. Rotate the model and select the vertex highlighted in Figure 6.40. Move it into the Van until it lines up with the vertex next to it (See Figure 6.41).

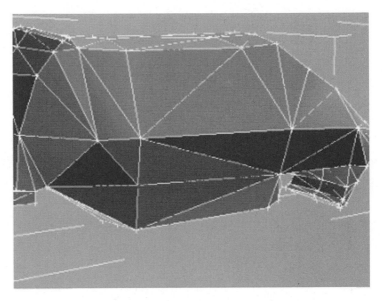

FIGURE *Perspective view with vertex selected.*
6.40

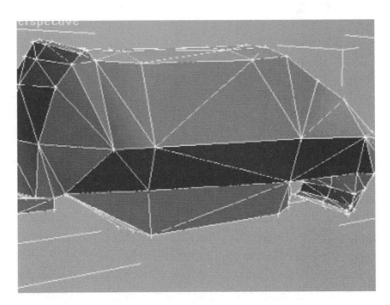

FIGURE *Vertex moved into the Van.*
6.41

16. Go to the front view and select the upper left vertex shown in Figure 6.42. Move it over so that it looks like Figure 6.43. This will start to create that top piece on the Van.

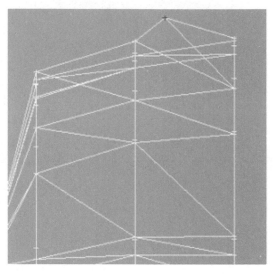

FIGURE *Vertex adjusted.*
6.43

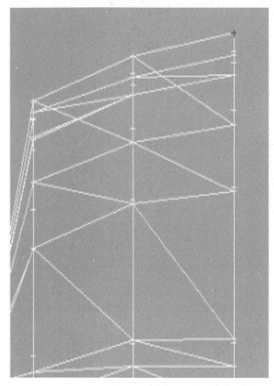

FIGURE *Front view with vertex selected.*
6.42

The body of the Van should look like Figure 6.44. Be sure to take time to tweak any other part of the Van before moving on to the booster.

17. If you have hidden or moved the booster, go ahead and bring it back (See Figure 6.45). Make sure to place it back in the original spot. If you're not sure where you had it last, use the sketches in the background to relocate the exact position.

18. We need to make a cone on the front end of the rocket. Rotate the model around until you can see the front of the rocket, as shown in Figure 6.46. Select the center vertex and pull it out, as shown in Figure 6.47.

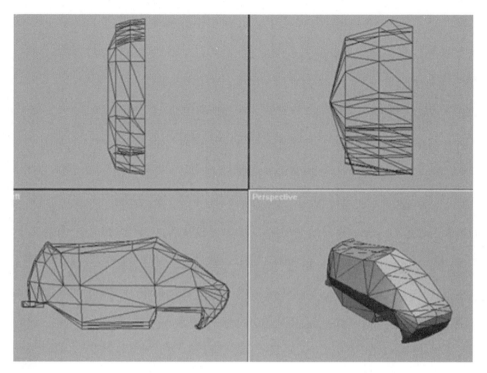

FIGURE *Multiple views of the Sci-Fi Van.*
6.44

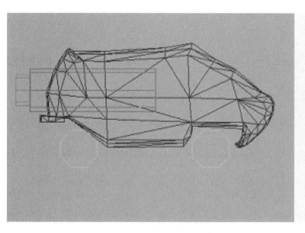
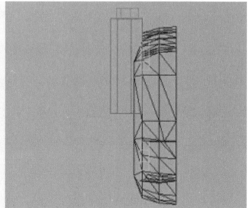

FIGURE *Rocket boosters moved back.*
6.45

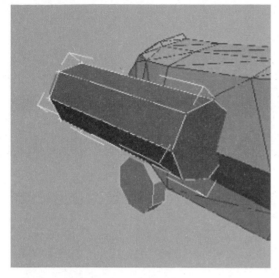

FIGURE *Perspective view of the rocket.*
6.46

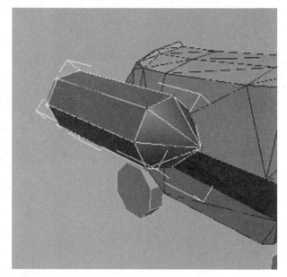

FIGURE *Vertex pulled out.*
6.47

Don't forget to use the sketches for most of your measurements.
The side view and top view will provide you with all the necessary
TIP *lengths.*

19. We need to move the tip of the rocket over to the side. Go to the top view of the Van and select the first vertex, (See Figure 6.48). Next, drag it over to the side of the Van so that it's just touching, as shown in Figure 6.49.

20. At this point, the rocket needs to be rounded out. The vertices highlighted will be the ones you need to adjust (See Figure 6.50). The outline behind the model is the drawing of the rocket. This was to help us get the correct curve of the rocket

21. Move each vertex to its proper place, as shown in Figure 6.51.

22. Rotate to the back of the rocket so that it looks like Figure 6.52.

23. Select the vertex of the rocket and pull it in to the end. Then pull the tail end into the rocket, as shown in Figure 6.53.

24. Rotate the model so you can see the inside of the Van (See Figure 6.54). Select the highlighted rocket faces and delete them (See Figure 6.55).

25. The Van is now complete and ready to be duplicated. Select the Van and rocket See (Figure 6.56). Now use the Duplicate tool to duplicate the model, as shown in Figure 6.57.

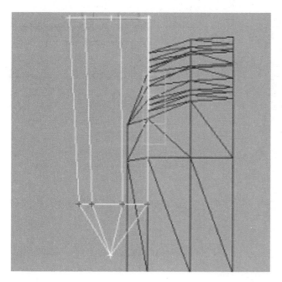

FIGURE *Top view of rocket.*
6.48

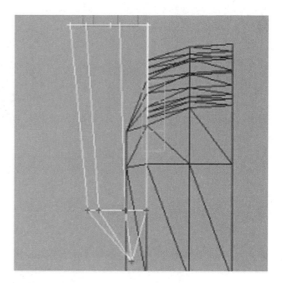

FIGURE *Vertex moved over.*
6.49

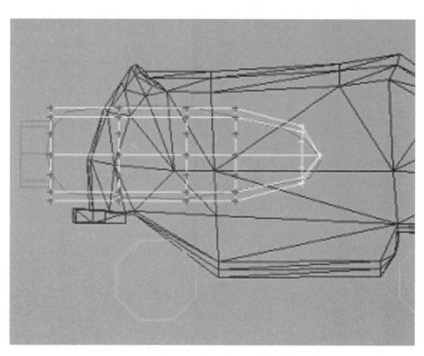

FIGURE *Front view of rocket.*
6.50

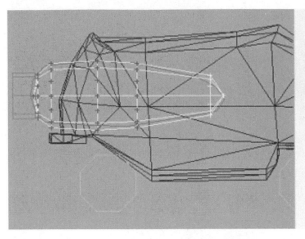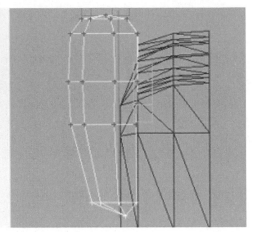

FIGURE **6.51** *Front and top views of vertices adjusted.*

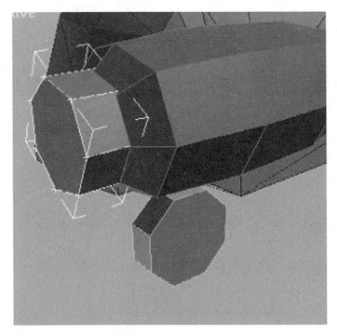

FIGURE **6.52** *Back end of the rocket booster.*

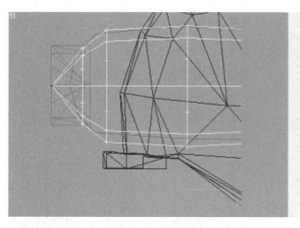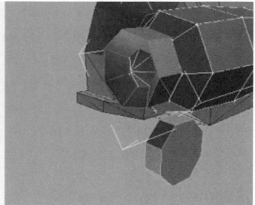

FIGURE
6.53
Side and perspective views of the rocket.

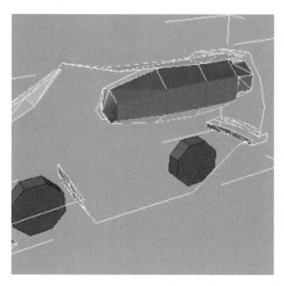

FIGURE
6.54
Inside view of rocket booster.

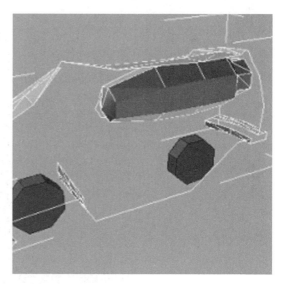

FIGURE
6.55
Faces deleted.

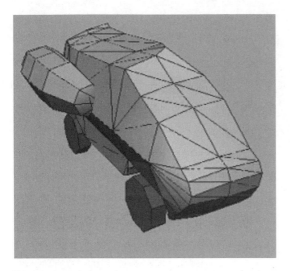

FIGURE *Van selected.*
6.56

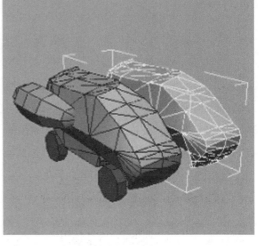

FIGURE *Van duplicated.*
6.57

26. With the Van copy still selected, use the Mirror tool to flip the model, around as shown in Figure 6.58. We are using the same type of steps here as we did for the characters because it allows us a perfect match for the other side and cuts the modeling time in half. That's a good thing.

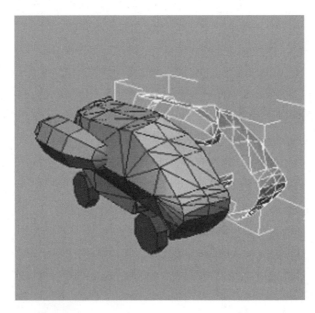

FIGURE *Van mirrored*
6.58

27. Go to the top view and move the Van pieces as close together as you can. Be sure to zoom in on the model if you can't see it clearly from our current distance (See Figure 6.59). Next, select the vertices on both sides of the Van and weld them together (See Figure 6.60).

28. Close in on the top hole of the Van, as shown in Figure 6.61. Now build two faces with the Face tool to seal up the empty space, as Figure 6.62 illustrates.

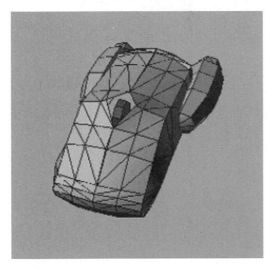

FIGURE **6.59**   *Van pieces moved together.*

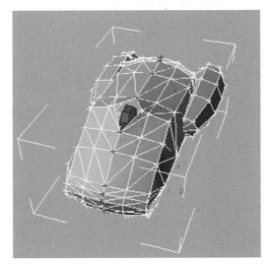

FIGURE **6.60**   *Vertices selected down the center and welded.*

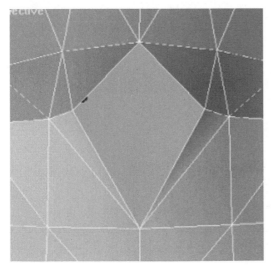

FIGURE **6.61**   *Top view of Van.*

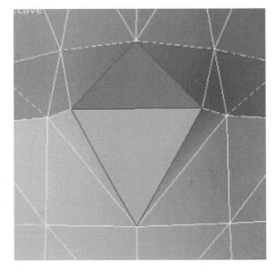

FIGURE **6.62**   *Faces built in hole.*

29. Now select the two highlighted edges in Figure 6.63. Next, use the Flip tool to flip the two edges so that they look like Figure 6.64. This will give us the front light piece for the Van.
30. Change to a top view and select the vertices on the front of the Van (See Figure 6.65). Next, use the Scale tool to scale the vertices in toward the center of the Van, as shown in Figure 6.66.

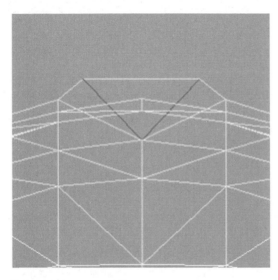

FIGURE **6.63** *Front view of Van, top piece.*

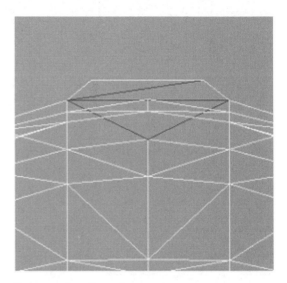

FIGURE **6.64** *Edges flipped around.*

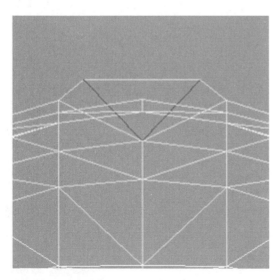

FIGURE **6.65** *Top view with vertices selected.*

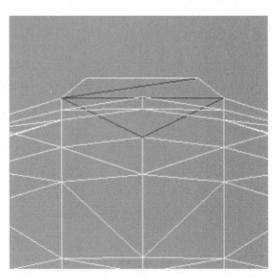

FIGURE **6.66** *Vertices scaled in.*

31. Now it's time to finish refining the wheels. Select both of the wheels, as shown in Figure 6.67. Pull the center vertices out, as in Figure 6.68. This will give the wheels a spacey sci-fi look and feel.

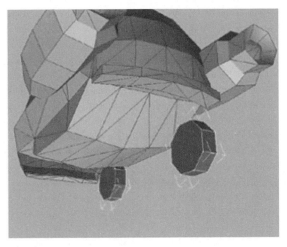

FIGURE *Perspective view with tires selected.*
6.67

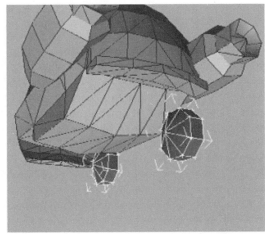

FIGURE *Vertices pulled out.*
6.68

32. Select the outside faces of the tire (See Figure 6.69). Once the faces are selected, move them in to give the wheels more depth. They should look like Figure 6.70.

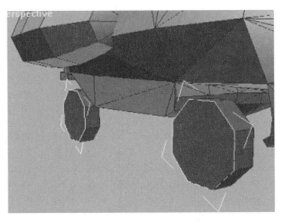

FIGURE *Tire faces selected.*
6.69

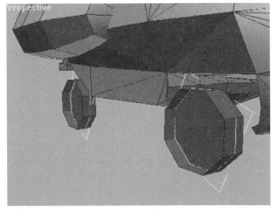

FIGURE *Faces moved in.*
6.70

33. With the tires selected, use the Duplicate tool to copy both tires. Be sure to drag them over to the other side of the Van, as shown in Figure 6.71. After they have been moved, go ahead and flip them around with the Mirror tool (See Figure 6.72).

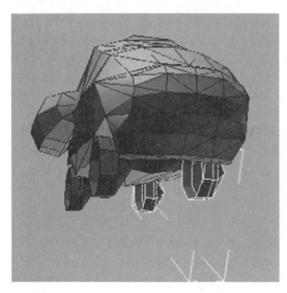

FIGURE *Tires duplicated and moved over.*
6.71

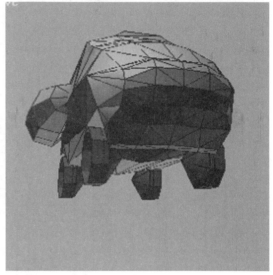

FIGURE *Tires mirrored.*
6.72

The finished Sci-Fi Van should look like Figure 6.73.

This completes the modeling end of the Sci-Fi Van. By now, you should have a pretty good grasp of making vehicles. With that said, let's create a Car that uses the same methods as this Van.

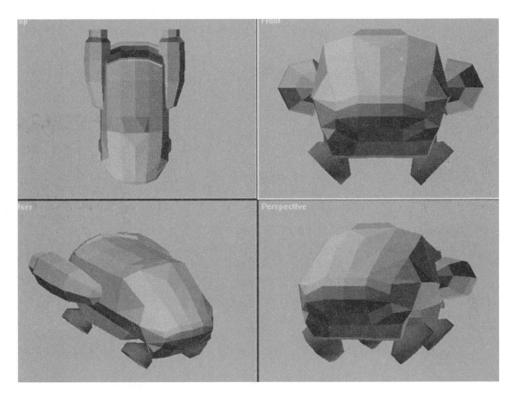

FIGURE   *Multiple shots of the finished Van.*
6.73

CAR

The Car is a straightforward and simple shape to create. It is a very blockish object with few extruding parts, unlike a human or an animal. Using the principles applied here, you should be able to model any type of car or truck with relative ease. In Figure 6.74, we have the finished outlining shape of the Car. As you can see, the vehicle is very similar in design to the Sci-Fi Van, and has only three outlining shapes.

The next step we need to accomplish is the extruding process. If you have already modeled the Van, then you shouldn't have any trouble properly extruding this Car. In Figure 6.75, we have the Car fully extruded and almost finished. The last thing that needs to be added is a line segment through the center of the Car, which will allow us to further round the edges (See Figure 6.76). At this point, you can either divide the Car again so that you will have one more set of polygons to work with, or you can keep it low and stick to the one line down the center. It just depends on how smooth you want your vehicle to appear.

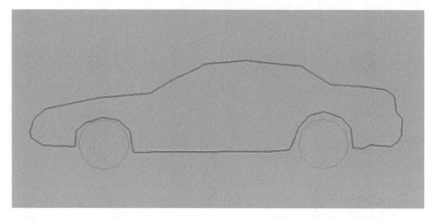

FIGURE *Outline of Car.*
6.74

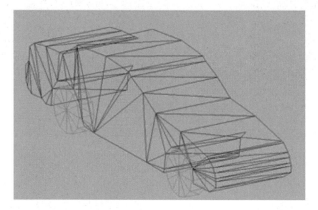

FIGURE *Perspective view of Car.*
6.75

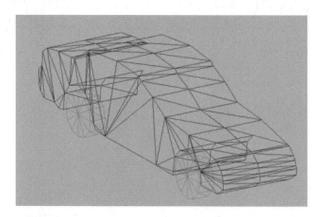

FIGURE *New line segment dividing Car body.*
6.76

Once you've extruded the shapes, we have one final step to go, which is re-fining the objects. In Figure 6.77, we have the finished version of the Car. It is very important to note that the Car and the Van were constructed in nearly the exact same fashion. So, if you are about to model the Car, be sure to follow the same process as the Van. This should get you through the refining stage without any problems.

Now we are going to push you to the next level of modeling — the Mech Robot.

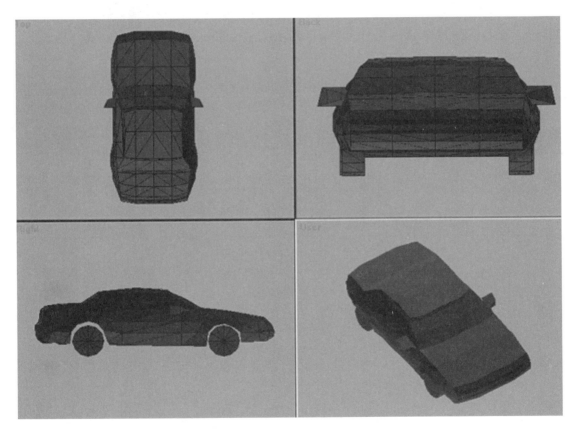

FIGURE   *Multiple views of finished Car.*
6.77

MECH ROBOT

The Mech Robot is going to be a good test of all the things we have learned so far. The one thing that will be different in modeling the Robot is it will be a hierarchy character instead of a full mesh character. When creating a robotic character or a model with sharp angles, it's a good idea to keep the pieces separate, which will help in decreasing the amount of polygons used and make the metal-like pieces hard and rough-feeling.

DRAWING THE SHAPES WITH THE LINE TOOL

There are a lot of shapes that have to be outlined for the Robot, so select your 2D Line tool, place your sketches of the Mech Robot in the proper view ports, and begin outlining the side view! In Figure 6.78, we have the finished outlining shapes for the Robot, which, by the way, is a lot. Every piece that has been outlined will vary in degrees of extrusion, so be sure that the outlining shapes you do are similar to the ones we have here.

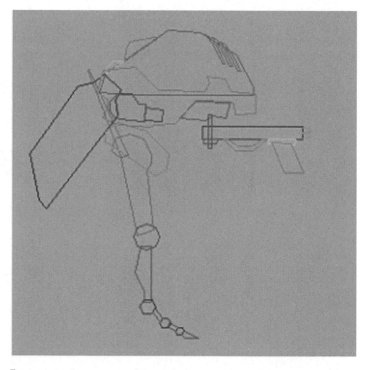

FIGURE   *Outline pieces of the Robot.*
6.78

EXTRUDING ALL YOUR SHAPES

Since we have so many shapes for the Mech Robot, we are going to show you the final extruded Robot and let you use your newfound knowledge of extruding to its fullest. Be sure to use the sketches provided on the CD-ROM to guide you along on this extruding bonanza (See Figure 6.79).

REFINING THE OBJECTS

Each shape that has been outlined and extruded on the Mech Robot now has the depth needed for this part of the process and is ready for us to begin refining. Since the Robot is made mostly of metal surfaces, there will be a bit of different refining to do, so take the time to refine and tweak each piece accordingly. Then you should be able to make-boring looking metal, exciting!

1. We are going to start with the foot, so rotate the model around so you can see the foot. (See Figure 6.80). Select all the parts of the lower toe and duplicate it two times. Make sure that the front two toes are rotated a little and placed right next to each other (See Figure 6.81). Place the third toe at the back of the foot, as shown in Figure 6.82. This will help to balance the Robot while he stands.

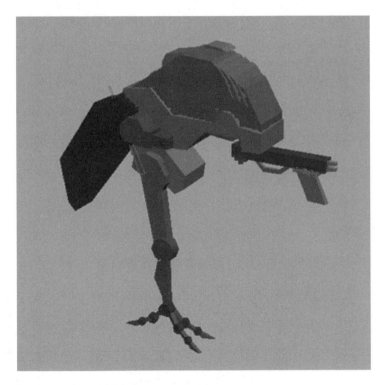

FIGURE *Robot extruded.*
6.79

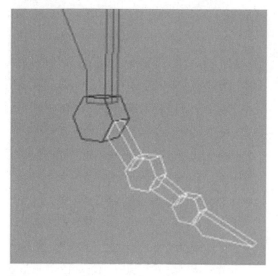

FIGURE **6.80**   *Toe.*

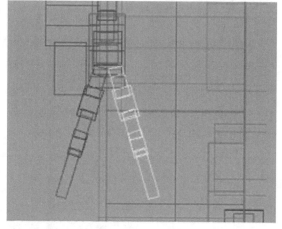

FIGURE **6.81**   *Toe duplicated and moved.*

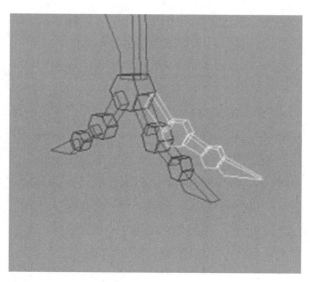

FIGURE **6.82**   *Back toe placed in.*

2. In Figure 6.83, select the vertices along the outside edge of the calf. Use the Scale tool to scale the vertices in toward the center, as shown in Figure 6.84.

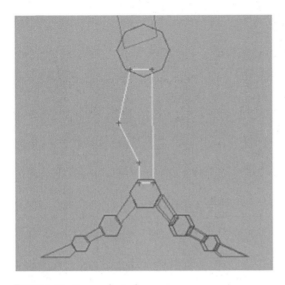

FIGURE   *Vertices selected.*
6.83

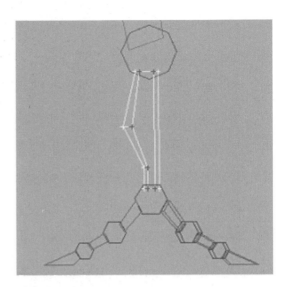

FIGURE   *Vertices scaled in.*
6.84

3. Go to the perspective view of the upper leg and select the vertices on both sides. Make sure not to select the inside vertices (See Figure 6.85). With the vertices selected, scale both sides in together, as in Figure 6.86 or just move each set of vertices inward until it looks correct.

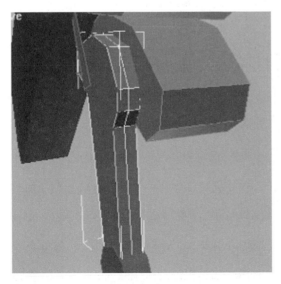

FIGURE   *Perspective view of the upper leg.*
6.85

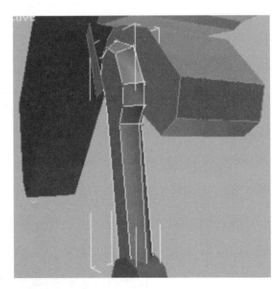

FIGURE   *Vertices pulled in.*
6.86

4. Select the middle and outside vertices, as shown in Figure 6.87. Either scale the vertices outward or move them separately to their proper places (See Figure 6.88).
5. Now select the two outside edges of vertices and scale them inward, as shown in Figure 6.89.

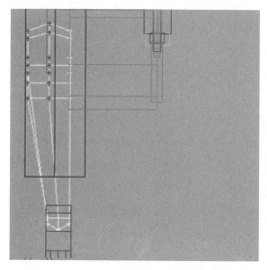

FIGURE
6.87
Top view of Robot leg.

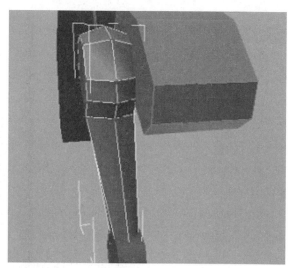

FIGURE
6.88
Perspective view of vertices enlarged.

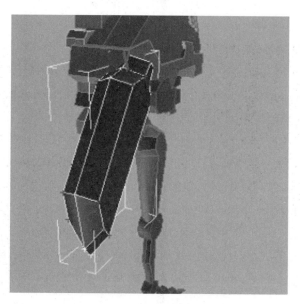

FIGURE
6.89
Vertices selected and scaled inward.

6. Rotate the model around so that the top of the thruster can be seen. Select the top row of vertices, as shown in Figure 6.90. Then, with either the Scale tool or by hand, move the vertices in toward the center (See Figure 6.91).
7. Now move down to the side gun. Select the vertices around the cover plate, as shown in Figure 6.92. Use the Scale tool and move the vertices in, as shown in Figure 6.93.

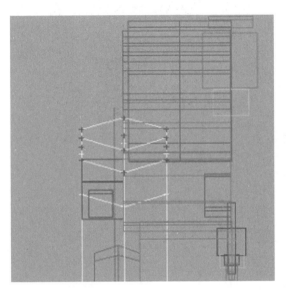

FIGURE *Vertices selected.*
6.90

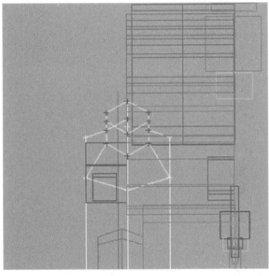

FIGURE *Vertices moved in.*
6.91

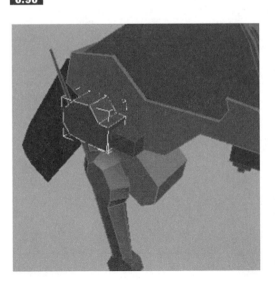

FIGURE *Vertices selected.*
6.92

FIGURE *Vertices scaled.*
6.93

8. Rotate the Robot to the back of the pod cover (See Figure 6.94). Select the vertices shown and scale them in. It should look like Figure 6.95 when it's finished.

9. Go to the top view of the model. Choose the front vertices, as shown in Figure 6.96. Now pull each set of vertices up so that you can create an angle for the front portion of the vehicle (See Figure 6.97).

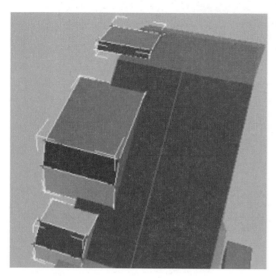

FIGURE **6.94** *Vertices selected.*

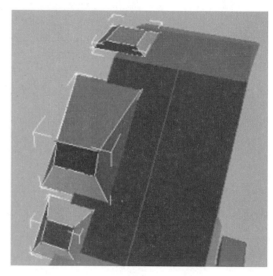

FIGURE **6.95** *Vertices scaled inward.*

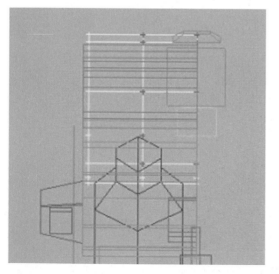

FIGURE **6.96** *Top view of Robot with vertices selected.*

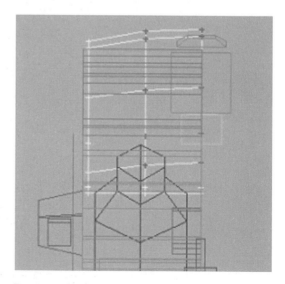

FIGURE **6.97** *Vertices moved upward.*

10. Rotate the model around, as in Figure 6.98, so that you can select the vertices shown. Then change the view again so that you can pull it toward the center of the Robot (See Figure 6.99).

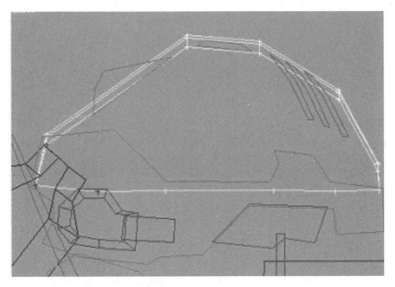

FIGURE *Side view of Robot pod.*
6.98

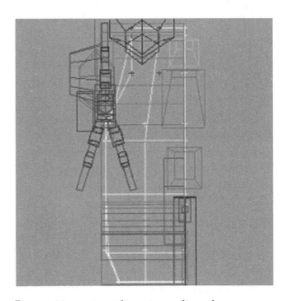

FIGURE *Top view with vertices adjusted.*
6.99

11. Rotate the Robot to a side view (See Figure 6.100). We need to make the cover piece a little rounder, so let's divide the side vertices once through the center, as shown in Figure 6.101.
12. Now straighten the vertices until it looks like Figure 6.102.

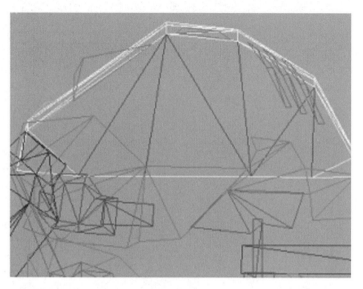

FIGURE   *Side view with edges selected.*
6.100

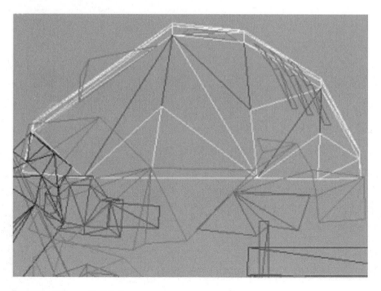

FIGURE   *Edges divided.*
6.101

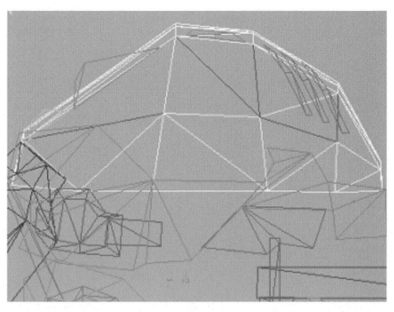

FIGURE   *Side view with edges straightened.*
6.102

13. Select the vertices on the top of the pod (See Figure 6.103). Pull them in to the center, as shown in Figure 6.104. This will help to create a rounder top to the Robot.

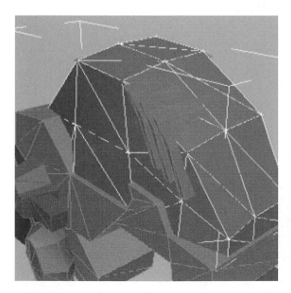

FIGURE   *Perspective view with vertices selected.*
6.103

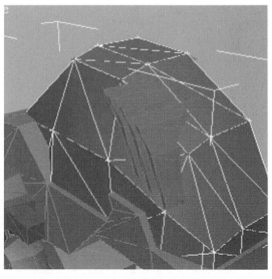

FIGURE   *Vertices moved in toward the center.*
6.104

14. Now let's start refining the cockpit. Change the view to a top view (See Figure 6.105). We need to round the front of it out some more by selecting the bottom left vertices and pulling them over to form a soft angle, as shown in Figure 6.106.
15. Rotate the model to the back view (See Figure 6.107). Select the back two vertices of the cockpit and move them in toward the center, as shown in Figure 6.108.

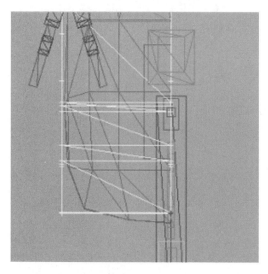

FIGURE **6.105**   *Top view of cockpit.*

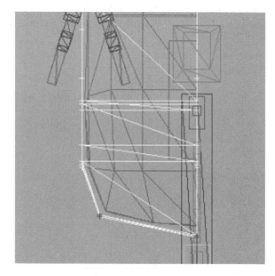

FIGURE **6.106**   *Vertices selected and moved.*

FIGURE **6.107**   *Back view with vertices selected.*

FIGURE **6.108**   *Vertices moved in.*

16. Select the highlighted vertex in Figure 6.109 and move it in until it resembles Figure 6.110.

Most of the corrections we are making simply refine the Robot as a whole. They are not huge adjustments, but by correcting each one, we are creating better-looking 3D models and becoming more professional in our attitude toward modeling.

17. While we are still at the back end of the cockpit, let's correct another vertex. Select the vertex highlighted in Figure 6.111. Move it up above the side gun so that it will look as though the gun connects inside (See Figure 6.112).

18. Now rotate the model around to the side view. Select the vertices shown in Figure 6.113. Pull the vertices out so that the cockpit begins to give a slight curve to the outlining shape (See Figure 6.114).

19. We need to flip one more edge. In Figures 6.115 and 6.116, we have flipped the side edge and created a softer curve for the outer line of the cockpit.

20. Move up to the barrel, as shown in Figure 6.117. Select the outside vertices and scale them in just a little. This will help the barrel to appear round (See Figure 6.118).

FIGURE **6.109** *Perspective view with vertex selected.*

FIGURE **6.110** *Vertex moved in.*

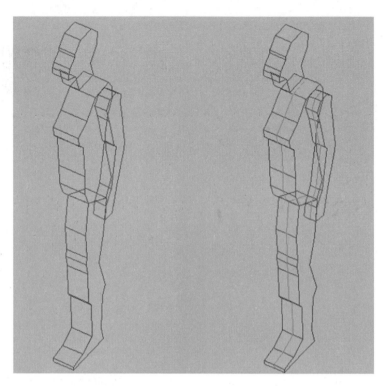

FIGURE *Perspective view with vertex selected.*
6.111

FIGURE *Vertex adjusted for side gun.*
6.112

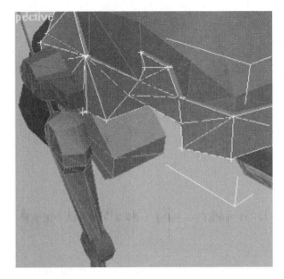

FIGURE *Vertices selected.*
6.113

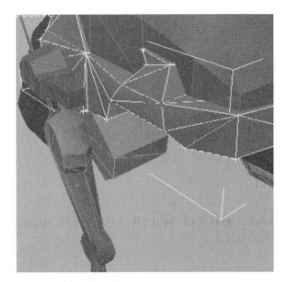

FIGURE *Vertices adjusted.*
6.114

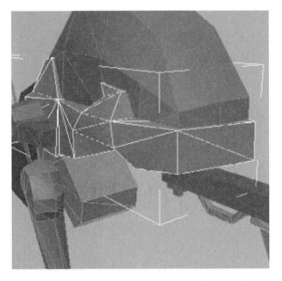

FIGURE *Perspective view with edge selected.*
6.115

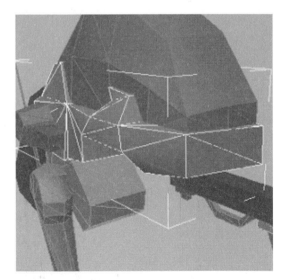

FIGURE *Edge flipped.*
6.116

21. Next, rotate the model to the front view (See Figure 6.119). We need to divide the grail pieces to match the angle of the pod cover. In Figure 6.120, divide all the pieces once through the center. Then select the vertices in the center and the outside edge and move them up, as shown in Figure 6.121.

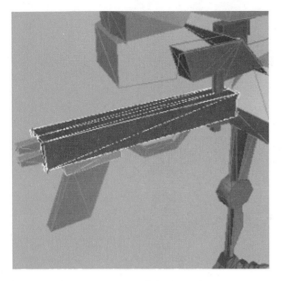

FIGURE
6.117   *Perspective view of the barrel.*

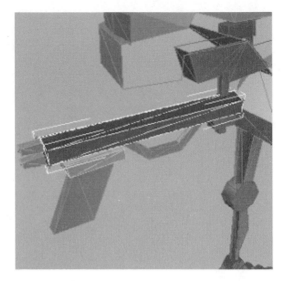

FIGURE
6.118   *Vertices scaled in.*

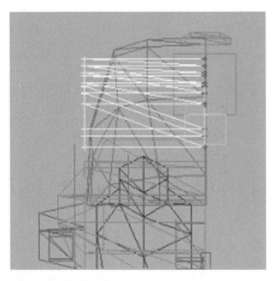

FIGURE
6.119   *Front view.*

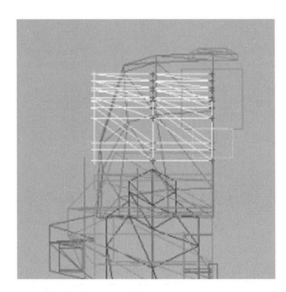

FIGURE
6.120   *Grail pieces divided.*

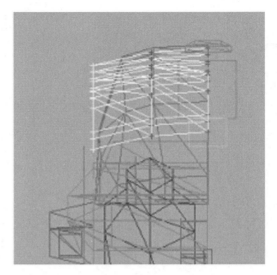

FIGURE *Vertices moved.*
6.121

22. We are now ready to duplicate the model. Select only the pod cover, cockpit, thruster, leg, front grail pieces, and side gun. The other pieces should remain as one (See Figures 6.122 and 6.123).

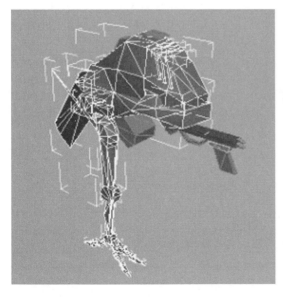

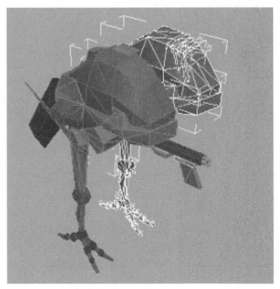

FIGURE *Perspective view of Robot selected.*
6.122

FIGURE *Robot duplicated.*
6.123

23. Next, with the copy of the Robot still selected, mirror the object so that we have an exact copy of the Robot (See Figure 6.124). Now move the Robot copy as close as you can to the original model. We will need to weld the pieces together, so be sure that they are very close together (See Figure 6.125).

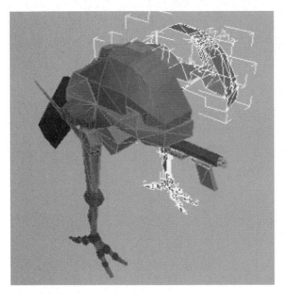

FIGURE *Robot copy mirrored.*
6.124

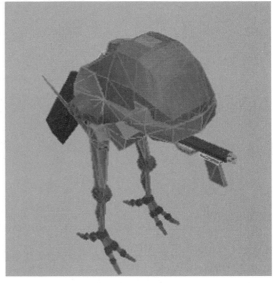

FIGURE *Pieces moved in close together.*
6.125

24. With the pieces next to one another, it is time to weld them. Make sure you have selected the Welding tool and select the vertices highlighted in Figure 6.126. Once you have them selected, weld the pieces together. It should look like Figure 6.127.

This completes the Mech Robot! In Figure 6.128, we have a final version of him for you to see.

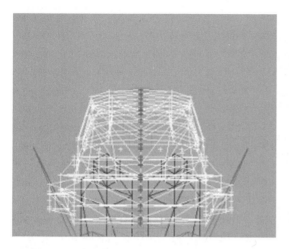

FIGURE
6.126 *Front view of vertices selected.*

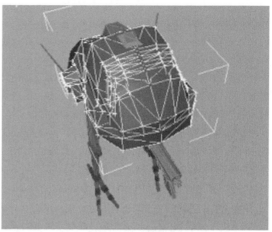

FIGURE
6.127 *Perspective view of vertices welded.*

FIGURE
6.128 *Multiple views of finished Robot.*

REVIEW OF MODELING

In the journey through the world of modeling, we have discovered many hills to climb, but fortunately, no mountains to scale. The understanding and ability to model a character or object in 3D has been laid out for you in an easy-to-follow manner. By remembering the major steps in modeling a character, you should gain the confidence needed to tackle any project. Modeling is only the first step in creating a complete 3D model; it is the understructure and basis for determining the life of the character. Creating a 3D model with the same enthusiasm and artistic interpretation as with a concept sketch will prove to be the benefactor involved in making the best models possible for the next great game. Remember to always use the side view sketch of the character to create the primary 3D shape. It will provide you with the greatest likeness and stature that the model should have. For all of your future modeling endeavors, be sure to stick with the five-step method that we have used on our models, which are: *Trace* the sketch with the 2D Line tool, *Extrude* all the objects, *Refine* the individual shapes, *Attach* the objects together, and lastly, *Add* any essential accessories to the character. Don't forget to reduce the poly counts in your models as needed. It will make your games more efficient. Follow these steps and model on a continual basis, and you should be on the road to becoming a modeling genius!

U.V. Mapping
Coordinates

In Part 3, we will look at what a U.V. map is, what it does, and how best to position your model's U.V. coordinates to fit on the textures used for the characters. Also, we will show how to properly manage the space, and explain the importance of each piece that's placed onto the map to ensure that every inch of the map is used to its fullest extent. All the U.V. mapping coordinates for each of the models have been included on the CD-ROM for your use when working on your layouts and textures.

CHAPTER

7 Mapping Characters

WHAT IS U.V. MAPPING?

U.V. Mapping is one method of texture mapping, the technique of applying textures to an object. In some cases textures are wrapped around the object like a blanket, while in others they appear as though they are being projected onto the object through a slide projector. In most 3D modeling software, there is a core group of texture mapping techniques: spherical, cylindrical, flat, cubic, and UV. We will be focusing on UV.

Most textures have two-dimensional coordinates, x and y that define the texture's horizontal and vertical positions. Many 3D applications, however, use U and V to define the positions. In most cases two coordinates would be sufficient, except that 3D has three dimensions, so in order to fix a texture in three-dimensional space, a third coordinate W is added. The three texture coordinates, U, V, and W represent the following: U is the width of the texture, V is the height, and W is used for depth, if you are using a 3D procedural texture. (Procedural textures are often referred to as shaders, and are the method of giving color to an object through mathematical formulas.) Almost every 3D application available today has UV mapping, because it is a powerful tool that recognizes more complex shapes and attempts to wrap itself around the various contours of the shape. When applying U.V. maps, the coordinates are measured on a scale of 0.0 to 1.0, with 0.0 and 1.0 at opposite sides of the texture. Numbers higher than 1.0 will make the texture tile, and negative numbers will mirror the texture. With most 3D modeling software, these numbers are usually hidden from the artist, and replaced by helpful visual representations of how the textures are projected. Planes, cylinders, and spheres help the artist align the textures in a visual way, but it helps to know that engines see only the UVW numbers (also called mapping coordinates) that these shapes create for the polygons. The best way to become comfortable with U.V. Mapping is to practice, so let's get started.

HUMAN CHARACTERS

MAPPING THE ANCIENT BARBARIAN

There are many different ways of mapping a model. In the following sections, we show you two examples of how to cut the map up to get the most out of your work space. The images simply give you a general idea of how to properly manage your space on a 256 to 512 map.

ON THE CD

1. First, we need to load the model of the Barbarian in a program that will let us map the U.V. coordinates. The Barbarian model and U.V. map are included on the CD-ROM under the Barbarian folder. If you haven't modeled

him yet, then just load the one from the CD-ROM. The objects done in this section have been mapped using UView, but any program capable of U.V. mapping should be able to correctly map a model. Now the model loaded in the front view, with the polygons highlighted, should look like Figures 7.1 and 7.2 below.

2. The next step is to separate the polygons in a conventional and organized manner. Remember: Our work space is going to be 256x256 pixels, which means that as we position the polygons onto the map, we'll need to place the most important pieces, such as the head or upper body polygons, onto the largest sections of the map. This first example of a U.V. map has a very clean and organized layout that places the pieces well within our limits.

Starting with the top left corner, you notice that we have the head (much larger than the rest of the pieces since it is highly essential). When mapping out the head, a good way to keep the skins from becoming seamed is to leave the side of the head and the front of the head together. The easiest way to achieve this, is to just pull the vertices of the side of the head over until it looks like the headshot in Figure 7.3. The other side of the head can just be flipped over and laid right on top of the first side view.

Moving down the side of the picture, we have the arms. Each arm is mapped out separately, just in case the texture maps are different for each of them (like our Barbarian). Look real close at the next step of the maps;

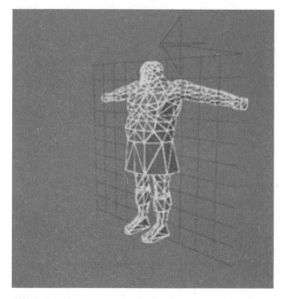

FIGURE **7.1** *Perspective view of Barbarian.*

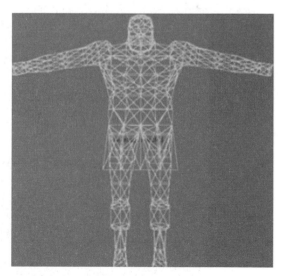

FIGURE **7.2** *U.V. map of the Barbarian in the front view.*

what we have basically done is pulled the vertices of the arms outward. This will allow you to place the texture maps (front view, side view, and back view) of the arm in one whole piece. By doing this, you won't have to divide your texture map and position it all over the place.

In the bottom left corner, we've placed the side views of the foot. Notice how it is much smaller than the others on the map since it isn't in a place where people would look at it all the time. Be sure that all four sides of the feet are placed on top of each other.

Let's move back up to the top center now. As you can probably tell, this section is the chest and upper abs. Be sure to pull the traps up and the neck out to the side. One of the most important things in mapping out a character is to keep the waistline as straight as possible. This is done so that when you place a belt or shirt across his waist, you will have no problem lining up the pieces. Do this for both the front and the back of your maps.

The next thing on your map is the front and back of the legs. Pull the vertices out to the sides so that you have every polygon showing. By making sure that every polygon is showing, you will lessen the chance for a texture to get stretched across a face. Keep the two polygons of the pelvis straight, as shown in Figure 7.3. The last step is to place all the minor objects into the scene. This would be the bottom and top of the feet, the top and bottom of the hands, the skirt, and any other objects that might be with your model (See Figure 7.3).

3. Our next example of mapping the Barbarian is shown in Figure 7.4. Here, we have moved the head down to the bottom center. It's still the same in terms of layout. The arms have been moved up to the top left corner and are still mapped the same as the example before. The biggest change to the actual mapping pattern of the model is the chest and the back. The top right side of the map is the full front and back of the upper body. Notice what we have done: The chest is in the center of the piece and the back has been split up and moved to each side of the body. This will help decrease the possibility of a seam on the model when it's completed. Below the body is the skirt. It has been increased from its previous example. The boots have also been enlarged on the map. The top and bottom of the boot have been placed right next to it. Keeping the same objects next to each other will help you maintain a nice organized map. The last things changed are the legs. Here, we have made them smaller and moved them to the bottom left corner (See Figure 7.4).

4. In Figure 7.5, we have a very isometric layout for our U.V. map. Everything in the map is close to the example in Step 3. Let's go over the biggest changes involved in this map. First, we have placed the arms on top of

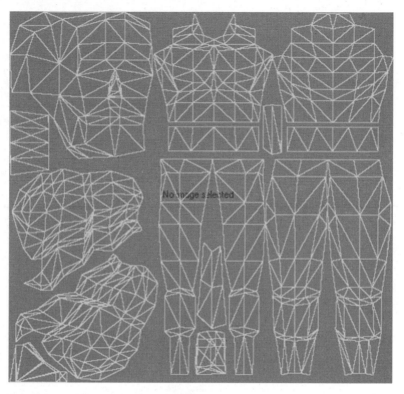

FIGURE   *Finished U.V. map coordinates of the Barbarian.*
7.3

each other in the top left corner. Next to it, we have the skirt, which has been squashed and stretched to fit in. In the right corner, the right side of the chest and the back piece connected to it have been flipped over and lined up with the left side. Are you seeing a pattern yet? What we are doing is placing all the objects that are of the same type on top of one another. This will let us enlarge all the shapes, and make the map simpler to work up. In the lower left corner, place all the leg pieces on top of one another. These are the major changes that take effect when you map your Barbarian this way.

Don't forget — this map layout is used only if you know your characters are going to be isometric. If you decide that one arm has purple dots going down it and the other arm has tattoos, then make sure to keep the U.V. maps separate.

FIGURE *Another layout of the Barbarian's U.V. mapping coordinates.*
7.4

These figures of maps are only representational of what you can do. For instance, if the colors of his clothes are solid colors, then you may want to shrink them way down in size, which will free up a lot of space for the head and accessories.

The U.V. coordinates for the other models will be shown once. Since we have provided you with a few iterations, we'll show you the maps that we have decided to go with for our characters. All the models and maps used for each character can be found on the CD-ROM and are used to generate the U.V. maps.

ON THE CD

Let's move on to the Female Marine!

MAPPING THE MARINE

ON THE CD

1. Pull in the Female Marine model that you have created, or open it from the CD-ROM. Just like with the guy, we are going to use a U.V. mapping program and work over the U.V. coordinates. She should look something like the Figures 7.6 and 7.7.

FIGURE   *Last layout for the Barbarian.*
7.5

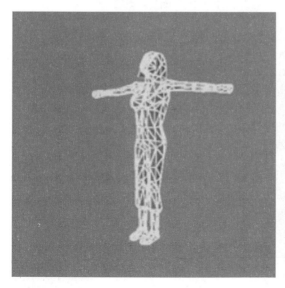

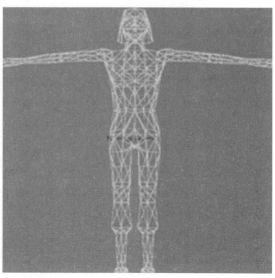

FIGURE   *Perspective view of the Marine.*
7.6

FIGURE   *Front view of the U.V. map.*
7.7

2. Let's run through what each part is (See Figure 7.8). First, the top left section is the leg. Here, we have done the same as we did on the Barbarian. Be sure that your vertices on the legs have been fully pulled out, as shown. Also, keep the waist straight, just like on the guy. If we keep moving over, you have the front and side view of the boot, then the side view of the hair in the right corner. The arms have been separated and placed right below the boots. The front of the arms have been overlapped with the back of the arms to allow you a little extra room. Down in the bottom left corner, the chest has been placed in between the center of each side of the back. Again, this will make texturing the character much more efficient. The head has been mapped out the same way as we did the Barbarian. This process should work for any type of head you wish to map.

The Princess model was created using the Marine, so when you get ready to map her, just use the same layout provided here, except be sure to leave room enough for the hat she wears. That and the dresses are the only extra things which need to be placed on the map.

FIGURE   *Finished U.V. mapping coordinates of the Marine.*
7.8

Let's work over the gun that the Female Marine uses.

MAPPING THE WEAPON

1. Open the weapon that we modeled for the Marine in a U.V. mapping program. The gun should look like Figure 7.9.
2. The gun is primarily mapped using the side view. In Figure 7.10, we have shown each piece of the gun mapped separately.

The pieces are all doubled over. Make sure that the inside polygons have been properly moved out. This will help reduce the stretching that could occur.

3. The map can be taken one step farther. In Figure 7.11, the pieces of the map have been laid over one another. It can look quite confusing, but when attempting to create more room on the map and increase the size of the pieces, this type of method can come in handy. It is not advisable to do it this way if you are handing the map off to another person to texture, as it may become confusing for someone else. But if you are also going to texture it, then it should not pose a problem.

   That's all there is to properly mapping a weapon. This is the same process you can use to map the sword and magic wand that we modeled earlier in Part

2. Try doing each of these before moving on to the Civil War Soldier. Also, if you run into any problems or get completely mixed up, the models and U.V. maps are available on the CD-ROM to help you out. Good luck!

ON THE CD

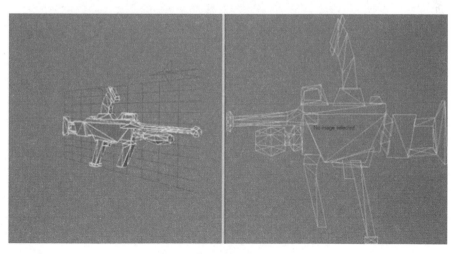

FIGURE *Perspective and front views of the weapon.*
7.9

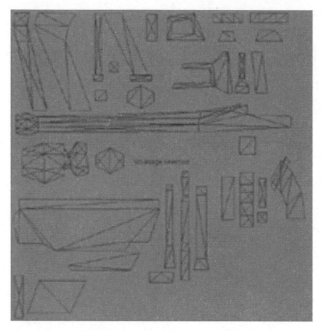

FIGURE
7.10   *Gun map separated.*

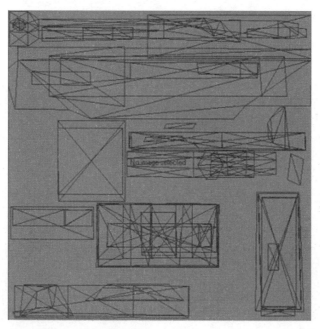

FIGURE
7.11   *Finished U.V. map of weapon with polygons moved.*

MAPPING THE CIVIL WAR SOLDIER

The Civil War Soldier is going to be mapped differently than the previous two because he is such a low polygon character and in the game, he will be seen at a distance. The best way to show how to make use of the allotted space is to use it several different ways. This allows you to choose which pattern will best suit your needs. For the Soldier, we are going to keep his individual pieces more whole. Check it out below.

ON THE CD

1. The first thing we need to do is load the model of the Civil War Soldier — either the one you created or the one found on the CD-ROM, into a program that will let you map the U.V. coordinates. The Soldier should look like Figure 7.12.
2. Select the front and back pieces of the body and legs (See Figure 7.13). With each piece pulled away from the rest of the body, stretch the smaller polygons out, as shown in Figure 7.14.
3. Figure 7.15 shows the head selected, split, and moved over. This is the basic process that you have done with the Barbarian and Marine. Even with a low polygon head such as this one, it can still be done.
4. In Figure 7.16, we have the finished U.V. maps for the Soldier. In the top left section, we have placed the side view and front view of the feet. Below the feet, the body and legs were placed together. Notice that the front and back views of the body were kept the same size. This will make it much easier to texture the figure's side planes versus having a different size front and back. A different size for the two would force us to expand or shrink our maps while trying to line up the texture pixels on the side of the

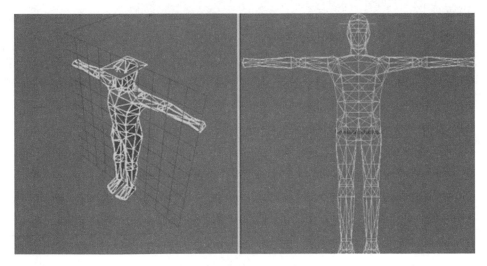

FIGURE *Perspective and front views with polygons selected.*
7.12

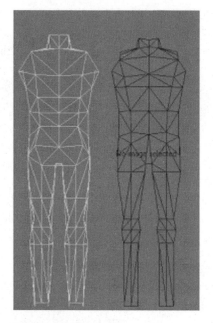

FIGURE
7.13   *Body map.*

FIGURE
7.14   *Stretched body map.*

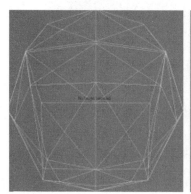
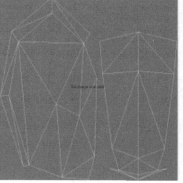
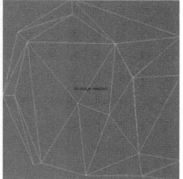

FIGURE
7.15   *Head selected, split, moved, and then connected to the side.*

character. Now, at the top right section of the map, the arms have been placed next to each other. Below the arms are the head and the hat. For an RTS (Real Time Strategy) style-based game, this is one of many good map patterns you could choose from.

FIGURE   *Civil War Soldier U.V. mapping coordinates finished.*
7.16

CARTOON CHARACTERS

Cartoon characters are mapped using the same techniques as the human figures. There is one benefit to these characters, though. The texture maps that we will be using have a simple color palette. This makes stretching marks almost nonexistent and lining pieces up very simple. The U.V. map itself can be saved as a 128x128, or possibly even smaller, without noticing any difference in the map itself.

MAPPING THE CARTOON VILLAIN

ON THE CD

1. Open the Cartoon Villain into whichever U.V mapping program you enjoy using. If you have not modeled the Villain, he and the U.V. map are on the CD-ROM that came with this book. The Villain should look like Figure 7.17.

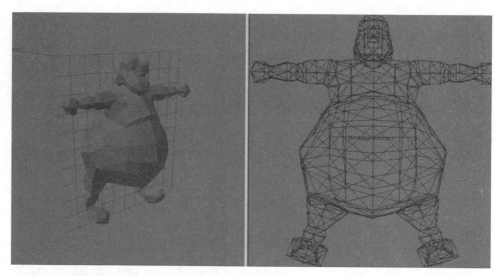

FIGURE *Perspective and front views of the Villain.*
7.17

2. Let's start off by selecting his body and legs (See Figure 7.18). Make sure that the side view has been chosen for the U.V. map, as shown in Figure 7.19.
3. Next, select the feet in the side view. By selecting them in the side view, we've placed each map of the feet one on top of the other with one simple selection. See Figure 7.20.

   Go ahead and place the feet polygons in the lower right corner of the map.

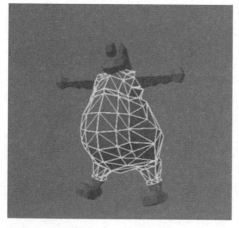

FIGURE *Perspective view of polygons*
7.18 *selected.*

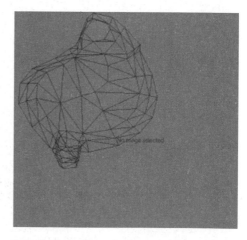

FIGURE *Side view of villains body.*
7.19

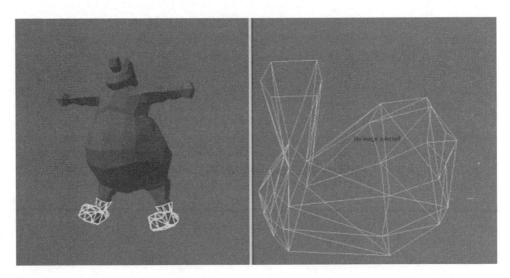

FIGURE   *Side view of the feet polygons.*
7.20

4. Select the head polygons as shown in Figure 7.21. Make sure that it is in the side view.
5. Now move the nose off to the side and select the front polygons of the face, as shown in Figure 7.22.
6. With the front view of the head polygons selected, move them over to the side of the head, as shown in Figure 7.23.

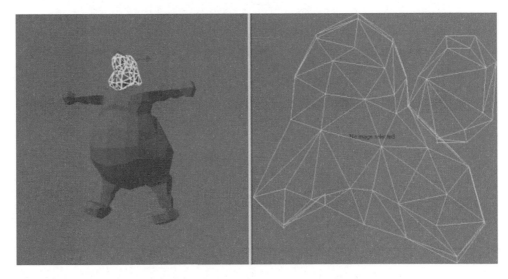

FIGURE   *Side view of head polygons selected.*
7.21

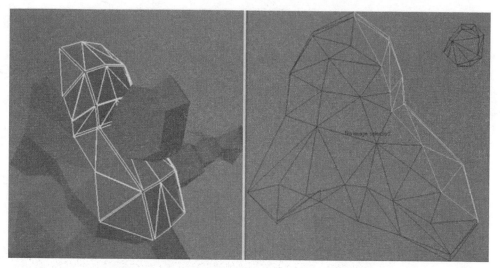

FIGURE   *Front view of polygons selected.*
7.22

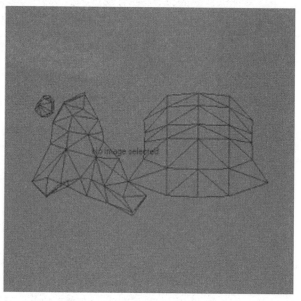

FIGURE   *Front view of head moved to the right of the*
7.23   *side.*

7. For now, the map should look like Figure 7.24. The face has been moved to the lower left corner and the feet are in the bottom right corner.

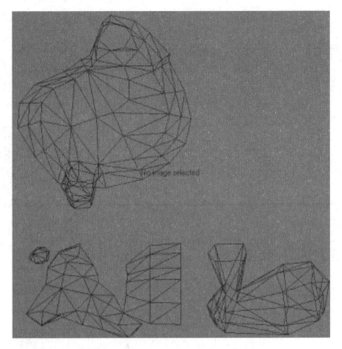

FIGURE   *U.V. map with face and feet pieces added.*
7.24

8. Select the arms, as shown in Figure 7.25. Then flip the left arm over to the right arm, as shown in Figure 7.26.

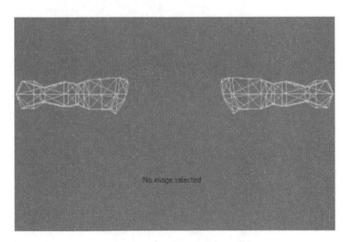

FIGURE   *Front view with arm polygons selected.*
7.25

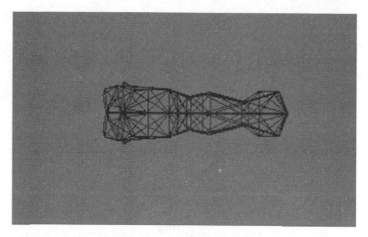

FIGURE *Left arm flipped over to the right arm.*
7.26

9. The finished map should look like Figure 7.27. This can be considered a completed map, but if you'd like to stretch and move him some more, then refer to Figure 7.28. Here we have placed the side view of the head in the top corner. Below that are the nose and the front view of the head. The front view has been stretched upward so that we can place a bigger eye on him. The square next to it is the mouthpiece. You don't have to separate

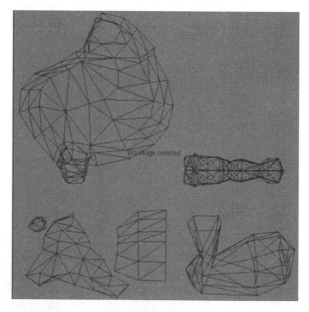

FIGURE *Map with finished pieces.*
7.27

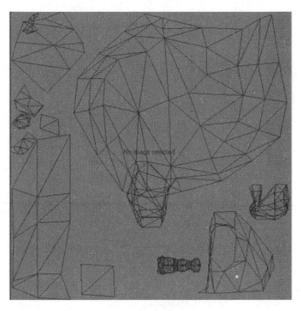

FIGURE   *Map with rearranged pieces.*
7.28

them, but it can help out when animating the mouth. Next, in the lower center of the map are the arm pieces. Then you have the chest and feet pieces. Both of these have been kept small since the texture map is going to be black.

The last thing we should point out is that the Cartoon Hero can be produced in the same manner as the Villain; so when you begin mapping the Hero, just follow the same steps shown above. The finished map of the Hero is available on the CD-ROM, in case you want to see how he was laid out.

ON THE CD

ANIMALS

MAPPING THE HORSE

1. With your U.V. program running, load the Horse model into the view port. The Horse model and U.V. map are both available on the CD-ROM for you to use (See Figures 7.29 and 7.30).
2. Use a straight side view of the Horse as the thrust of the map. Be sure to move the vertices around the head out, until they look like Figure 7.31. Once the head is correct, pull the vertices around the body and the legs out. Notice there isn't really a need to separate these polygons from everything else. If we were dealing with a higher-count model, then it might be a good idea to separate everything. Now place the tail over on the bottom right side of the map. Then place the bottom of the hooves in between the horse's legs. That's it!

MAPPING THE STEGOSAURUS

1. Open the file for your Stegosaurus, or the one from the CD-ROM, into your U.V. mapping program. Once he is in your View Port, we want to determine what kind of mapping system we will use. Most of our dinosaur detail is in the side view. Therefore, it is important that the majority of the map be used for the side of his body. Figures 7.32 and 7.33 show the dinosaur before any polygons have been moved.

FIGURE **7.29**   *Perspective view of the Horse.*

FIGURE **7.30**   *Side view of Horse's U.V. map.*

FIGURE   *Finished U.V. map of the Horse.*
7.31

FIGURE   *Perspective view of the Stegosaurus.*
7.32

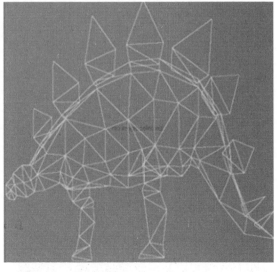

FIGURE   *Side view of the U.V. map.*
7.33

2. To keep an organized map, let's start by selecting all of the scales across his back. Be sure to place all of the scales on top of each other, as shown below. In the top left corner, we have positioned our scales upside down, which allows for more space to be used and lets us keep the size of his scales larger so we can add a higher amount of detail with the textures (See Figures 7.34 and 7.35).

3. Since we have the sides of our dinosaur mapped out, we need to select the underbelly. This is a very important selection. Many times, people will just let it slide and allow the texture to pull through these polygons without properly mapping them. But, if you're going to do it, you might as well do it right. So, select the belly as shown in Figures 7.36 and 7.37.

4. Place the belly piece in the top right-hand section of your map (See Figure 7.38). As you can tell, we are taking full advantage of all the space allotted us.

5. We can't forget the bottom of our Stegosaurus's feet now, can we? Go ahead and select those polys and put them on top of each other, as shown in Figures 7.39 and 7.40. Be sure to enlarge them as far as you can between the spaces allowed.

6. The last step we want to do is to separate the legs from the body. Pull them apart, as shown in Figure 7.41. Since the legs are relatively on four sides, you should just be able to spread out all four sides so that they are showing (See Figure 7.41).

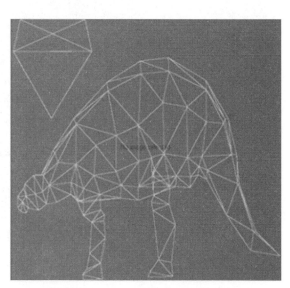

FIGURE **7.34**   *Scales selected.*

FIGURE **7.35**   *Scales placed in the top left corner.*

FIGURE
7.36   *Perspective view of underbelly selected.*

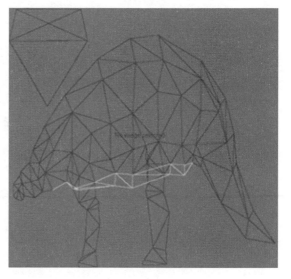

FIGURE
7.37   *Side view of selected polygons.*

FIGURE   *Bottom side moved to upper right corner.*
7.38

FIGURE
7.39   *Feet selected.*

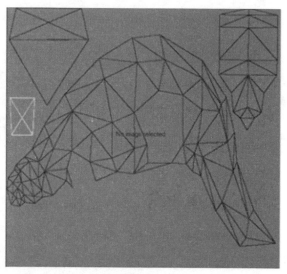

FIGURE
7.40   *Feet polygons on the map.*

FIGURE
7.41   *Finished U.V. map of the Stegosaurus.*

We put the front legs on top of one another, and we put the back legs together. If you feel like the front legs and back legs will be textured in the same fashion, then go ahead and stick them together. This way, you can increase the size of the legs.

This completes the study of the human figures, cartoon characters, and animals. Next on the list are the vehicles and robots. See you in Chapter 8.

8

U.V. Mapping
Vehicles

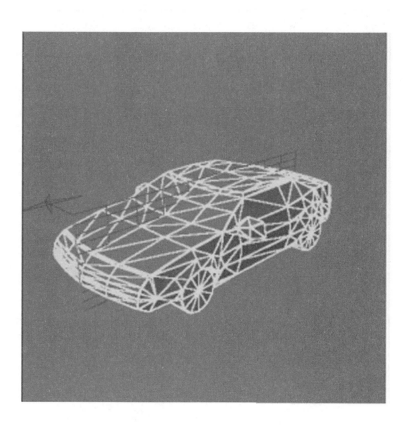

VEHICLES

In this chapter we will be applying U.V. maps to our vehicle models. The techniques used are very similar to those used on the characters, so let's get started.

MAPPING THE SCI-FI VAN

ON THE CD

1. Open the Sci-Fi Van model that we created into your U.V. mapping program so that we can begin making some sense of all these polygons. Once you have the Van opened, it should resemble Figure 8.1. The model and U.V. map for the Sci-Fi Van are available on the CD-ROM, in case you need to use them for reference or if you haven't modeled the Van.
2. Next, select the body of the Van (See Figure 8.2). Make sure that the bottom of the Van and thrusters are not selected.
3. Select the top of the Van, as shown in Figure 8.3. Be sure that you have it in the top view. This will make the shape easier to work with.
4. Next, select the underside of the Van and place it next to the top piece (See Figure 8.4).
5. Select the side view portion of the tires (See Figure 8.5). Then, with the left tire selected, move it on top of the right tire, as shown in Figure 8.6.
6. Now let's select the outside of the tires (See Figure 8.7).

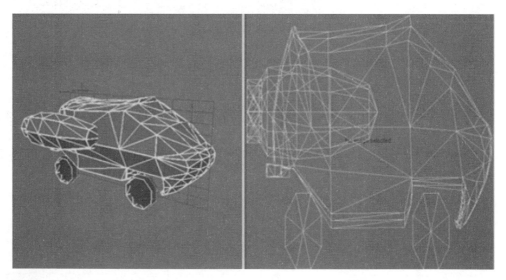

FIGURE *Perspective and side views of Van.*
8.1

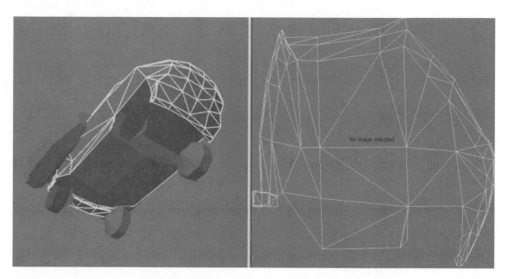

FIGURE *Bottom and side views of the Van.*
8.2

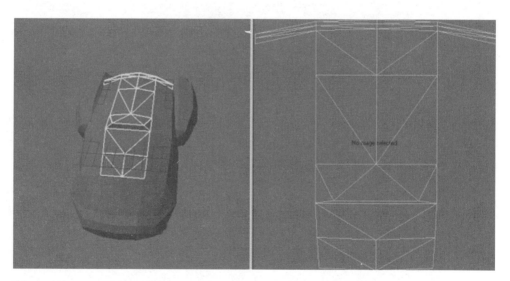

FIGURE *Top view of Van with polygons selected.*
8.3

FIGURE
8.4
Van polygons selected and moved to the top right corner.

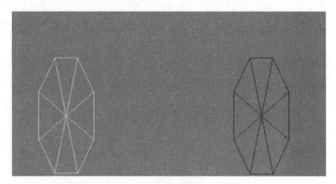

FIGURE
8.5
Side view of tires selected.

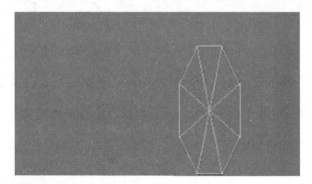

FIGURE
8.6
Tires moved in together.

7. In Figure 8.8, the two pieces have been placed on top of each other. Next, we move the top and bottom set of polygons to the center, as shown in Figure 8.9.

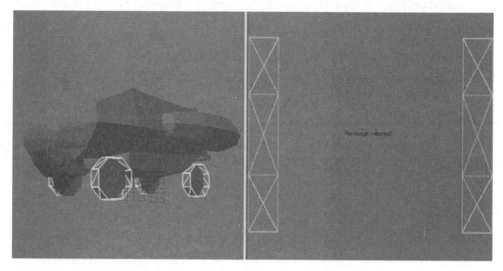

FIGURE *Outer polygons selected on the tires.*
8.7

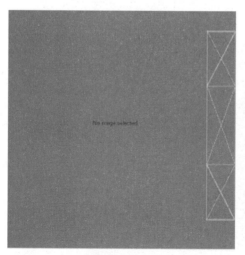

FIGURE *Tires moved on top of each other.*
8.8

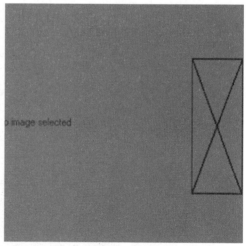

FIGURE *Polygons moved over one another.*
8.9

8. The last pieces we need to get are the thrusters. Be sure to select the polygons in the side view. By doing so, they should already be doubled over. If they are not, then move one on top of the other (See Figure 8.10).

Be sure to separate the front and back pieces of the thruster from the main hull.

9. The finished U.V. map should look like Figure 8.11. Starting in the top left corner, we have placed the tires. Going to the left are the side view of the tires, back of the thrusters, back outside rim of the thrusters, and then the bottom of the body piece. Below these pieces are the main thrusters stretched out. The bottom row of polygons is the side and back of the Van. These pieces have been stretched out so that the texture map can be properly placed on the Van. The last piece is in the lower left corner, which is the top of the Van.

MAPPING THE CAR

1. The Car is one of the easiest objects to map (next to a refrigerator), since it is made up of basic block shapes. It has a lot of parts, but taken in individual pieces, we will be able to create a very good map. The beginning look of the Car should look like Figures 8.12 and 8.13.

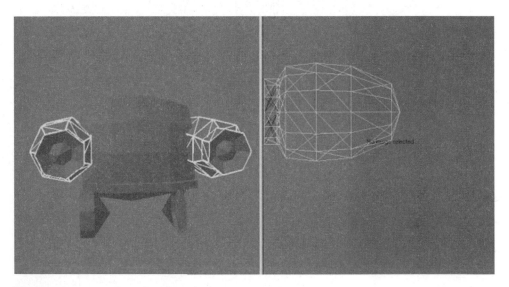

FIGURE *Thrusters selected in the side view.*
8.10

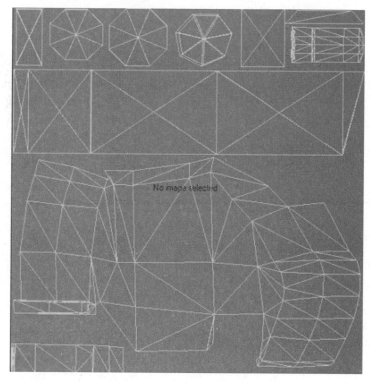

FIGURE
8.11
Finished U.V. map of the Sci-Fi Van.

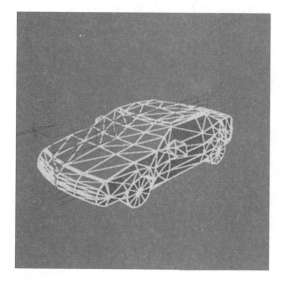

FIGURE
8.12
Perspective view of the Car.

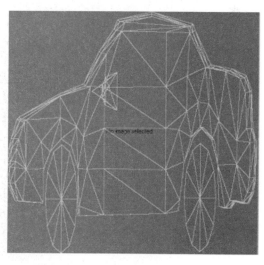

FIGURE
8.13
Side view of the Car's map.

2. In Figure 8.14, the map is finished. Starting from the left side of the map and working our way over, we see the top of the Car. Now move to the center of the map and notice the full side view of our Car, which is both sides of our vehicle. In the space where the tires are, we have put the outside mirrors. Right next to that we have a half circle; this is all of our tire wheels. Since the tires are symmetrical, we can simply divide the tires and overlap all the shapes. The hood and the trunk are the last of the two pieces. Leave them separate just in case you want to put numbers or a logo on the hood, but not on the trunk.

MAPPING THE MECH ROBOT

ON THE CD

1. Open the Robot in a U.V. mapping program, as shown in Figure 8.15. If you do not have the Robot model, that's okay. The Mech Robot model and U.V. map are both available on the CD-ROM for you to use.
2. Let's start by selecting the joints and the thrusters. Place each set on top of one another. Move the thrusters over to the right upper corner. Then move each set of joints over to the top left side (See Figure 8.16).

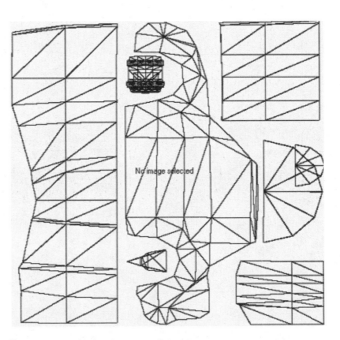

No image selected

FIGURE *Finished U.V. map of the Car.*
8.14

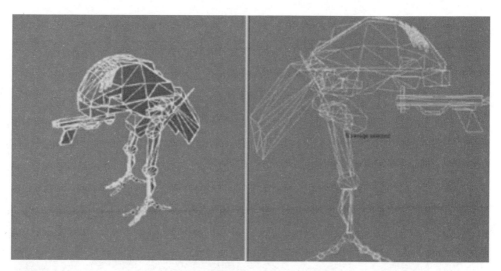

FIGURE   *Perspective and side views of the Mech Robot.*
8.15

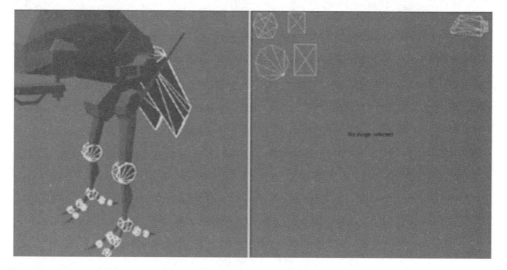

FIGURE   *Joint and thrusters selected and moved.*
8.16

3. Now select the side view of the legs and place them underneath the joint pieces. Then select the toes and place them in the lower left corner (See Figure 8.17).

4. Select the pod cover in the top view and place it next to the joints (See Figure 8.18).

5. Next, select those square pieces on the pod (See Figure 8.19). Be sure to place them in the lower right corner of the map.

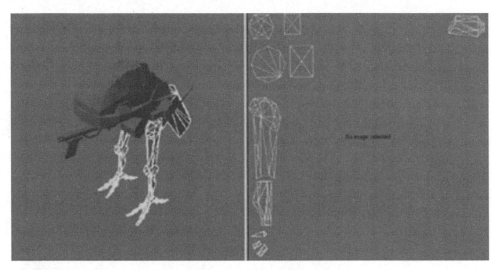

FIGURE *Legs and toes selected and placed on map.*
8.17

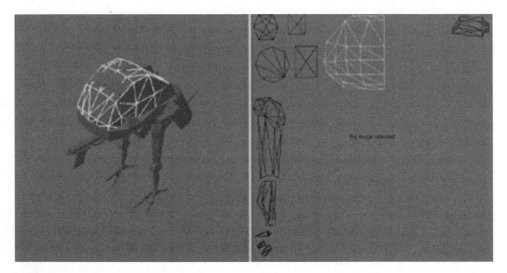

FIGURE *Pod cover selected and placed on the map.*
8.18

6. Select the waist piece of the Robot. Be sure and separate the front and side pieces so that it looks like Figure 8.20.

7. Go to the back of the Robot and select the polygons indicated in yellow. Move these pieces over to the lower right side of the map as shown in Figure 8.21.

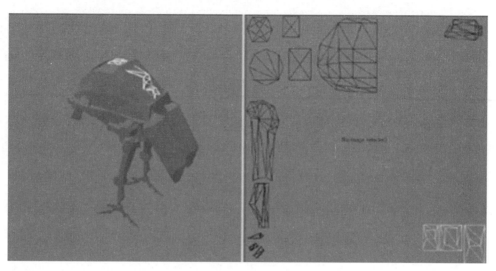

FIGURE *Cover pieces selected and placed on the map.*
8.19

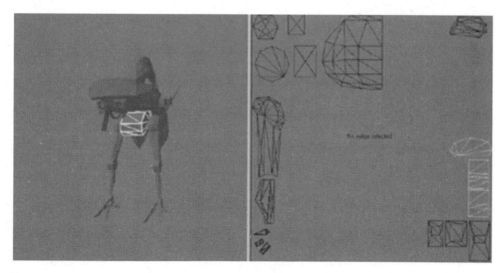

FIGURE *Waist polygons selected and placed on the map.*
8.20

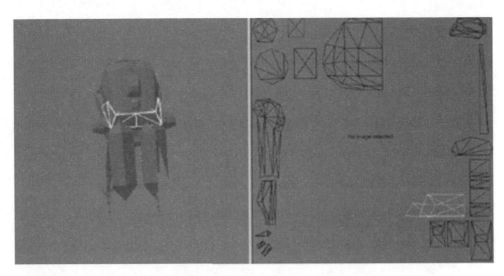

FIGURE *Back pieces selected and moved over.*
8.21

8. The side guns need to be mapped out next. Select and divide each piece as shown below in Figure 8.22. The barrel, gun mount, and the front of the barrel have been separated and moved to the upper right side of the map.

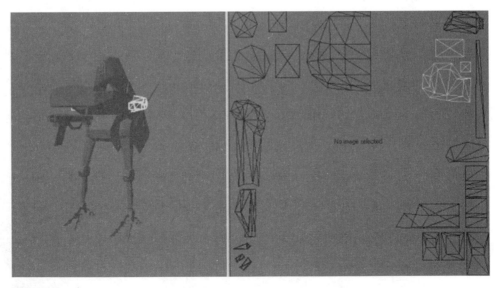

FIGURE *Side guns selected and moved to the map.*
8.22

9. Choose the bottom side of the pod, as shown in Figure 8.23. Place it in the upper portion of the map.

10. Now select all of those grail pieces we made. Place them in the center of the map. Then select the barrel at the front and place it down at the bottom of the map (See Figure 8.24).

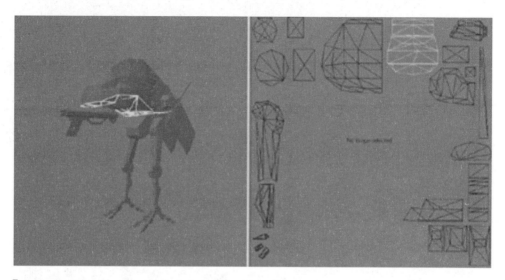

FIGURE   *Bottom side of pod selected and placed on the map.*
8.23

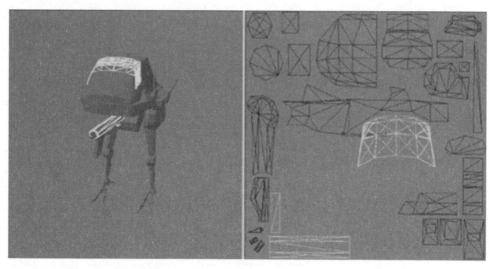

FIGURE   *Grail and barrel selected and placed on the map.*
8.24

11. The last pieces that need to be selected are the clips on the guns and the box holding the gun on. Notice that the boxes have been split open so that we can texture each side (See Figure 8.25).

REVIEW OF U.V. MAPPING COORDINATES

By now, mapping a 3D model should be an understood process. As you have seen in Part 3, there are many ways to correctly map a model so as to generously make room for the textures, or skins. We have shown you just a few examples of what kind of U.V. maps are possible, but the actual placement of pieces is truly limitless. This section is here to provide a direction with which to start. By using the techniques present, there should be no problems in properly mapping out an organized and simple-to-use map. Remember: When creating a U.V. map, it's not a process that can always be done alone. Creating texture maps along with the U.V. maps can and often will be done together simultaneously. Usually, switching back and forth between the two processes will generate a map that is more refined and better understood than by doing it alone.

FIGURE *Finished Mech Robot U.V. map.*
8.25

P A R T

4

Textures

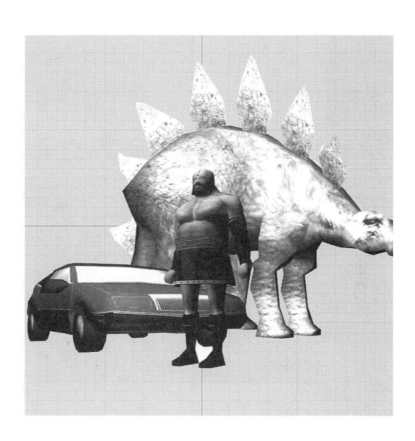

In Part 4, we will learn what a texture is, and how someone would go about collecting, cleaning, sizing, and placing textures on a map. There are many steps involved in creating a proper texture map, from the texture list you'll write down, to the type of programs needed for making texture maps, to other tools that are necessary for creating high-end, professional texture maps. Also, all the textures for each character are included on the CD-ROM for you to use on the 3D models.

9 Introduction to Textures

TEXTURES

Textures, skins, seamless tiles, particle materials, shaders, bump maps are all one in the same. Each one is a way to make a seemingly lifeless set of polygons jump off the screen with realism. Textures are sort of like a veneer that go over the polygons and bring objects to life through the use of colors, shapes, and tones. Without textures, viewing computer models would be like seeing a movie with just silhouettes.

Textures can come from photographs you take or you can design your own. The style of the 3D model being developed helps determine what kind of textures will be created and used. Whatever type of textures you choose to use, they are all basically a set of colors on a map, which create a volumetric form in a 2D space.

TOOLS OF THE TRADE

Before we get started with texturing, there are a few things you should have. The following is a list of programs, tools, and gadgets that can aid in creating texture maps:

- Adobe Photoshop (Basically, any version can work.)
- Painter
- Paintshop Pro
- Corel Draw
- Camera (Digital would be the easiest, but a good film camera will also work.)
- Scanner
- Lighting equipment (Flashlights, spotlights, or even just the sun.)
- Cloth (Some kind of really big cloth. Go to your nearest fabric store and by a few yards of material in either white or blue. This is excellent to place behind objects that you are photographing.)
- Scissors, knife, tape, etc.

All of these items are excellent for setting up and shooting any textures that might come your way. Many people spend hours surfing the Web or reading books in search of the right textures, but in reality, sometimes all you need to do is step outside with a camera and take a picture. The best textures you'll ever find are more than likely the ones you see everyday.

MAKING A PHOTO LIST

A photo (texture) list is similar to the sketch list we did at the very beginning This list helps you get organized and prepared for the actual textures you'll need, so that you don't spend a lot of time searching aimlessly. The first thing to do when preparing this list is to review all of the models you've created and then write down the pictures you need for each one.

- A male figure, tight but somewhat overweight. A good face with a beard.
- A female face and an upper body shot, plus camouflage pants and a white t-shirt.
- Civil War outfit and a male face.
- A hand, preferably just palmar and dorsal side.
- A horse. Get a good close side shot, and multiple shots of the head and body, if needed.
- A dinosaur skin. Find something scaly. (Lizards, snakes, elephants, alligators)
- A car. Get pictures of a sporty, fun car. Side shots, close-up of tires, hood, front, and back.
- Robotic textures like grids, panels, plates, etc.
- A large tree with a bunch of leaves on it.
- An elephant ear (plant).
- A sunflower.

This is a general list of what we need. For example, with the car we included a close-up of the tires, but we can also write down a detailed list. For instance, we need a close-up shot of the inside seats, the engine, the steering wheel, and what not, to be able to texture map the car to the smallest detail. With a list, you'll be able to know what you should have and accomplish the task in only an hour or so, getting exactly what is required. These pictures will provide the right colors, tones, and surfaces that you need to use in order to finalize your models and make them lively, and realistic.

MAP SIZES FOR TEXTURES

The texture map size is part of the texture-making process. This determines the amount of space or pixels you get to work with while creating a skin.

Why is this important? The map size is very important because it directly relates to how the object will be viewed — Whether it's clear, fuzzy, has harsh angles, or even is one big blur.

The size of the map can be any dimension. The following are sizes typically used:

8x8
32x32
64x64
128x128
256x256
512x512
1024x1024

A variation of the maps can also work, such as a 256x128 or 64x128 map size. The larger the map size, the more detail you will have. A map size determines if you will have a crisp and clear picture or a blurry and dotted picture. In Figures 9.1, 9.2, and 9.3, the different map sizes have been provided in order to show the difference in clarity between the pictures.

Most maps are done at a 128x128 or 256x256 map size. They are very close to the look of a 1024 map, but as you can tell, they are still a little blurry. Remember: It won't be long before we can put whatever size texture maps we want on our objects. But for now, be sure to test the performance of your computer and engine using the different map sizes before deciding on what dimensions to work with.

CLEANING PHOTOS AND TEXTURES

Once you have taken some photos and brought them into your computer, don't forget the most important part — cleaning them up! It's time to start pixel pushing! You can use Adobe Photoshop or any of the paint programs listed previouslyto get the job done. At this stage, you need to clean up the photos, cut edges, and straighten the pictures so that are refined enough to go into a game. When creating textures for 3D models, the cleanup doesn't usually take too long, but with 2D models or sprites, the process can be very slow and time-consuming. The important steps in cleaning maps aretaking your time and zooming in good and close. In Figure 9.4, we have a photo of a window that was taken. As you can see, the picture is slightly concave and has excess things around it that need to be removed. The first thing we need to do is select the window and frame and then delete everything else around it, as shown in Figure 9.5. After you've clean that up, take a moment and straighten your image by pulling the corners of the window out and then slightly sinking the center of the picture inward, as shown in Figure 9.6. You may have to do this process a few times until the window is properly corrected. Once that is done, be sure to sharpen your

FIGURE **9.1** *128x128 map size.*

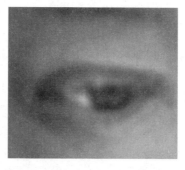

FIGURE **9.2** *256x256 map size.*

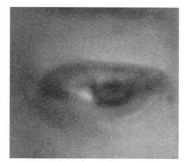

FIGURE **9.3** *1024x1024 map size.*

image at least once to bring back any detail that may have been lost while play-ing with it. The window should look like Figure 9.7 when you get it finished.

BLENDING TEXTURES

Blending textures is a way for us to create a smooth and seamless color transfer from one texture to the other. In the next example, we will show you a few techniques for creating a seamless-looking head texture. The best programs for doing this are those that allow the user to use layers, such as Photoshop.

FIGURE **9.4**   *Photo of window.*

FIGURE **9.5**   *Window cut out.*

FIGURE **9.6**   *Correcting window warp.*

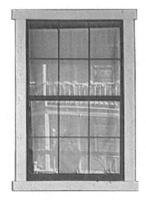

FIGURE **9.7**   *Window corrected and finished.*

1. Let's start with a photo of someone's head (See Figure 9.8). Here we have a picture of a front and side view of a male head. Once you have the photos, place each one into a map as separate layers and make sure that they are equal in size and similar in color tone.
2. Next, choose the side view head. Move it in so that the features of the face line up with the front view (See Figure 9.9). Once they match, cut the front part of the face off, as shown in Figure 9.10. The cut should reside on the side plane of the head.

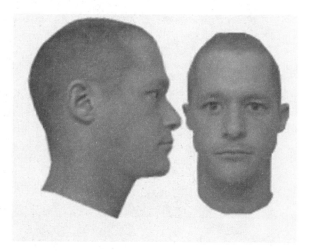

FIGURE   *Front and side views.*
9.8

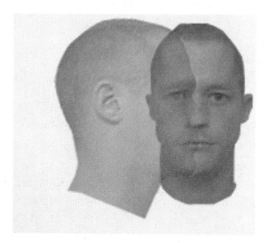

FIGURE   *Side view moved and transparent.*
9.9

FIGURE   *Side view cut out.*
9.10

*After you have cut the image and the pieces are lined up with
each other, flatten the layers together so that we can blend the*
TIP *face pieces together.*

3. The final step is to smudge the two skin tones together. Make sure to use
a small brush when smearing the tones. It now looks like we have the side
view and front view welded together (See Figure 9.11).

> *Tip: If your model has different hair or features on each side of
> the face, then make a copy of half the face and just flip it over to
> the other side. This will allow you to do whatever you want on
> both sides of the face.*

FIGURE *Side and front views smudged together.*
9.11

PULLING TEXTURES

Pulling textures is another essential method for making texture maps solid and
refined. The process is simple, yet very effective. The following steps explain
this process.

1. In Figure 9.12, we have a photo of the underside of a hand. What we are
going to do is create more flesh around the fingers to use while mapping.
2. We have two options for how we can pull the texture. In Figure 9.13, we
have selected the side of the finger and pulled the texture upward using
the transform option. In Figure 9.14, notice that we have used the Smudge
tool and just pulled the texture up. These two options are virtually the

same. But if you look closely, you can see that in Figure 9.13, we have a crisper-looking picture compared to Figure 9.14. This image can appear a little blurred, but it is still just as effective.

3. For our final step, we have smudged the hand and fingers (See Figure 9.15). This is a very useful technique for doing many forms of textures.

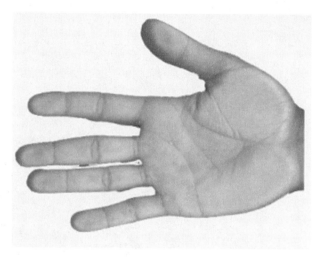

FIGURE   *Hand picture.*
9.12

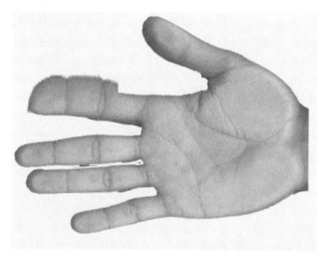

FIGURE   *Texture pulled.*
9.13

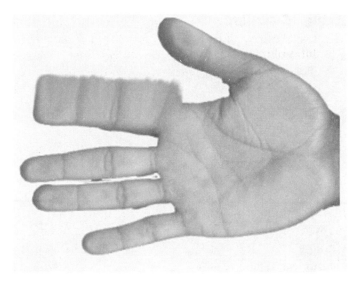

FIGURE *Texture smudged.*
9.14

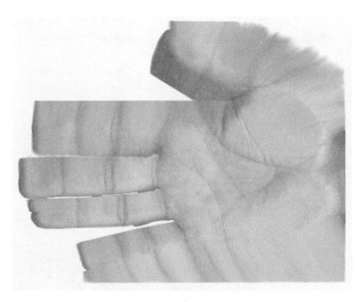

FIGURE *Finished hand smudge .*
9.15

ALPHA CHANNEL

The last thing we need to cover is the alpha channel. This is a texture map applied with an existing map, and is generally used to define how translucent parts of an image should be and where they are located.

 This can also be a pre-multiplied image saved with the .tga file format.

You can use an alpha channel to make an image slightly transparent or completely invisible by choosing values between white (visible) and black (invisible). Typically, an alpha channel is defined by importing a gray-scale image that maps over the specific color to be alpha or by specifying a flat alpha for the whole texture. In Figure 9.16, we have three images of a plus sign that are alpha channeled. The first image has only a slight indication of black, while the second one is 50-50, and the last image is 100 percent black.

Now let's apply each of these maps to a square box, as shown in Figure 9.17. Notice how the gray tones have become translucent and the black tone completely hides the pieces.

This is an excellent method for creating objects such as trees, bushes, wheels, rough edges, hair, and anything else that requires more than you can provide with polygons. Make sure to take full advantage of this and all the other techniques listed when you begin working on your own texture maps.

Let's move on to Chapter 10, where we'll start applying textures to our models.

FIGURE *Three images of an alpha channeled map.*
9.16

FIGURE *Boxes with alpha maps applied.*
9.17

10 Texturing Characters

CREATING TEXTURES FOR MODELS

Our 3D models are done and now we have the task of making them lifelike. The first texture we need to apply to achieve this is skin. It's time to put everything that we learned about textures to work, so let's get started by applying a texture map to the Ancient Barbarian!

HUMAN CHARACTERS

Applying Textures to the Ancient Barbarian

The first, step isto get the color guides of our Barbarian, which we did in Part 1. This will help provide the costume and colors that we want to use for the Barbarian. You can find our color guides on the CD-ROM, but if you came up with a different color design for the Barbarian, be sure you have it next to you as a reference. Open your 2D program and then open your U.V. map of the Barbarian found on the CD-ROM in the Barbarian folder.

ON THE CD

1. In Figure 10.1, we see the burned copy of our U.V. map. This is where the basic placement for our textures will be. We will start filling in the pieces from the top left and work our way around.

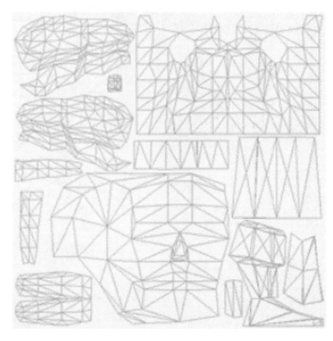

FIGURE *Copy of U.V. mapping coordinates.*
10.1

When making the actual map, create it on either a 512x512 or 256x256 map size. It's easier to simply shrink the map down farther, than to start with a small map and make it look good on a larger map. You will also have a map that will look good for rendering screen shots and movie clips.

2. The first sections of the map are the arms. As you can see in Figure 10.2, we have put a skin tone down for the shoulders and biceps. The back pieces of his costume have also been placed in. Be sure that you include the stripes down his arms. Now, in Figure 10.3, we have the chest and the back. As you can tell, the back has been split through the center. This is just one way you can cut it up. Notice we have applied our blending technique to connect the back pieces and the chest.

3. Once you have the chest and back finished, we can go ahead and place the skirt on. In Figure 10.4, we have designed his skirt with single tone colors. For the belt, we have a piece of grainy-looking brown. Next, we are going to place the head on. The head was done just like the blending technique above. Notice that we have applied the dots on his head and given him a dark beard (See Figure 10.5).

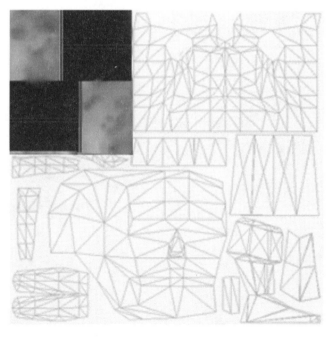

FIGURE *Arm texture.*
10.2

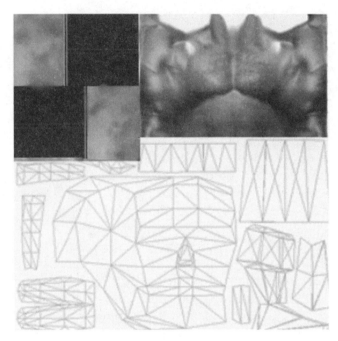

FIGURE
10.3   *Chest and back textures.*

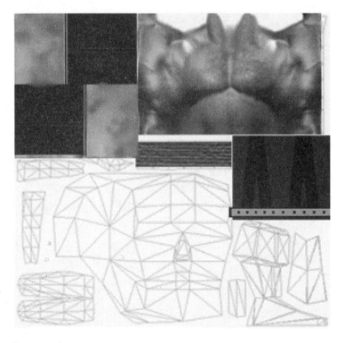

FIGURE
10.4   *Skirt and belt textures.*

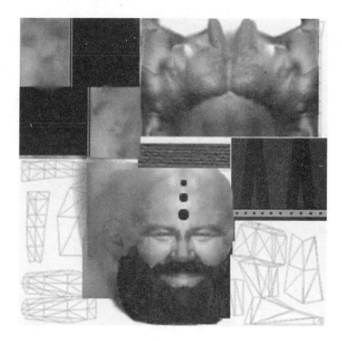

FIGURE *Face texture.*
10.5

4. Now let's place some leg textures on our map. On the bottom left side, we have a row of leg textures. Notice that we have used the blending and pulling techniques on the legs. We have also placed the hand textures next to the legs (See Figure 10.6). The last step in our texture map is blocking in the boots. In Figure 10.7, we have covered it with a black color tone and then placed a pattern piece on his boot.

This finishes up the Barbarian skin. Save the texture map as a .bmp or other usable file name and then open your 3D program. Load the 3D model of the Barbarian and apply this new texture to your model. Figures 10.8, 10.9, and 10.10 show how the Barbarian looks rendered with the texture map. Check the CD-ROM for the full colored version of the Barbarian.

ON THE CD

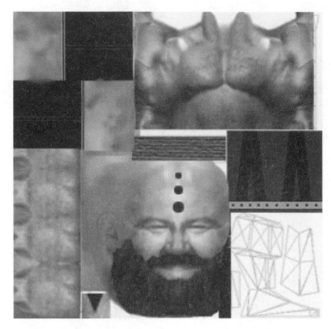

FIGURE *Leg textures.*
10.6

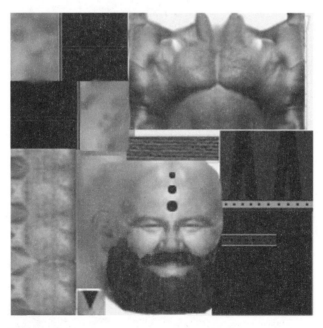

FIGURE *Boot texture.*
10.7

FIGURE **10.8** *Finished Barbarian.*

FIGURE **10.9** *Barbarian back view.*

FIGURE **10.10** *Barbarian side view.*

Texture the Female Marine

The Marine texture process will be similar to the Barbarian, except, of course, the textures themselves will differ greatly. Be sure to have the color guide next to you for a quick reference of what we want the Marine to look like. Once you have the guide, open the U.V. map of the female Marine that's provided on the CD-ROM.

ON THE CD

1. In Figure 10.11, we see the burned copy of our U.V. map. This is basically the placement for our textures. During the process of making the textures, you may have to change or move some of the coordinates around, which is okay. Don't ever feel like you are stuck with this one map. We will start filling in the pieces from the top left and work our way around. Let's start with the camouflage pants (See Figure 10.12). Be sure that the pants cover the entire area.

2. Place the pieces of the boot in now. Notice that we have one boot on the map. Since they were similar, we put both of them together (See Figure 10.13). Now place the hair and the arm textures on. The arms have been extended outward to catch the U.V. mapping coordinates, as shown in Figure 10.14.

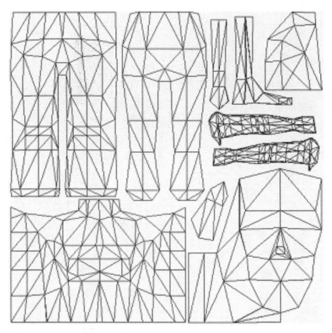

FIGURE
10.11   *Copy of U.V. mapping coordinates.*

FIGURE
10.12   *Pant textures.*

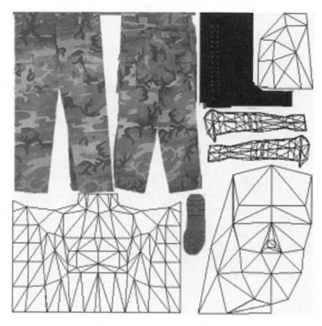

FIGURE   *Boot textures.*
10.13

FIGURE   *Arm and hair textures.*
10.14

3. In Figure 10.15, we have placed the head in. Use the blending technique to blend the side view and front view together so that it looks like the picture. Our last step is putting an upper body on the Marine (See Figure 10.16). The body has been done the same way you did the face, with the blending technique. Just like on the Barbarian, we have divided the back on each side of the front piece, which makes placing the skins on the models much easier.

The Marine texture map is finished. Now save it and load the 3D model of the Marine. With the Marine loaded, go ahead and apply the texture map to her. In Figures 10.17, 10.18, and 10.19, we have a few shots of what she looks like. To see a color version of the Marine with the textures, refer to the CD-ROM.

The Princess that was modeled can also use the same style of texture map, but just be sure to add the hat and dress colors to her, so that she will stand out differently in an eloquent way. In Figure 10.20, we have two pictures of the Princess with a new texture map applied to her.

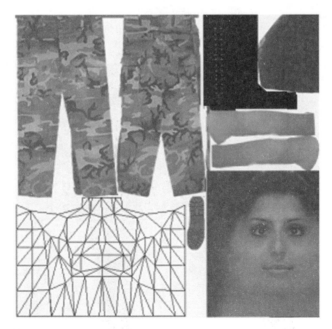

FIGURE *Head texture.*
10.15

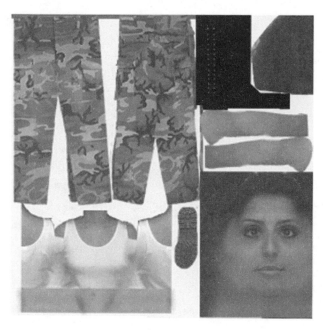

FIGURE   *Body texture.*
10.16

FIGURE   *Finished textures*
10.17   *of Marine.*

FIGURE   *Back view of*
10.18   *Marine.*

FIGURE   *Side view*
10.19   *of Marine.*

FIGURE *Finished Princess.*
10.20

Applying Textures to the Weapon

ON THE CD

Since the most complicated weapon we have is the gun, we will demonstrate the steps necessary to create a good texture map for it. Make sure that you have the color guides for the Weapon and the U.V. maps that are both provided on the CD-ROM inside the Weapons folder.

We have modeled a Weapon, which is intended to be used by the Female Marine. But to show the power of a texture map: we are going to design two different styles of maps; one that can be turned into a real gun and the other, a cartoon gun. The first texture map we will devise is the cartoon map, which will show how a real-looking object can be transformed with flat colors into a cute, fun-loving, toy gun.

1. In Figure 10.21, we have the U.V. map of our cartoon weapon. The first thing we can do, is place a blue and gray color across the butt of the gun as shown in Figure 10.22.

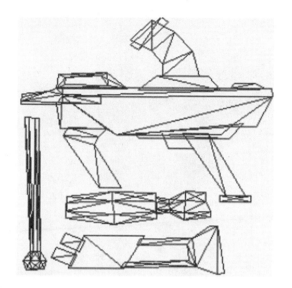

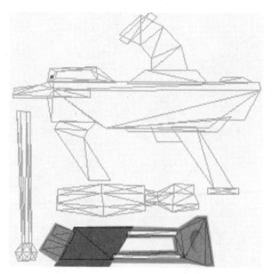

FIGURE **10.21**   *Copy of U.V. mapping coordinates.*

FIGURE **10.22**   *Butt of gun textured.*

For the next several steps, we will be working with the U.V. map as the top layer. This will allow us to see the U.V. coordinates while the map is being placed on.

2. Fill in the body of the gun with blue, green, and gray colors, as shown in Figure 10.23. Now we want to add a few effects to the weapon. In Figure 10.24, the empty areas have been filled in with a shadow box. This will help to give a little depth to the gun and still keep it looking like a cartoon.

When creating a cartoon Weapon, make sure to use bright, solid colors. Try not to go into high detail, as that would distract from its simplicity.

3. Add a bunch of small circles around the gun, as shown in Figure 10.25. Then finally place a silver gray color for the barrel and a bright red and yellow color for the bottom barrel (See Figure 10.26).
4. Take off the U.V. map so that we can see the Weapon clearly, as illustrated in Figure 10.27.

Now open the 3D model of the Weapon, and apply this new and colorful texture map to it. In Figure 10.28, 10.29, and 10.30, we have several shots of the 3D model with the cartoon texture map.

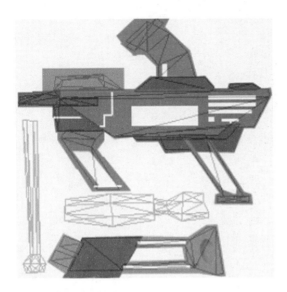

FIGURE
10.23
Body of gun textured.

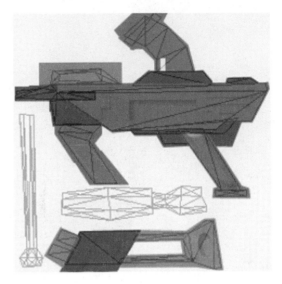

FIGURE
10.24
Shadows created.

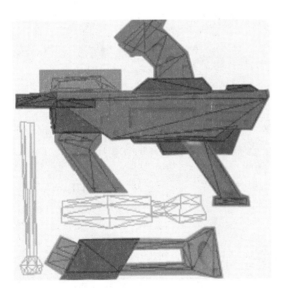

FIGURE
10.25
Small circles added.

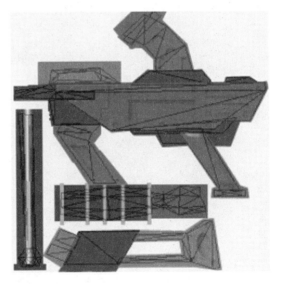

FIGURE
10.26
Top and bottom barrel textured.

FIGURE **10.27**   *Finished cartoon Weapon texture.*

FIGURE **10.28**   *Finished Weapon with texture.*

FIGURE **10.29**   *Front view of Weapon.*

FIGURE **10.30**   *Side view of Weapon.*

Now let's transform this Weapon into a futuristic-looking gun for the Female Marine. In Figure 10.31, we have the new map that will be applied to the gun. See Figures 10.32, 10.33, and 10.34 for several shots of the 3D model with the new texture map. This is a great example of how important the texture map is for the overall look and feel of the Weapon or any model. The model itself has a lot of shape and form, but only after you add the texture map do you give it an identity.

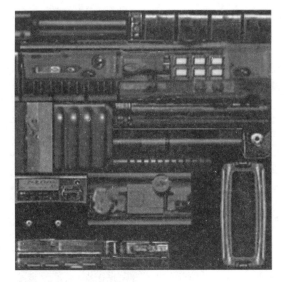

FIGURE **10.31**   *Gun texture.*

FIGURE **10.32**   *Back view of gun textured.*

FIGURE **10.33**   *Perspective view of the gun.*

FIGURE **10.34**   *Side view of gun.*

*Be sure to study the differences between the cartoon and real gun
map. You should be able to see the distinction in terms of detail
and color for each map, as well as the U.V. mapping coordinates
layout style.*

Applying Textures to the Civil War Soldier

The Civil War Soldier is the last human map we are going to work with. The
map we designed for the Soldier is very different from the others, so let's take a
moment to go over where the new pieces are and just how we are going to
place the textures in.

1. In Figure 10.35, we see the burned copy of the U.V. map. Take a moment
   to examine this new layout. You can see that we have simply divided the
   polygons in half (front and back) for the body, which allows us to have a
   very straightforward map to work on. The other biggest change on this
   map is the direction of the head. In order for us to have a large head map,
   we had to turn it sideways. Now, in Figure 10.36, we have placed a bluish
   tone color in for the arms, which we've stretched across the entire arm
   section.

*The texture map we are creating for the Soldier is being designed
on a 128x128 map. If you would like to make a larger map, that's
fine. But we just want to show you how much detail you can get
into a character on a map size this small.*

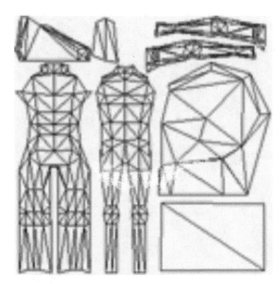

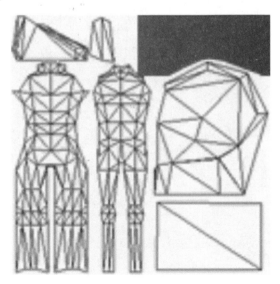

FIGURE **10.35** *Copy of U.V. mapping coordinates.*

FIGURE **10.36** *Arm texture.*

2. The next sets of textures we are going to place on the Soldier are the pants and the shirt. In Figure 10.37, the backside of the Soldier has been textured. Even though this map is small, the texture itself can have a wide variety of shades, so be sure that you don't just place a flat blue across the character. In Figure 10.38, we have added the front shirt and pants to the map, as well as some smaller details like several buttons and a belt buckle to the front view.

3. Choose a golden brown color and make a set of gloves for the Soldier's hands (See Figure 10.39). Then make a pair of black boots and add a few lines for the bottom of the boot, as shown in Figure 10.40.

4. Let's place a brownish color across the bottom right square to fill in a texture for his hat, as shown in Figure 10.41. The last thing we need to color in is the Soldier's head. In Figure 10.42, the face texture has been placed in, along with a brown color across the top of his head, which is going to be the top of the hat he is wearing.

5. The last thing we need to add is an alpha map to his hat. The hat needs to look round and not like a rectangle, so apply an alpha map, as shown below, to give it a softer, more realistic appearance (See Figure 10.43). If you don't quite remember how to do an alpha map, go back to Chapter 9 for a quick review.

The gray line around the image is present so that the map size can be seen.

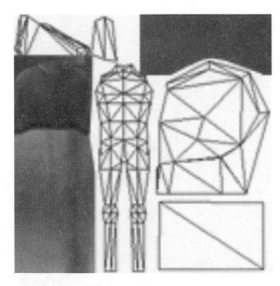

FIGURE **10.37** *Back of Soldier textured.*

FIGURE **10.38** *Front of Soldier textured.*

FIGURE
10.39   *Gloves added.*

FIGURE
10.40   *Boots textured.*

FIGURE
10.41   *Hat texture.*

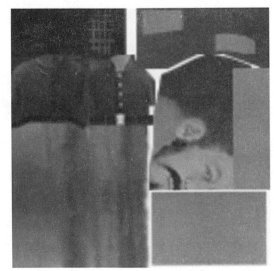

FIGURE
10.42   *Face texture.*

Once the Soldier is finished, open the 3D model of him and apply the texture map, which is shown in Figures 10.44, 10.45, and 10.46.

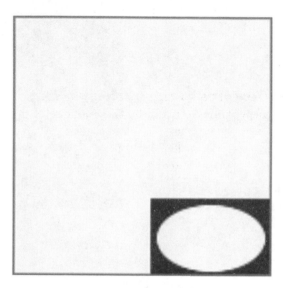

FIGURE
10.43　*Alpha channel map on the hat.*

FIGURE
10.44　*Top view of Soldier.*

FIGURE
10.45　*Three-quarter shot of Soldier.*

FIGURE
10.46　*Back view of Soldier.*

CARTOON CHARACTERS

Let's venture into the colorful world of cartoons! Here in cartoon land, we will show you how to texture characters so that they resemble the look and feel of 2D animated cartoons from television, using one or two tones of color for each shape. The most important rule when creating toon textures is to "keep it simple," because we want to make it seem inviting and playful, like a toy for a little kid.

Applying Textures to the Cartoon Villain

To texture the Villain, we need the color guides of the Villain that we did in Part 1. This will help remind us what colors we used. If you came up with a different color design for the Villain and would like to use it, make sure you've got it somewhere near you for reference. Now open whatever 2D program you like working with. Next, get the U.V. map from the CD-ROM for the Villain. This is a copy of the actual U.V. mapping coordinates and a great guide to use for texturing a model.

ON THE CD

1. In Figure 10.47, we see the burned copy of the U.V. map. This is where the basic placement for the textures will be. Now draw the side of the Villain's face, as shown in Figure 10.48. Add whatever color hair you had in mind and then draw a cute cartoon ear. Remember: The face has been doubled over, so only half the face has to be drawn.

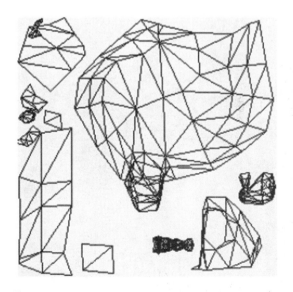

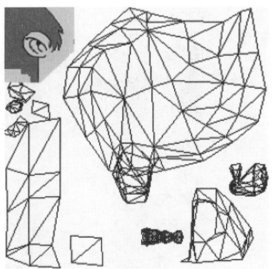

FIGURE **10.47** *Copy of the U.V. mapping coordinates.*

FIGURE **10.48** *Side of the face textured.*

2. In Figure 10.49, the eye and the eyebrow have been drawn. We have put big cute eyes on him, but if you feel he should have squinty, mean eyes, then just draw them. Next, square off another section of flesh tone at the bottom to cover the arm, and draw the mouth, as shown in Figure 10.50.

3. Place a section of black at the lower right corner for the boots and the chest. Make sure to add two yellow buttons at the top of the boots (See Figure 10.51). Then, just like you did with the Hero, add a big belt and some camouflage-looking pants, as shown in Figure 10.52.

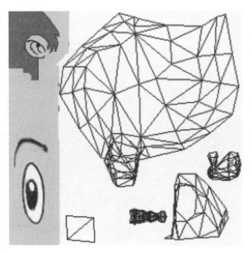

FIGURE **10.49** *Eye and eyebrow drawn.*

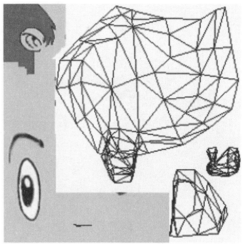

FIGURE **10.50** *Mouth and flesh texture for arm.*

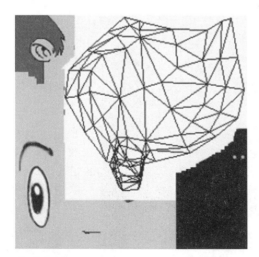

FIGURE **10.51** *Eye and eyebrow drawn.*

FIGURE **10.52** *Mouth and flesh texture for arm.*

This completes the cartoon texture for the Villain. Pull up the 3D model and apply this new texture to him. Take a look at Figures 10.53, 10.54, and 10.55 to see it applied to the 3D model.

This is really going to make a fantastic-looking art set. Now let's take a quick glance at how the finished skin of the Hero looks. In Figure 10.56, we have the finished map of the Hero, which, as you can see, closely resembles the Villain texture map. The biggest differences between the two maps are the arrangement of pieces and the color of camouflage they are wearing.

FIGURE
10.53   *Finished Villain.*

FIGURE
10.54   *Side view of Villain.*

FIGURE
10.55   *Back view of Villain.*

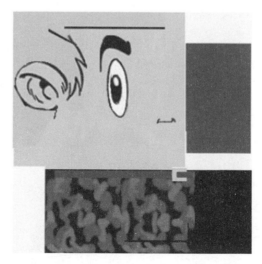

FIGURE
10.56   *Finished texture map for the Hero.*

Figures 10.57, 10.58, and 10.59 show the texture map applied to the 3D model of our Cartoon Hero, as he would look finished.

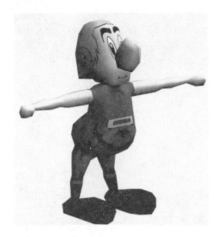  

FIGURE **10.57** *Finished Hero.*

FIGURE **10.58** *Side view of Hero.*

FIGURE **10.59** *Back view of Hero.*

ANIMALS

Applying Textures to the Horse

So far, we have textured humans and cartoon characters. The next model we are going to texture is the Horse. This is one of the easier models to texture map, since most of its shape is found on the side view. We will use the pulling technique around the edges of the Horse to create its skin from a picture of a nicely colored brown horse.

1. In Figure 10.60, we have the U.V. map showing the side view of the Horse, which we did in Part 3 of this book. Be sure to use this when creating the texture map for your Horse, since it has the outlining shape of where the textures need to be placed. With the map set, go ahead and place the photo of the Horse in, as shown in Figure 10.61.

In Figure 10.2, look at how the Horse was cut. All of the dark shadows have been cut off of the Horse. This will make it easier to use the pulling technique.

NOTE

2. Next, we want to start pulling the outlining shape of the Horse out and away. Be sure that when you are done, the Horse's texture covers the full shape of the U.V. map, as shown in Figure 10.62. The last step involved for the Horse is placing his tail on the map (See Figure 10.63).

FIGURE
10.60   *Copy of U.V. mapping coordinates.*

FIGURE
10.61   *Side view of Horse texture.*

FIGURE
10.62   *Texture pulled to cover the U.V. map.*

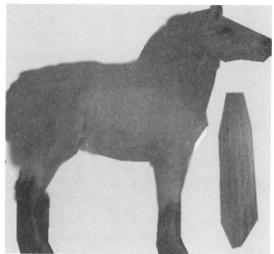

FIGURE
10.63   *Tail textured and light tone background applied.*

Congratulations! The Horse's skin is now complete. Pull up your 3D model of the Horse and apply the texture to it. Look at Figures 10.64, 10.65, and 10.66 to see what the Horse and his newfound skin look like.

FIGURE **10.64** *Horse texture finished.*

FIGURE **10.65** *Side view of the Horse.*

FIGURE **10.66** *Back view of the Horse.*

Applying Textures to the Stegosaurus

The Stegosaurus is one creature that could have many types of scaly, rough textures. Make sure to continue the same process we did for the Horse skin on the Stegosaurus and you should do fine. If you feel creative and want to design your own texture for the dinosaur, then go ahead. But if you'd like to get some real-looking textures, you should use an alligator, lizard, snake, or even an elephant skin. These animals should give you what you are looking for.

ON THE CD

1. In Figure 10.67, we have the U.V. map showing the mapping coordinates of the Stegosaurus. The map has been provided for you on the CD-ROM in the Stegosaurus folder. This should help you in placing the textures on the map correctly and quickly.

TIP

We have altered the U.V. map of our Stegosaurus. This is something that may happen when working with texture maps and U.V. coordinates at the same time. It's nothing to worry about; you actually want to work with both at once, in case changes like this have to be made.

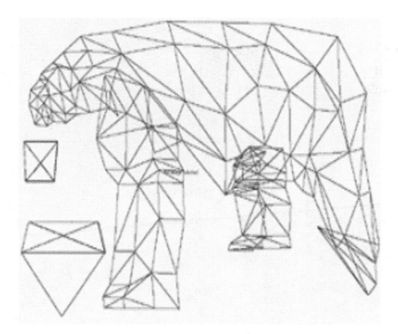

FIGURE   *Copy of U.V. mapping coordinates.*
10.67

2. The next step will be to place the texture map across the dinosaur. In Figure 10.68, we have several pieces of a skin texture. Let's blend the pieces together, as shown in Figure 10.69. Notice that we have a very close resemblance to an elephant texture.

3. The last thing we want to do is make it a little scalier-looking (See Figure 10.70).

FIGURE   *Texture pieces.*
10.68

FIGURE   *Pieces smudged together.*
10.69

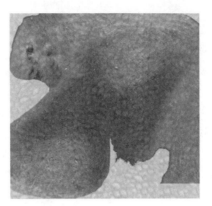

FIGURE *Scales added to the texture.*
10.70

That wraps up the Stegosaurus skin. Let's apply it to the 3D model and render a few shots. Load the 3D model of the Stegosaurus and apply the new texture map to it. Look at Figures 10.71, 10.72, and 10.73 to see what the Stegosaurus looks like.

Now that we've applied textures to our characters, we need to move onto texturing techniques for the vehicle models.

FIGURE *Front view of the*
10.71 *finished Stegosaurus.*

FIGURE *Side view of the Stegosaurus.*
10.72

FIGURE   *Back view of the Stegosaurus.*
10.73

11

Texturing Vehicles

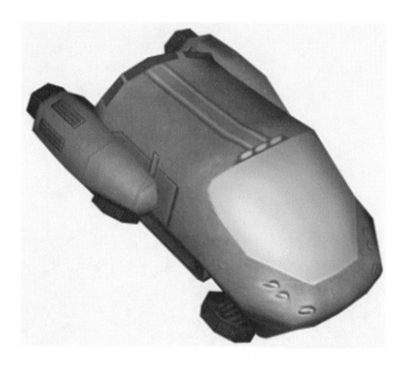

APPLYING TEXTURES TO THE VEHICLES

In this chapter we will cover texturing for our vehicles, beginning with the Sci-Fi Van. The texture map of the Sci-Fi Van is going to be made up of some photos and some Photoshop touch-ups. When we get done with this map, be sure to study the way the real-world textures are mixed with some made-up textures. This pattern of texturing is one that will often be used when creating science fiction or fantasy models and characters.

ON THE CD

1. In Figure 11.1, we see the burned copy of the U.V. map, which is from the CD-ROM in the Van folder. The map shows the basic guidelines we'll want to use for the placement of textures that will be applied. Let's start with the top row of shapes and work our way down. In the top row, the textures for the tires, the thrusters, and the bottom of the Van have been placed in. In the top right corner, we have also placed three glowing lights, which are for the top of the Van (See Figure 11.2).

2. Next, we have placed a metal-looking texture across the rocket boosters. Also, in Figure 11.3, the back ducks have been added. In Figure 11.4, we have placed a yellowish - orange color to represent the pod cover.

NOTE *The pod cover has not been taken to the full extent of the U.V. coordinates. Instead, we have curved the edges of the cover at the top to make the shape a little softer and rounder-looking.*

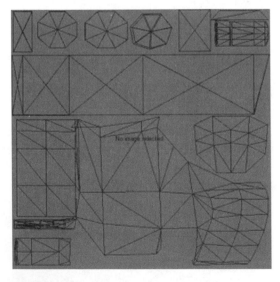

FIGURE
11.1 *Copy of U.V. mapping coordinates.*

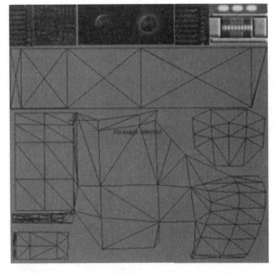

FIGURE
11.2 *Tires and thruster textures.*

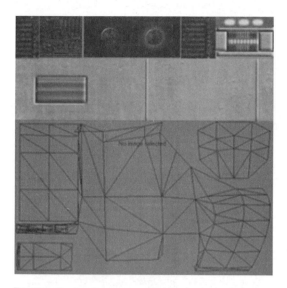

FIGURE
11.3   *Rocket booster texture.*

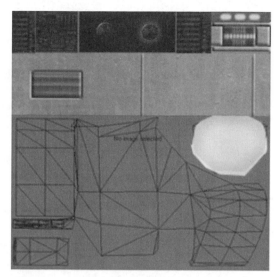

FIGURE
11.4   *Pod cover texture.*

3. Now add the lights, door panels, and the bumpers onto the side of the Van, as shown in Figure 11.5. Once you have the pieces laid in, place a large gray texture across the entire bottom portion of the map (See Figure 11.6).

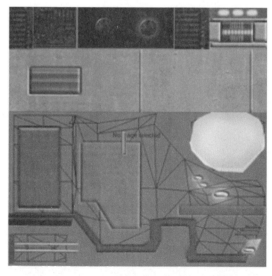

FIGURE
11.5   *Panels and bumpers textured.*

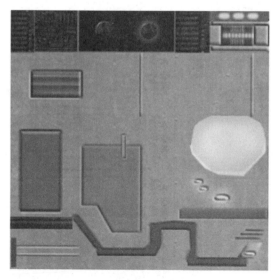

FIGURE
11.6   *Gray texture piece placed in.*

This completes the futuristic space map for the Sci-Fi Van. At this time, open up the 3D model of the Van and place the finished texture map on it. In Figures 11.7 through 11.10, we have rendered a few shots of the Van to show you what it looks like finished.

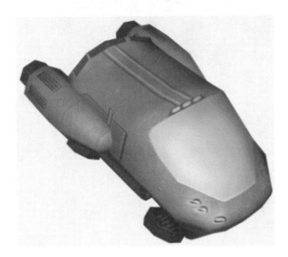

FIGURE
11.7   *Perspective view of the Van.*

FIGURE
11.8   *Perspective view of the Van.*

FIGURE
11.9   *Front view of the Van.*

FIGURE
11.10   *Back view of the Van.*

CAR

The second vehicle we are going to texture is the Car. So, get the color guide you did of it from Part 1 of the book, and then open a 2D paint program. Now open the U.V. map copy, which is on the CD-ROM in the Car folder.

1. In Figure 11.11, we see the burned copy of the U.V. mapping coordinates that will serve as the general guide to place the textures. When designing textures for a vehicle, you can use flat tone colors for the paint job and then add reflective properties to the Car when we render it. If you have done your own Car design, then make sure that you have all of the necessary photos of the lights, knobs, tires, and reference material you may need.

2. Let's work our way from left to right on this texture. In Figure 11.12, we have placed a shade of blue for the hood and trunk. The next thing we need to do is place black for the roof of the car. After that has been done, place the photo of the side view of the Car on the map (See Figure 11.13).

When working with a vehicle, be sure that you have crisp edges and clean cuts for the body pieces. Since a vehicle is very inorganic, the shapes are much easier to texture.

NOTE

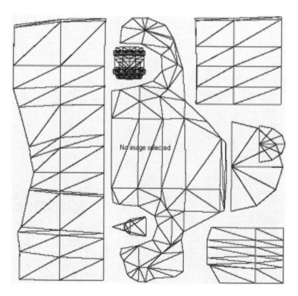

FIGURE *Copy of the U.V. mapping coordinates.*
11.11

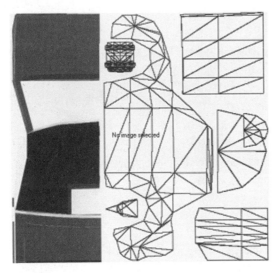

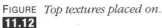

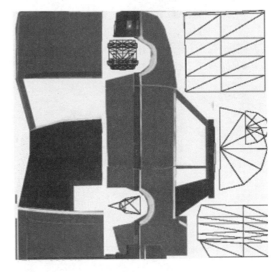

FIGURE **11.12** *Top textures placed on.*

FIGURE **11.13** *Side textures placed on.*

3. Once the two main body pieces have been placed in, go ahead and do the minor parts of the vehicle (See Figure 11.14). In the last step, we want to place the bumper, the front end, and the tire onto the map. Notice that all three of these textures are cut in half, since the U.V.'s have been flipped on top of each other. This allows us to make it larger on the map and get more detail out of our pictures See (Figure 11.15).

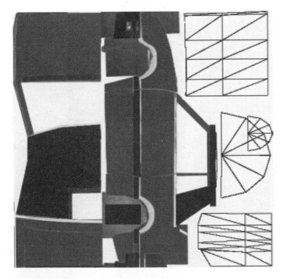

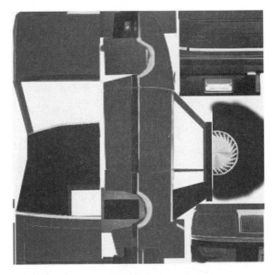

FIGURE **11.14** *Lights and smaller texture pieces placed on.*

FIGURE **11.15** *Bumper, tire, and front end textured.*

All right, that completes the texture map for the Car. Now it's time to pull up the 3D model of the vehicle and apply our new stylish texture map to it. Check out Figures 11.16 through 11.19 to see what it looks like.

FIGURE *Finished texture map of the Car.*
11.16

FIGURE *Top front view of the Car.*
11.17

FIGURE *Back rear view of the Car.*
11.18

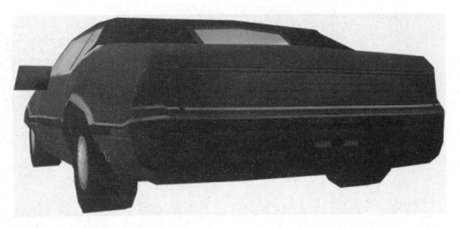

FIGURE *Rear view of the Car.*
11.19

MECH ROBOT

The Mech Robot will be textured similar to the Van, except that it will use more handmade pieces. Being able to make good textures can be a little difficult, but using Photoshop features and plug-ins can make the task much easier than it appears. Make sure that you have your color guide next to you for reference while we create the texture map for the Mech Robot.

1. In Figure 11.20, we see the burned copy of our U.V. map. In the top left corner of the map are two circles and a roughed-up texture (See Figure 11.21). These are the sprockets on the sides of the Robot's legs.

The textures that are being placed on the map will usually cover more than just the required area. This allows us to have a cleaner map, and is a good precaution for keeping background colors off of the actual map pieces.

2. Next, add the pod cover texture, as shown in Figure 11.22. It has a slight highlight on the lower left side to create a more spherical shape. The pod cover can also be colored flat and later you can add a reflective map to it in your 3D application. After the cover has been placed on, we need to apply the cockpit textures. In Figure 11.23, the green metal pieces have been added, along with the grail piece for across the top of the pod cover.
3. Now place the side gun and the thrusters in the upper right portion of the map (See Figure 11.24). In the lower right corner, the waist textures and the cover plates have been added (See Figure 11.25). When you are creating your own textures, be sure to add filters or other layers that will keep the textures from looking lifeless or dull.

FIGURE
11.20   *Copy of the U.V. mapping coordinates.*

FIGURE
11.21   *Leg pieces textured.*

FIGURE
11.22   *Pod cover texture.*

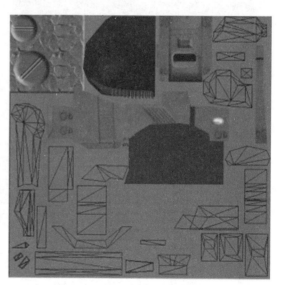

FIGURE
11.23   *Cockpit textures.*

4. In Figure 11.26, the black texture for the gun has been placed on the texture map, which we have used several times for different parts of the guns. The last things we need to texture are the legs of the Robot, as shown in Figure 11.27. Many of these pieces are difficult to line up on the first try. A good

idea would be to keep your U.V. program running while you are texturing the object. This way, you can go back and forth between the two stages and make sure everything is lining up and being placed in the correct areas.

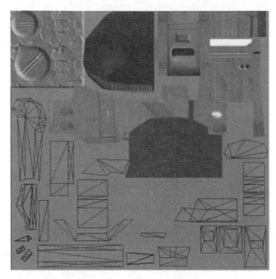

FIGURE
11.24 *Thruster and gun textures.*

FIGURE
11.25 *Waist and cover plate textures.*

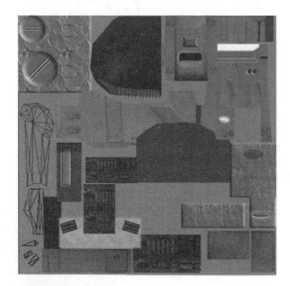

FIGURE
11.26 *Gun textures.*

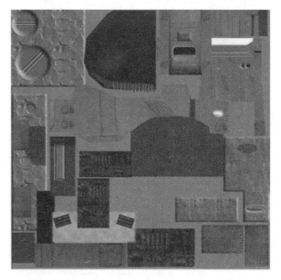

FIGURE
11.27 *Legs textured.*

This completes the texture map for the Mech Robot. Congratulations! Now load the Mech Robot in a 3D application and apply the new texture map to him. Also, if you want to make a reflective map on the pod cover, this would be a good time to apply that. The Mech Robot should look like Figures 11.28 through 11.31 when it's completed.

Now you should be ready to tackle any type of mechanical robot or flying spaceship with the greatest of ease. Be sure to use the techniques illustrated in this chapter to help in creating those next fantastic vehicles!

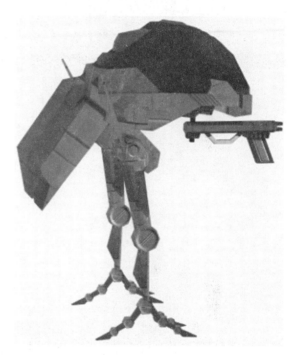

FIGURE **11.28** *Perspective view of the finished Mech Robot.*

FIGURE **11.29** *Side view of the Mech Robot*

FIGURE **11.30** *Top view of the Mech Robot.*

FIGURE **11.31** *Perspective view of the Mech Robot.*

REVIEW OF TEXTURING

As you have seen in this section, textures play a huge role in how the models will look and feel. A texture map can really change the appearance of a lifeless 3D model. In the previous chapters of texturing a 3D model, we have learned many useful techniques, two of which are blending and pulling. These two procedures are simple and very effective for creating a texture map that looks seamless and smooth around its edges. By producing a fluid texture, your model will become more believable and its overall shape and form will be further strengthened. These textures are what give life to your models and worlds. They must be well thought out from the very beginning stages and executed with the utmost care and patience. A thought to remember would be: "A model is only as good as its skin." The next time you are sitting in front of your computer screen, pixel pushing some image, or out taking a picture of somebody's car, thinking. "why am I doing this?", remember that you are doing it because you know what it takes to make a great texture map. Good luck, and be sure to keep a camera by your side. Who knows when you'll come across a texture that you'll want to get a picture of for one of your models!

Now you're ready to move on to the final part of the book, Final Assignments.

Final Project

P art 5 is the final step to the lessons. With your newfound knowledge, it's time to step out on your own and gain the experience necessary to create characters, models, and worlds from your own imagination. This section will cover all the things we have discussed, and let you apply them to one more model.

12 Putting It All Together

ONE LAST TIME

Hopefully you made it here without too many problems and you're ready to put all that you've learned to work. To put your newly developed skills to work, we are going to put your skills to work and create an evil villain to go against our Ancient Barbarian and the Female Marine. To begin, we'll use the evil guy that we drew for the front cover. This guy is crazy, mean, and definitely ready to take over the world and then destroy it. This is his entire motivation and purpose for living. Sounds perfect for a villain, right? Following is a concept sketch of Mr. V (villain), who, by the way, is decked out in all sorts of techno wires and metallic armor (See Figure 12.1). At this point you can color the image using maybe a dark blue tint for the outfit and gray tones for the metallic parts.

Now that we provided the front sketch of Mr. V , it's time to take all the skills and techniques you learned and apply them to finish the drawings. Use the generic male picture and sketch the side view and the back view. Take your time, and remember that the side view is the most important view, so concentrate on making itgood!

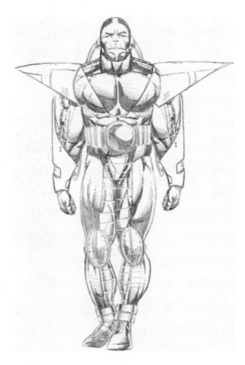

FIGURE   *Villain front sketch.*
12.1

Once you finish this stage, you'll have your own menacing bad guy, who's ready to put fear into the universe... If you'd like to make a terrifying weapon for him to use, go for it. Just use the basics of the gun modeled in Chapter 5 to get a good start on a weapon that he can use to put the universe into submission!

Now that you have sketched Mr. V, it is time to use our new knowledge of 3D modeling to flesh him out. At this point, youhave practiced modeling a number of characters and objects, so this will be very simple for you. Take your side view sketch of Mr. V and place it in the background Viewport of a 3D modeling program. Once you have it placed in there, take your time and outline the side view of the character just as we did with the other models. This is a very important step in the modeling process because, just like the sketch, it defines the look of the model. Be sure that you catch all the major angles and curves during the outlining phase so that he will be just as great as the drawing! (See Figure 12.2).

After Mr. V has been successfully outlined it's time for you to extrude, refine, attach, and add what ever accessories you feel he needs. The model without any accessories should look like Figure 12.3. This model is available on the CD-ROM for use if you are having any problems. When modeling Mr. V remember to use

ON THE CD

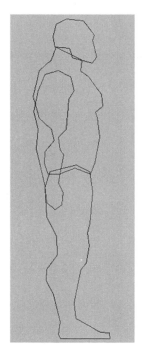

FIGURE *Outlining shape*
12.2 *of Mr. V.*

FIGURE *Finished Model.*
12.3

the exact steps we used for the Barbarian. As you'll see from this exercise, this is an excellent way to see how well the process works for any character you choose to model in 3D. If you find yourself having difficulty with Mr. V, just flip back to the beginning of chapter 5 and review the Ancient Barbarian lesson.

The next thing you will need to do is create a U.V. map for the Villain. This, as we learned, is open to many interpretations of the best placement for the map pieces, but this is your chance to layout a U.V. map the way you think it should be done. But before laying out the map, remember to take a moment to decide which are the most important features and polygons on Mr. V. As you saw in the other characters, a map layout can change depending on the style of game you choose to make or where the major camera view will be placed. If you think all the body parts play an important role in this character then give each piece a descent size on the U.V. map. If you are having trouble coming up with just the right map, we have provided a few different examples of how Mr. V might be mapped. (See Figure 12.4). Use these as guides only; the final decision is yours.

The last step we need to concentrate on is the texturing of Mr. V. The character at this point has a lot of potential for being really good so let's be sure to finish him off with just as much effort as when we started him! A texture map for Mr. V has been started and is included on the CD-ROM in case you need a little help with him. We did the most difficult parts of the texture for you, but the rest is up to you.. This is the chance to test "your new abilities" on texturing If you do not have any references or photographs to use, then spend some time looking for anything that could work for Mr. V. Go to your local gym and take a picture of a body builder or someone wearing leathery clothing. You may also want to take pictures of glossy things like shiney new metal, or a silver bike. If

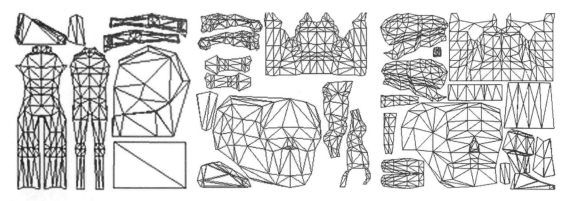

FIGURE
12.4   *Multiple examples of how to layout a U.V. map.*

you want to try developing your own skins from scratch, then do it. It's up to you to decide how the final texture map will appear. Follow the order and steps, which we laid out and you should have no problem designing, modeling, and texturing your next 3D modeling assignment, not matter what it is. Good luck and have fun!

13 Tips and Techniques List

QUICK REFERENCE

We have put together the top points from each section so that you can have a quick reference guide. Keep this guide handy for your future projects until, ultimately, you become one with the quick reference.

CONCEPT ART/DESIGN

The major points to remember are:

- **Write down the ideas and descriptions of your game.**
- **Make a concise list of what you want drawn.**
- **Keep reference material readily available.**
- **Use the generic male and female pictures provided for the basics of characters.**
- **Sketch front, back, and side views of characters.**
- **Put your characters in a few action poses if you want to create an attitude.**
- **Color in your characters in to provide an idea for texture maps.**
- **Always do several variations of an idea, to get the best one.**

3D MODELING

When modeling, be sure that you follow these steps:

- **When doing a model, it's best to use the side view of the character to get the initial shape. It always provides the greatest likeness.**
- **Use the sketch for your background image.**
- **Trace it with the Line tool . (Remember: The more points you put on it while outlining it, the higher count your model will end up being.)**
- **Extrude all the objects.**
- **Refine the individual shapes.**
- **Attach the objects together.**
- **Add accessories.**
- **Reduce the model for L.O.D. testing.**

U.V. MAPPING COORDINATES

When mapping out models for textures, follow these rules:

- **Keep it organized.**
- **Think of it as a puzzle.**
- **Use the space wisely; make the important parts of a model bigger on the maps, and overlap and shrink the less important parts.**
- **Make sure all the major pieces stay together.**

TEXTURES

Follow these rules for making a skin, or texture, for the model:

- **Write down all the textures you will need (photo list).**
- **Take a camera and get the images you need.**
- **Clean up the pictures.**
- **Use the blending technique.**
- **Use the pulling technique.**
- **Use a copy of the U.V. map to see where to place the textures.**
- **Go back and forth between U.V. maps and texturing to tweak the maps.**

About the CD-ROM

WHAT'S ON THE CD-ROM

Game Modeling Using Low Polygon Techniques book is accompanied with a CD-ROM which has everything needed to complete the tutorials throughout the chapters. It also includes all the images from the book in full color for you to use as you work on the 3D models and textures.

CD FOLDERS:

- **IMAGES:** All images found in the book are stored here for the reader to use. Each picture is saved in its Part and chapter sections.
- **TUTORIALS:** All the files necessary to complete each 3D character. This includes the textures, several 3D model steps for each model, alpha channel maps, and sketches for every character in the book. They are set up in Character name folders.

General Minimum System Requirements: In order to use this CD you need to have a computer that can run Windows (95/98/NT/2000) or Mac with a CD-ROM drive and a mouse. Also needed are a 2D program that will import .tiff files and a 3D application that will import a .3ds file.

Index